William Bedell

A True Relation of the Life and Death of the Right Reverend Father in God William Bedell,

lord bishop of Kilmore in Ireland. Ed. from a ms. in the Bodleian library, Oxford, and amplified with genealogical and historical chapters

William Bedell

A True Relation of the Life and Death of the Right Reverend Father in God William Bedell, *lord bishop of Kilmore in Ireland. Ed. from a ms. in the Bodleian library, Oxford, and amplified with genealogical and historical chapters*

ISBN/EAN: 9783337324100

Printed in Europe, USA, Canada, Australia, Japan

Cover: Foto ©ninafisch / pixelio.de

More available books at **www.hansebooks.com**

A TRUE RELATION OF

THE LIFE AND DEATH

OF

THE RIGHT REVEREND FATHER IN GOD

WILLIAM BEDELL,

LORD BISHOP OF KILMORE IN IRELAND.

EDITED FROM A MS. IN THE BODLEIAN LIBRARY, OXFORD,

AND AMPLIFIED WITH GENEALOGICAL AND HISTORICAL CHAPTERS,

COMPILED FROM ORIGINAL SOURCES,

BY

THE REPRESENTATIVE OF THE BISHOP'S MOTHER'S FAMILY OF ELLISTON,

THOMAS WHARTON JONES, F.R.S.

PRINTED FOR THE CAMDEN SOCIETY.

M.DCCC.LXXII.

COUNCIL OF THE CAMDEN SOCIETY
FOR THE YEAR 1871-72.

President,
SIR WILLIAM TITE, C.B., M.P., F.R.S., V.P.S.A.
WILLIAM CHAPPELL, ESQ. F.S.A , *Treasurer.*
WILLIAM DURRANT COOPER, ESQ. F.S.A.
F. W. COSENS, ESQ.
JOHN FORSTER, ESQ. D.C.L.
SAMUEL RAWSON GARDINER, ESQ.
ALFRED KINGSTON, ESQ.
SIR JOHN MACLEAN, F.S.A.
SIR FREDERIC MADDEN, F.R.S.
FREDERIC OUVRY, ESQ. Treas. S.A.
EDWARD RIMBAULT, LL.D.
EVELYN PHILIP SHIRLEY, ESQ. M.A. F.S.A.
WILLIAM JOHN THOMS, ESQ. F.S.A., *Secretary.*
THE VERY REV. THE DEAN OF WESTMINSTER, F.S.A
SIR THOMAS E. WINNINGTON, BART.
SIR ALBERT W. WOODS, Garter, F.S.A.

The COUNCIL of the CAMDEN SOCIETY desire it to be understood that they are not answerable for any opinions or observations that may appear in the Society's publications; the Editors of the several Works being alone responsible for the same.

PREFACE AND DEDICATION.

THE true Relation of the Life and Death of Bishop Bedell, of Kilmore, here printed, is contained in Volume cclxxviii. of the Tanner Collection of MSS. in the Bodleian Library, Oxford. The Manuscript was formerly in the possession of Archbishop Sancroft, and bears marks of his Grace's revision. How it came into the Archbishop's hands appears from the following correspondence:—

DR. WILLIAM PALLISER TO CAPTAIN AMBROSE BEDELL.*

Trinity College, Dublin,
Oct. 5, 1680.

SIR,

The great motive of my writing to you is the great honour I bear to your most worthy Father's memory, and that I hope will make it more kindly received. It seems the present Archbishop of Canterbury was of the same College with your Father in Cambridge, and most highly esteems him an eminent Ornament of the Place; and therefore designs as soon as may be to print whatever he can procure of your Father's in writing. Some excellent letters of your Father's while he was Chaplain to the Ambassador at Venice † I have sent over, and am now sending a large discourse of your Father's against one Alabaster, a Papist,‡ and a very

---

* Tanner MS. xxxvii. 147, Bodleian Library.

† These appear to be the letters from Venice to Mr. Adam Newton, mentioned and quoted from in Supplementary Chapter iii. pages 103-4.

‡ In the Archiepiscopal Library at Lambeth there is a MS. (Codex 772), entitled "A Defence of the Answer to Mr. Alabaster's four Demands against a Treatise entituled 'The Catholic's Reply upon Bedel's (afterwards Bishop of Kilmore) Answer to Mr. Alabaster's four Demands.'" This is perhaps the Discourse here referred to. Alabaster was a pervert, but returned afterwards to the Church of England.

learned Sermon he preached here in Christchurch * when he was Bishop. But possibly, Sir, you may help me to many other excellent Pieces of his. If you can, I am confident you will not be so so much wanting in your duty to his memory as to deny me a transcript of them. The term is now near, and I believe you may safely send them to me, and I do faithfully promise you that after I have transcribed them, which I shall do immediately upon the receipt of them, I will be careful to restore them unto you. You see I am very bold with you, but the zeal I have that Bishop Bedell's name and work may be better known to the world causeth this boldness, and I hope will excuse it too. The remarkable passages of your Father's life and the circumstances of his death I desire to be very particularly informed in, that the most excellent Archbishop may be able to give your Father his due character in the account that he intends of his life to be printed before his works.† Your answer is desired by the first convenience, that I may be sure you have received my letter; and if you contribute what you can towards the satisfying this just request of mine you will much oblige, Sir,

Your reall friend and servant,

WM. PALLISER.‡

For Captain Bedell, to be left at Mr. Frenches
house in Bal-Turbet, Ulster.

Indorsed:—To Capt. Ambr. Bedel at Carnhill
in yᵉ county of Cavan.

To be left at yᵉ Post Office in Dublin, and thence
directed to yᵉ Post Office in Bell-Turbut (a great
market toun).

---

* Before the Lord Deputy and Parliament in 1634, on the text, "Come out of her my people," Revelation xviii. 4. This sermon Dr. Nicholas Bernard has printed in his "Certain Discourses," &c. (Chapter VII. p. 147,) and tells us that he heard it preached.

† Archbishop Sancroft never carried out his intention of publishing the Life and Works of Bishop Bedell, probably on account of being anticipated by Burnet in 1685. The political troubles in which the Archbishop became soon after involved may have finally banished the subject from his mind.

‡ William Palliser, D.D., was born in Yorkshire about 1641, but received his University education in Dublin, and became Fellow of Trinity College in 1668. He was admitted to Holy Orders in 1670, appointed Professor of Divinity in Trinity College, Dublin, in 1681, consecrated Bishop of Cloyne March 5, 1692-3, and translated to the Archbishopric of Cashel in 1694. He died January 1, 1726-7, in the 85th year of his age.

DR. HENRY DODWELL TO THE ARCHBISHOP OF CANTERBURY.*

MAY IT PLEASE YOUR GRACE,
I understand by a late letter from Mr. Took that your Grace has received a parcel designed for you by Dr. Palliser. I am glad it is come safe to your hands. By the letter which came with it I guess it to be the Life of Bishop Bedel, written by his son Mr. Ambrose Bedel. Dr. Palliser does further proffer to get those letters of Bishop Bedel from Venice † anew transcribed which I had transcribed for your Grace's use, but have since lost my copy. If your Grace be resolved to go through with the design of publishing the works of that excellent Prelate, your Grace will be pleased to let me know your pleasure concerning it. No more, but that I beg your Grace's Prayers and Blessing for
Your Grace's, as in duty bound,
HENRY DODWELL.‡
Cookham, Sept. 16, 1682.

CAPT. AMBROSE BEDELL TO THE ARCHBISHOP OF CANTERBURY.§

The first of 9^{ber}, 1682.

MAY IT PLEASE YOUR GRACE,
As in all Gratitude I am Oblidged, I return to your Grace my humble and hearty Thanks for your Grace's last favour, of which (I bless God for it) I injoy the Benefitt‖ in a large measure, having my health fully restored. In obedience to your Grace's Command, I have made a search for the Life and Death of my Father, and have had an account from one Mr. Palliser (in whose hands it was left to be sent to your Grace) that he had it transcribed and sent it to one Mr. Dodwell, to be delivered to your Grace, who hath given a return that he hath sent it to your Grace. If otherwise I humbly beg that your Grace will be pleased to let me know, and I shall not fail to send it over with all expedition; and what else your Grace shall

---

* Tanner MS. xxxv. 94, Bodleian Library.
† See Supplementary Chapter III. p. 104.
‡ Dr. Henry Dodwell, born of English parents in Dublin in October 1641, was admitted of Trinity College in 1656, and obtained a Fellowship in 1662. This he resigned in 1666. He did not enter into Holy Orders, but in 1688 was elected Camdenian Professor of History in the University of Oxford; refusing, however, to take the oaths to William and Mary, he was deprived three years after. He died at Shottisbrooke, June 7, 1711.
§ Tanner MS. xxxv. 121, Bodleian Library.
‖ The explanation of the allusion here made by Captain Ambrose Bedell to his health will be found in Supplementary Chapter XVIII. p. 226.

impose I shall esteem it both my honour and happiness to obey, as I am realy, may it please your Grace,

Your Grace's most Obleadged and most humble Servt.

Ambr Bedel

Dr. Henry Dodwell in his letter to Archbishop Sancroft, it is seen, speaks of Captain Ambrose Bedell as the author of the work before us. This, however, appears to have been a mere inference on the part of Dr. Dodwell, from the fact that it was Captain Ambrose Bedell from whom the manuscript was obtained for transcription. It was not Captain Ambrose Bedell, but his eldest brother the Rev. William Bedell, Vicar of Kinawley, in the Diocese of Kilmore, from 1634 until the Rebellion in 1641, and afterwards Rector of Rattlesden in Suffolk from 1644 till his death in 1670, who was, there is every reason to believe, the author of the " Relation of the Life and Death " of the Bishop their father.

In William Bedell's letter to his Godfather, Dr. Samuel Warde, given in Supplementary Chapter XIX. may be recognised the quiet, subdued, and scholarly style which characterises the "Relation" under notice. Amongst other things, the expression in the letter, " had courteous usage, in comparison of what other Englishmen found " (p. 230), may be instanced as very similar to one which occurs in the Relation, viz. " the courtesy of the Irish, which (in comparison to what others met withall) was very much " (p. 68). It need scarcely be observed that Ambrose Bedell's letter to Archbishop Sancroft presents little resemblance in style either to the Relation or to his brother William's letter. Besides this, the account given of the Bishop's incumbency of Horningshearth in the "Relation" is evidently the composition of one who had a personal knowledge and vivid remembrance of the occurrences he was writing about. Now, Ambrose, being only ten years old when the family left for Ireland, could scarcely have had much knowledge and remembrance of their residence at Horningshearth; whereas William, who was fifteen years of age at the time, must have had his experiences of the parish well fixed in his mind, to say nothing of his renewed acquaintance with the place when he came to reside close by at Whepsted and Rattlesden.

The "Relation," in short, is altogether such as might have been expected from William, the English Rector, but scarcely from Ambrose, the soldier and country gentleman in Ireland.

The place where the "Relation" was written is not directly mentioned, but that it was in some part of England is proved by the following passage at page 62: "The only considerable Town in the whole County was Belterbert, which yet was but as one of our ordinary Market Towns here in England." This of itself might, indeed, be also taken as decisive of the question of authorship between William and Ambrose, for it was William only who was resident in England.

As to the time when the work was written. This no doubt comprised many of the earlier years of the Rev. William Bedell's incumbency of Rattlesden, when he probably had little else to occupy his leisure but literary composition, and when he enjoyed the advantage of near neighbourhood to Dr. Despotine,* his father's old Venetian

* In the eleventh Classical Presbytery of Suffolk, meeting at Bury, the name of Mr. William Beadle of Ratlesden occurs among the Ministers, and that of Dr. Jasper Despotine of Bury among the elders. See a 4to. Pamphlet published in London, 1647, entitled, "Novr. 5, 1645. The County of Suffolke divided into 14

PREFACE AND DEDICATION.

friend, from whom so much information was derived. Dr. Samuel Warde, of Sydney College, Cambridge, William Bedell's godfather, who could have supplied still more information from the Bishop's numerous letters to him, was dead before William's settlement at Rattlesden. This accounts for the absence of any mention of Dr. Warde or contributions from him in the text of the Relation.* The reference at page 40 to Dr. N. Bernard's book shows, as remarked in the note, that the passage was written subsequently to 1659. Altogether, there is reason to believe that the materials for the work were collected and arranged in the course of the years from 1645 to 1660, but that the Relation was not finally written off in the form in which it now stands until after the latter date.

From the preceding correspondence it is seen that the MS. of the Relation of the Life and Death of Bishop Bedell in the Bodleian Library is a transcript from one which was in the possession of Captain Ambrose Bedell. What became of the original manuscript does not appear. A transcript of the Bodleian MS. has been used as copy to print our text from. In revising it for the press the spelling† has not been interfered with, but some alteration has been made in the employment of capital letters, and the numbering of the paragraphs into which the text is divided has been omitted. A few verbal alterations have been ventured on, such as the Author himself

---

Precincts for Classical Presbyteries," &c. to be found in the British Museum Catalogue under the heading of "Suffolk."

* Bedell's letters to Warde, now in the Bodleian Library, Tanner MSS., it will be found, have been made use of in the compilation of some of the Supplementary Chapters.

† The spelling as it stands may not, however, be exactly the same as it was in the original.

no doubt would have made in correcting the press, and explanatory footnotes have been added here and there.

Whilst the Relation of the Life and Death of Bishop Bedell here printed appears to have been, for the most part, a sketch from memory, the Supplementary Chapters which I have added comprise recorded facts of Bishop Bedell's history, gathered from parish registers ; wills ; manuscripts and books in the British Museum ; manuscripts in the Bodleian Library, Oxford; State Papers, Venetian and Irish, in the Public Record Office; entries at the Colleges of Arms in London and Dublin; a manuscript in the Diocesan Registry of Norwich; and last, though not least, documents in the Library of Trinity College, Dublin, and in the Archiepiscopal Library of Armagh.

For special contributions I am indebted to that distinguished ecclesiastical archæologist the Rev. William Reeves, D.D., LL.D., Rector of Tynan, Prebendary of Armagh, and Chaplain to His Grace the Archbishop of Armagh; and to William Stokes, M.D., D.C.L. Oxon., F.R.S , the eminent Regius Professor of Physic in the University of Dublin.

In acknowledgment of which assistance, and of the sympathy shown by them in the object of my Editorial labours, I beg these gentlemen to accept the Dedication of this Volume with my best thanks and sincerest respect.

T. WHARTON JONES.

35, George Street, Hanover Square, London.
August 1, 1871, being the three-hundredth year
since Bishop Bedell's birth.

CONTENTS.

	PAGE
Preface and Dedication	
A True Relation of the Life and Death of the Right Reverend Father in God, William Bedell, Lord Bishop of Kilmore in Ireland	1
Birth and Parentage	1, 2
School education at Braintree	2
University education at Emmanuel College, Cambridge . .	3
Studies in Divinity	4
Entrance into Holy Orders—Preacher at St. Mary's, Bury St. Edmund's	5
Manner and Method of Preaching	5, 6
Strictness in conforming to the Doctrine and Discipline of the Church of England	6, 7
Held in high estimation at Bury St. Edmund's	7
Appointed Chaplain to the English Embassy at Venice . .	8
Acquaintance with Father Paulo, the Servite	8, 9
Intercourse with the Jews in Venice	9
Dr. Jasper Despotine	10–12
Return to England, and resumption of his Ministerial employment at Bury St. Edmund's	13
Introduction of Dr. Despotine to Medical Practice at Bury St. Edmund's	13
Mr. Bedell's marriage	14
His children	15
Presentation to the Rectory of Great Horningshearth . . .	15
Objects to pay the fees demanded for his Institution and Induction as Simoniacal	16
Settlement and mode of life at Horningshearth	16–20
Suit for the recovery of lands belonging to the Rectory of Horningshearth	21
Elected Member of Convocation for Suffolk	22, 23

CONTENTS.

	PAGE
Appointed to be Provost of Trinity College, Dublin	23, 24
Sir Henry Wotton's letter to King Charles I. in recommendation of Mr. Bedell	25
Bedell's Provostship	26-28
Made Bishop of Kilmore and Ardagh	29
His Consecration	30
Endeavours to reform abuses in the Episcopal jurisdiction	32
Opposition raised up against the Bishop's good intentions	33
His suit with the Chancellor of his Dioceses	34, 35
The Bishop holds his Courts in person	36-40
His Diocesan Synod	41
His efforts to restrain pluralities	43
Labours to spread the Gospel through the medium of the Irish Language	44, 45
Resigns the See of Ardagh	46, 47
Misappropriation of the Episcopal lands by his predecessors	48
Blamed for signing the Petition of the Protestants of the county of Cavan against the charges for soldiers	49-51
Persecution of Bishop Adair of Killala	52
Bishop Bedell extenuates the charges against Bishop Adair's conduct, and is blamed for so doing	53, 54
Final issue of the Chancery Suit between Bishop Bedell and the Chancellor of the Diocese, Mr. Alane Cooke	55, 56
Subsequent moderation of Mr. Cooke's conduct	56
Bishop Bedell's correspondence with Dr. Despotine	23, 57-59
Building and repairing of Churches in the Diocese of Kilmore	59, 60
Translation of the Old Testament into the Irish tongue	60, 61
Description of the Episcopal House of Kilmore and of the country around	62
Outbreak of the Rebellion	65
The British Protestants, stripped and driven from their homes by the Rebels, find refuge in the Bishop's house	65, 66
The Rebels filch away the Bishop's cattle	67
Molestation of the Bishop by the Rebels	67, 68
The Bishop refuses to abandon his post	69

	PAGE
The Rebels at last invade the Bishop's house	71
The Bishop taken prisoner and his household goods seized by the Rebels	72
Imprisonment in Loughoughter Castle	73-75
Liberated from imprisonment	75
Takes up his residence in the Rev. Denis Sheridan's house	76
The Sheridan Clan	76
The MS. Hebrew Bible which Bedell brought from Venice saved by Mr. Denis Sheridan	76
His Library scattered	77
Divine Service in the Rev. Denis Sheridan's house	77, 78
The Bishop falls ill of typhus fever	78
His last moments	79, 80
Death and burial	80, 81
The Bishop's Seal	81, 82

SUPPLEMENTARY CHAPTERS, GENEALOGICAL AND HISTORICAL, *compiled from original sources.*

CHAPTER I.

Birth and Parentage 85

CHAPTER II.

Education and entrance into Holy Orders—College Contemporaries 92

CHAPTER III.

Residence in Venice—Sir Henry Wotton—Father Paulo . 100

CHAPTER IV.

Return to England from Venice—Dr. Despotine . . . 124

CHAPTER V.

Marriage—Incumbency of Horningshearth—Literary labours—De Dominis—The Diodati Family 128

CONTENTS.

CHAPTER VI.
Removal to Ireland and Provostship of Trinity College, Dublin   142

CHAPTER VII.
Elevation to the Episcopate as Bishop of Kilmore and Ardagh—
Extortions of the Court Ecclesiastical—Resignation of Ardagh   147

CHAPTER VIII.
Family bereavements   160

CHAPTER IX.
Diocesan Synod   162

CHAPTER X.
Efforts to spread the Gospel through the medium of the Native
language—Irish translation of the Old Testament . .   171

CHAPTER XI.
The Irish Rebellion of 1641   181

CHAPTER XII.
Last illness and Death   189

CHAPTER XIII.
Bishop Bedell's last Will and Testament . . .   192

CHAPTER XIV.
Funeral and Tomb   195

CHAPTER XV.
Departure of Bishop Bedell's Sons from the county of Cavan   201

CHAPTER XVI.
The Sheridan Family   203

CONTENTS. xvii

	PAGE
CHAPTER XVII.	
The Rev. Alexander Clogie	211
CHAPTER XVIII.	
Captain Ambrose Bedell	221
CHAPTER XIX.	
The Rev. William Bedell and his Family	226
CHAPTER XX.	
Publication of the Old Testament in the Irish language . .	240

APPENDIX No. I.
Letter from Bedell to Sir Nathaniel Riche on the state of Trinity College, Dublin 253

APPENDIX No. II.
Letter from Bedell to Sir Robert Cotton about Ricemarcus' Psalter 256

APPENDIX No. III.
Pedigree of the Bedell and Elliston Families of Essex . . 258

Index 261

ERRATA.

Page 86, third line from the top, for "Johanne" read "Johanea."

P. 105, foot-note, fifth line from bottom, for "by Sancroft" read "by the deprived Bishops of Norwich, Peterborough, and Ely."

P. 140, seventeenth line from the top, for "initio" read "initia."

P. 146, sixteenth line from top, for "furthermore" read "furtherance," and after "lines," insert a period.

P. 175, ninth line from the top, for "to read" read "to be read."

P. 193, foot-note, fourth line from the bottom, for "possessed" read "professed."

A true relation of the Life and Death of the Right Reverend Father in God William Bedell, Lord Bishop of Kilmore, in Ireland.

Though the writing of Lives is subject to be abused both by author and readers, yet experience testifieth the usefullness and benefit of such compositions. And tho' the Genius of the person whose Life I write, and the Rule he seem'd to walk by all his daies, was *Bene qui latuit*, &c. yet two reasons especially seem to plead for this that here ensues: 1st, That some reparation may be made for the hard entertainment the world gave to this Bishop while he lived; and 2ndly, That his example may have the advantage of commiseration (usually granted to sufferers and the dead) to commend it the more to the imitation of others.

This eminent Servant of God, William Bedell, late Bishop of Kilmore, in Ireland, was born in the County of Essex, in England, in a village called Black-Notley, in the year 1571, of a stock or family of ancient continuance in that countrey, allthough of no great eminency for worldly greatness, his Father and Grand-father not exceeding the stile of Yoman.* His Father and Grand-father were both noted in their time for Love to true Religion. His Grand-father (upon that account being forced for some years to fly the lands,) was a man of extraordinary severity, insomuch that

* The year of William Bedell's birth is here correctly given as 1571, but a statement, which I have omitted, as to the time of the year is erroneous. It was his older brother John, who was no doubt born on Michaelmas Day, seeing that he was baptized on the 23rd of October, whereas William, who was baptized on the 14th of January, 1571-2, had most likely been born at Christmas time, possibly on Christmas day. See Supplementary Chapter I.—T.W. J.

CAMD. SOC. B

He had this rare faculty, that whatsoever art or language he would set himself to acquire, he would reduce it into a body, or method of his own contrivance: and of languages he would usually draw up a Grammar. So far did he descend in this kind, that on the desire of some Italian friends he compos'd an English Grammar: thereby letting them see our language to be reducible to the bounds of art, and not obscure and barbarous, as commonly they accounted it then beyond the seas, but elegant and copious, and easy enough.

But to return from this digression: During his abode at Cambridge (which was not fully the time allowed by the Statutes of the House) he had gain'd the repute of an eminent scholar, and a very grave and pious man. Much esteemed he was by Dr. Chaderton, then Master of the Colledge; and by the famous Mr. William Perkins,[*] tho' both were Fathers in comparison of him. The latter took a very great affection to him, and judg'd him worthy of his more intimate acquaintance: and in answer hereof Mr. Bedell likewise bare a filial respect to him, communicating his studies, and submitting them to his approbation and direction.

And now we must conceive him full-pace entred into the study of Divinity; wherof his first essay was in the discharge of the Office of Catechist in the Colledge. In the study of Divinity (as being the scope of all his other studies) 'tis hard to say whether he was a more hard student or a greater proficient. His excellent skill in scholastical and positive Divinity was highly commended by that miracle of all learning, Padre Paulo the Venetian, as we have it attested by the hon[rble] and memorable S[r] Henry Wotton in a letter to King Charles the First of blessed memory; expressing to his Ma[tie] his judgement of the said Mr. Bedell and his abilities.[†]

Mr. Bedell being thus furnished, 'twas easy to perceive to what course of life God had destinated and his own inclinations led him;

---

[*] Mr. William Perkins, Fellow of Christ's College, and Incumbent of St. Andrew's Church, Cambridge, was of a Puritanical turn, and much esteemed as a preacher. He died in 1602, aged 44.—T.W.J.

[†] See this letter, *infra*, p. 25.

which was the ministry. His entrance into Holy Orders was before he had left the University : concerning which he would complain of the greedy gaping for money by the officers and servants of the Bishop, without heeding so much the sufficiency or insufficiency of the man, as of money. Yet his Orders * he esteemed nevertheless religiously, tho' cumbred with some faults in the men that conferr'd them. His first call to the Ministerial work was to St. Edmundsbury in Suffolk : where the great esteem he gain'd for his grave, humble, and diligent discharge of that employment is yet surviving in the mouths and memories of many. His Auditory there was very much consisting of men of the best quality, and best abilities of Judgement and Learning, who yet ever received ample satisfaction in his sermons; being such both for matter and method as gave no occasion of slighting, but alwaies affording even to the most knowing some farther information.

It will not be amiss here to give a description of his manner and method of preaching, wherin then he was in a manner alone. His prayer before sermon was not set, nor fixed allwaies to the same form of words, but various in expressions, as the time and present occasions most required ; but ever in the plainest and easiest phrase of the English tongue, according to the capacity of the weakest understanding; so as the most unlearn'd hearer might say Amen. Yet he never affected tedious prolixity or needless verbosity; he allwaies avoided light expressions, and all words unbeseeming the spirituality and weightiness of the duty of prayer to God. No man less stinted in his gift of utterance, and yet no man more carefull in the government of his tongue.

His voice was low, his action little ; but the gravity of his aspect very great, and the reverence of his behaviour such as was more affecting to the hearers than the greater eloquence and more pompous pronunciation of others. In the handling of his text no

* Mr. Bedell was ordained Priest by Dr. John Stern, Bishop Suffragan of Colchester, on the 10th of January, 1596-7, being at that time twenty-five years of age.—T.W.J.

man in his time was more exact, whether in opening the coherence, or the words themselves. His greatest excellency was in making plain the hardest texts of Scripture, wherin scarce any man was comparable to him. His way was first thoroughly to scann the force of the words in the original languages, Hebrew, Syriack, Greek, &c. Next he would compare other places with his text, and such words or phrases of other texts, as were like those of his text in hand; and to be sure if any such were, he would never, through his familiar and perfect acquaintance with the Scripture, miss them. By this means 'twas wonderfull how great light he brought not only to the text in hand, but all other texts of Scripture which he had occasion to quote. And in no one respect is the loss of his writings more deplorable than in this.

Though his Library was large and choice (*sc.* that of Mr. Perkins,* with his own additions), yet he seldom or never used to cite any Author or Interpreter, in his sermons: but his Expositions ever appeared to be the results of comparing other texts, and of the force of the Original, and of the mind of the Holy Ghost. The sence being traced out, often was found to differ from the common interpretations: According to that of an ancient author, *Aliud est ad internos recessus veritatis in Sacrâ Scripturâ pertingere; aliud secundum vulgarem opinionem definire, vel explicare.* And divers of good knowledge and judgement in the Scriptures (even Divines) would wonder, first at the unusuallness of his expositions; secondly, that themselves had not seen it before, as he had rendred it. Where others would pass over words and sentences *sicco pede*, there would he discover rich springs of heavenly Doctrine most naturally flowing from the text.

Neither yet (for all this) was he ever the author or broacher of any novel opinion dissonant from the Doctrine of the Church of England; wherof no man was either a more able maintainer, or a more obedient observer. No, nor in the matter of Discipline was he any Innovator; though privately, and to those of chiefest emi-

* After Mr. Perkins' death in 1602, Mr. Bedell purchased his library.—T.W.J.

nency in the Church, no man ever more bewaild or opposed the abuses therin. But the peace of the Church was that which he ever held precious; and therefore he was tender of uttering anything that might give occasion to turbulent spirits.

What he chiefly sought in diving into the depths of Scripture was to find out all possible conviction of the Evilness of Sin, as also to store himself and his auditors with all possible motives to Virtue and Holiness of Life, judging those motives and arguments the best (not which man's art inventeth and fixeth to a text, but) which the Holy Ghost hath laid down in the Scripture it self: which to discover, and then to improve upon the consciences and minds of his hearers, he judged the duty and main business of preaching.

His doctrinal observations were commonly two or three in a sermon; which he needed not much to stand upon either for proof or illustration, having done that work before in the exposition of his text. Finally, his uses ever were very naturally flowing from his text, and (as he manag'd them) very moving, their force lying more in the clearness and evidence of their ground from Scripture (especially the text) and in the matter of them, than in the loudness or contention of his voice or vehemency of his gesture.

He was able to preach (and often did) upon very little warning; and his manner most what was to prepare himself only by meditation, yet allwaies writing down his Sermons after he had preach'd them. In short, for a preacher, he was the Substance of this poor shadow here set down.

Mr. Bedell thus furnished and call'd to the publick exercise of the Ministry in the Town of St. Edmund's Bury (where he succeeded Mr. Geo. Estey, one of incomparable learning, godliness, &c. who died there in the flowr of his age,) had not been long there, 'ere he had gain'd a great reverence, as well from all that savoured of the power of Godliness as from the Gallants, Knights, and Gentlemen, who reverenced him for his impartial, grave, and holy preaching and conversation, and heard him gladly. As for his esteem among the Ministers, it will appear in due place hereafter.

Having continued five years at Bury, he was, in 1607, chosen and appointed to join Sr Henry Wotton, Ambassador to the State of Venice, as Chaplain to the Embassy, which employment he willingly embrac'd, desiring to concoct his knowledge and learning attain'd at home by the observations of travel and the experience of forraign countreys. This employment being publick, his engagement at Bury could not detain him, especially promising at his return to fix there. After a difficult journey (especially in his passage over the Alps) he arriv'd safe at last in the City of Venice. It happened to be in a time of very weighty transactions between the then Pope, Paulus V. and that State; which was a singular opportunity for him to be throughly acquainted with the mysteries of Papal iniquity : for by occasion of the controversy just closed, between the Pope and the State of Venice, many corruptions and much of the Pope's nakedness became more publick than might well suit with the credit of the common cause of Popery. As King James (of famous memory) was very inquisitive into those affaires, so his Ambassador there found means to give his Majestie a full and punctual account from time to time: and Protestant Princes (he especially the most considerable) were not so coily entertain'd in their Embassies there, as the manner of that State had been in former times.

And as the time was extraordinary, so there was also then flourishing in Venice an extraordinary person, that Oracle of the Christian world, Father Paulo, a Friar of the Order of the Servi, a man of miraculous learning, prudence and integrity, as fully may appear both by his works, and specially by the History of his Life and Death now published in the English tongue;* though that

* The Life of the most Learned Father Paul, of the Order of the Servie. Councellour of State to the most Serene Republicke of Venice, and Author of the History of the Counsell of Trent. Translated out of the Italian by a Person of Quality. London, 1651.

From this statement it may be inferred that the MS. of the "Relation of the Life and Death of Bishop Bedell" before us, was written after 1651, though perhaps not much more than ten years.—T. W. J.

History is compos'd with more partiality to the Roman Religion than verity, as to the persuasion and judgement of the man. This man, besides his acquir'd and natural parts, God had enlightned with the knowledge of his truth so farr, as to see the detestable enormities of the Papacy, and Court of Rome, and to loath the same. So as it cannot be doubted but God rais'd him up and fitted him for such a season, and such a juncture of affaires. This was the man employed by the wisest State of Venice to draw up their Letters and Rescripts that passed between the Pope and them : Wherin, as also in his whole deportment in that business, he hath more solidly, tho' less bitterly, detected and confuted the fundamental corruptions of the Papacy, then ever any Protestant Writer before his time. This eminent Instrument, tho' hard to be seen or spoken with by men of best quality * (some that came in a manner for little else to that City, than out of admiration of his fame), yet with the English Ambassador and his Chaplain had entred into a strict familiarity, which to Mr. Bedell was a singular advantage : For by controverse with the Father he both armed himself against the Papists with their own weapons, and became. more polite in all his other learning.

It might, indeed, have been a dangerous thing to him (then a young man) to be in such a place; as some others, then and since, by travelling and converse among the Italians have shewed by their sad example : But, by God's mercy, he was better grounded in piety and good learning than to be easily subverted. He would often say that he could never meet with any thing among them of that side that did not rather confirm him than shake his persuasion of the truth of the Protestant reformed Religion.

During his abode in Italy he found opportunity of converse with some of the learneder sort of the Jews, wherin he intended these two purposes, the bettering himself in his skill in the Hebrew, and the drawing some of them to the embracing of Christ. In the former the success answered, but not so in the later, that people being

* See an instance of this in the anecdote of the Prince of Condé's visit to Father Paulo in 1622, in " The Life," *ut supra*, p. 152.—T. W. J.

extraordinary stiffnecked, as the Scripture foretold us. Some account we have of the reasons they alledge for themselves, in Mr. Bedell's letters to Mr. Wadsworth, now reprinted, together with this present History of his Life.*

Before we leave Italy we must not omitt his acquaintance there contracted with Dr Jasper Despotine, a Gentleman of noble extraction, who, tho' a younger brother, yet was in a fair way of raising himself by his eminent learning, and the great fame he had gain'd by his singular skill and judgement in Medicine. One thing which was a great hind'rance to his rising in his own Countrey was his judgement in Religion, varying from that of his Ancestors, and from the falsly called Catholick. His great learning and much reading was to him an occasion of seeing more into the true state of the controversy between us and the Romanists than is permitted to ordinary Papists. The change of his judgement was not suddain, nor without very strong endeavours to maintain and defend within himself the Religion wherin he had been educated. But still in process of time, and by degrees, God sent in more light into his mind, which he was not able to avoid. The unquietness of his mind was very great in this pendulous condition, and the greater because 'twas a matter of life and death to discover himselfe. A long time therefore it was before he could get clear and come to a resolution.

One notable passage concerning him is not to be conceal'd. It happen'd in Venice that a Lady of great quality fell sick, and, her sickness proving very dangerous, a consultation of Physitians was call'd to consider of her estate, who, upon enquiry and view of the patient, having resolved what was to be done, appointed two of their number (of whom Dr Despotine was one) to be constantly with the patient. But in short space neither the care nor art of the Physitians, nor the dignity of the person, availing against Death's approaches, all hope of recovery was taken away, and then spiritual

---

* The meaning of this appears to be that the author of this present History of Bishop Bedell's Life intended, in the event of its being published, to reprint along with it Bedell's Letters to Wadsworth.—T. W. J.

Physitians began to flock about her, some Jesuites, and some of other Orders. Dr Despotine still attending, observed diligently the demeanour of these religious men towards the dying Lady; she being now allmost senseless (for it was the last night of her life), the Jesuites and others her Confessors abode continually at her bed's side. The Jesuites were very urgent with her, that she would bestow liberally to religious uses, and namely upon their own Order; alledging the great reward of such good works, and the benefit of the prayers of their Fraternity; presenting unto her a Crucifix, moving her to call on Our Lady, the Patroness of women, and more especially of ladies. On the other side of the bed was a Capuchin Friar, and he (not in so many words, but more to the purpose) put the lady in mind of the Death and merits of Jesus Christ, and exhorted her to believe and trust in him, and committ her soul to his mercy. This different manner of proceeding us'd by these religious men mov'd the D^r much; and the more in respect of the weakness of the patient: Wherefore in all respectfull manner he besought the Fathers to suffer her to depart in as much quiet as might be, she being now incapable of farther comfort. Notwithstanding they (the Jesuites) with their tapers and crucifixes, and their calling still to the dying lady, left her not till her life had left her first: And then (it being past mid-night) the company with-drew into other rooms, the D^r into a gallery: To whom being there (whether accidentally or on purpose 'tis uncertein) the Capuchin Friar resorted; and so considering it was not farr from day, they agreed to abide there and discourse. The Friar, tho' till then unknown to the D^r, did presently fall upon discourse of the lady, and the manner of the Jesuites addresses to her, blaming their so urging her at the point of death to call upon Our Lady, without once mentioning Jesus Christ; and asking his judgement, if he did not then think it an undiscreet and unseasonable thing. The D^r, though his heart was full, yet durst not vent himself to a man of that profession, and a stranger; fearing some designe to draw forth his opinion and so to accuse him. And, therefore, with all his skill and diligence, he laboured to put off that discourse. But the Friar so much the more urgently press'd upon him, giving all assurance possible of his ingenuity and candour of moving that discourse: Wherupon the D^r could no longer hold, but freely spake his mind; and the Friar and he jump'd so just in their thoughts about that point, that from thence in their discourse they proceeded to some farther abuses then prevailing; in the dislike wherof their judgements did no less concurr than in the former. But still the D^r was very jealous. On the other side, the Friar opened himself so freely that he thank'd him most heartily for his company and discourse, and earnestly desir'd his farther acquaintance, inviting him in most affectionate manner to his cell, that so they might have farther conference; And so, the day being come, they parted upon terms of extraordinary love and familiarity. The D^r communicated this passage to his friends, who would by no means would advise him to goe any more to the Friar; assuredly gathering that all this openness and profession of love was but a trap. Wherupon, tho' he was confirmed in his persuasion of the truth of the Reformed Religion, yet his apprehensions of the dangers impending over his person and life were no whit abated. So that still he was fain to be upon his guard, retiring himself into privacy as much as possible.

In which condition God's providence brought him to the acquaintance of Mr. Bedell, by whom being made acquainted fully with the state of Religion in England, for the more free enjoyment of his conscience he came over to this countrey with Mr. Bedell at his return out of Italy. The labours and studies of this Dr. and his profund judgement in Divinity, are little known to the world, and especially his great zeal and courage in defence of the Truth against Popish and all other innovations. So tender was he in the doctrinal part of Religion that oftentimes he hath taken very great offence at certain passages and words falling from some of our English Preachers, neither ill-meant by them, nor ill-taken by others, only because they seem'd to him, tho' but by some remote consequence, to abett the Popish or Pelagian opinions. It had been happy, if in time ourselves had been as cautious; and if that Apostolical Canon,

1 Tim. i. 3, had been more strictly given in charge, and better observed among us.

But we must now return from this digression to Mr. Bedell. His stay in Italy was for some years, where he gain'd much experience and knowledge both in Divinity and the Oriental tongues, but especially in the state of Religion as it then stood in most parts of Christendom, having a farr better advantage for this at that time and there, than the bare reading of ecclesiastical History was able to afford. He was also there much improv'd in point of prudence and moderation, meeting there with men, tho' of another persuasion from himself in many points of Religion, yet very conscientious and unblameable in life and conversation, and no less detesting the tyranny of the Papacy, and the gross points of Popery, than the Protestants themselves.

Before his return he gain'd the Italian tongue, and so with his dear friend Dr. Despotine he came safe again into England. Being landed, he repaired with all convenient speed to his former Charge at St. Edmunds-Bury, where he wanted no wellcome from his many dear Christian friends, who could not but look upon him as a return of their prayers; those prayers which at his departure he publickly crav'd in his farewell-sermon to them on Heb. xiii. 18, 19: Pray for us, and the rather, that I may be restored unto you the sooner.

Having disposed of his friend Dr. Despotine and himself for some time, as sojourners in the house of one Mr. Nunne, he settled himself to his Studies and Ministerial employment, and the Dr. fell to Practice. But a very great difficulty was in the Doctor's way, namely, his want of the English tongue. But his friend Mr. Bedell would not see him suffer for this, but voluntarily took upon him to be his interpreter at any time whensoever any patient should resort unto him. But as entire friendship made this labour easy to Mr. Bedell, so to the Dr. the trouble and difficulty was hereby the rather encreased, for he was exceedingly perplex'd and griev'd to be thus troublesome to his friend, and thus to interrupt his studies.

And considering his condition, being a stranger wanting language, being unfit for humane society, and burthensom (as he accounted) to his friend, he was at first even weary of himself, so strong was the reciprocation of love between these two friends. Such examples of entire friendship were ever counted memorable and commendable, even by the greatest persons, tho' seldom found amongst them, through the inconsistence of greatness and ambition with such friendship. But between this pair this their love continued firm to the last; some other notable passages whereof we shall have occasion to touch in the sequel. In process of time difficulties grew less, and the Dr. gaining upon the English tongue, the need of an interpreter began to cease. Upon which occasion these two, Mr. Bedell first, and Dr. Despotine some years after, betook themselves severally to a stricter kind of friendship, namely, conjugal, as that which might afford each of them an helper more meet, than they were able to be one to another.

Mr. Bedell entred into the holy estate of Matrimony with a very pious, grave, and every-way-accomplish'd Gentlewoman, Mrs. Leah Maw, widow, daughter of John Bowles, Esqr, of Ersham in Norfolk, and late wife to Robert Maw, Esqr, Recorder of the Town of St Edmund's-Bury. There were diverse things on either side that might seem to disswade from this match: on her side that she must now come down from that gallantry in which she had been mainteined, according to the place and profession of her former husband, and that now she must marry a Minister, a noted contemner of the world's pomp: on his part, that she had five small children, and but a slender estate. But these weightier considerations (as his piety and ability for heavenly knowledge, as also his conscientious integrity, and again her no-less eminent endowments of nature, education, and grace, for a woman), mov'd them to consent together in Holy Wedlock, setting aside all secular considerations that might disswade. And well it were if such weightier considerations did more preponderate in marriages, and worldly respects less. By this

match Mr. Bedell became now charged with the care and education
of 5 orphans. The eldest Nicholas Maw, by his own labour, and
the benefit of that then-famous school of Bury, he brought up to
learning, who, after being sent to Cambridge, was taken into the
special care of Dr. Maw, then Master of Peter-house, and by him, as
he was capable, preferr'd to be first Scholar, and after Fellow of
that House, where he liv'd diverse years in good esteem for learning,
being both an acute and able scholar. But not fancying the study of
Divinity, to which his step-father much incited him, he fell to the
study of Physick, wherin he profited very much, and after a good
time for furnishing his mind with the Theory, he married and
settled in Practice in the City of London, where he grew in a short
space into great esteem. But God was pleas'd to call him away in
the spring of his daies and first rise of his worldly advancement.
Of the others, two departed in their childhood; the other two were
dear to Mr. Bedell as his own, and were by him provided for over
and besides their own portions. It pleased the Lord also to bless
him with four children of his own, 3 sons and a daughter: In whose
education, next to Godliness, his earnest care was to make his sons
Scholars: and he would often tell them, if he knew which of them
would not be a Scholar, he would not leave him a groat.

He pass'd thus some 4 or 5 years more at Bury, as Preacher there.
The weakness of his voice, however, was found a great defect in so
large a Church as St. Mary's, as himself (with no small grief) did,
from his very first setling there, apprehend. He, therefore, was
resolv'd, when God should offer an opportunity, to remove and give
way to some of more audible voice; And God's providence was not
wanting. For among those worthy Knights and Gentlemen, that were
lovers and honourers of Mr. Bedell, Sr Thomas Jermin more especially
did study, and wait to doe him all good offices possible. And the
Rectory of Great Horningshearth, of his donation, falling void, S^t
Thomas freely presented Mr. Bedell to this charge. The place being
near Bury, and the congregation there not very great, but such as
his voice might reach, he accepted the presentation; not indeed to

the full satisfaction of his Bury friends, tho', the disproportion of his voice to their great assembly being considered, they could say no great matter against it. But, however, to give them all possible satisfaction, Mr. Bedell engaged himself to supply their Fryday Lecture for a year or longer as they should think fit : which he performed with advantage after his remove to Horningshearth.

But his first entrance upon his charge was not without some rubbs: For, being to repair to the Bp of Norwich, Dr Jegon, for Institution, altho' no scruple was made against his person or title, yet the demands of the Bps. Officers for his Instruments were very high; insomuch that Mr. Bedell, first to the Officers though all in vain, and then to the Bp. also himself, protested against the illegality of demanding such fees; and alleadg'd it to be no less than Simony on his part as well as theirs, if he should give them their demands. And in conclusion the Bp. being unmoveable from the principles of himself and his officers, alleadging that they demanded no more than what others were us'd to give in that case, Mr. Bedell profess'd his resolution never to take a living on those terms, so unwarrantable either by the Word of God, or ancient Canons of the Church; and so was fain to come away without his living. This accident did not a little trouble both the Bp., Sr Thomas Jermin, and Mr. Bedell himself: The Bp. in regard to the eminency of the man, whom he had sent home *re infectâ* ; Sr Thomas in regard of the frustration of his good intentions to the people of Horningshearth ; and Mr. Bedell himself was much troubled that it was his hap to be forc'd to this so publick appearing against the corruptions of the Bishop, and his Officers. And, therefore, he addressed a letter to the Bp. more fully showing the reasons, why in conscience he durst not yield to the paying of those illegal exactions: by which letter the Bp. was so farr mov'd that he caus'd the Instruments of his Institution and Induction soon after to be sent unto him: leaving it to his choice to pay what he thought fit.

And now we are to conceive Mr. Bedell settled at Horningshearth : where we shall consider him in a 3-fold relation : to his own Family;

to his Parishioners, and to his Neighbour Ministers. In his family-relation, his example and authority were such as to command the reverence of all. His children he had in very great subjection and nurture; wherin God had given him a Helper conformable and answerable to himself; both of them, as in all things, so in this happily concurring. And tho' oftentimes, where children of two several companies are in one family, discords arise either between the Children or Parents, or both; yet their impartiality and joint care for the good of all was such that no considerable emulation or variance was ever found among the Children, nor the least difference between the Parents.

His manner was, to rise very early (commonly at 4 winter and summer) and so to retire presently to his study; where he would be so fix'd till Prayer-time, that if any thing (as business of the family, or some stranger or neighbour comming to speak with him,) did happen to call him down, he would be even angry with the messenger (wife, child, or servant) of any such occasion of interruption.

For prayer he observ'd three seasons, Morning, Noon, and Evening, never tedious or prolix: At noon, his manner was to read and expound some chapter of the Bible befor prayer. His expositions were methodical, concise, and substantial.

As his children grew up (their mother having taught them to read English, and give an account of the heads of the Catechism,) he took them under his own teaching; and two of his sons he thus instructed for some years. But his other many occasions, as hereafter will appear, and his studies especially, not allowing so great a distraction, he was fain to give that task over.

Some little recreation he used to take before dinner or supper: which, for the most part, was planting, transplanting, grafting, and inoculating, and sometimes digging in his garden.

In his dress he was a great lover of plaineness, both for the matter and fashion; never changing the fashion in all his life. His rules were easiness for the stirring of his body and serviceableness;

avoiding all vanity and superfluity. And in his Children he still laboured to have the same rules observed; wherein onely he differ'd something from the disposition of his wife; she, according to her education, sex, and the quality of her former husband, affecting elegancy and neatness of habit, which also she did sometimes endeavour to observe in her children. But his will and authority bore the sway. Some of his friends would blame him for this carelessness and neglect (as they counted it). But among other grave answers he usually gave, this was one: That in our Baptisme we had all avow'd to forsake the pomps and vanities of this wicked world.

When his Friends came to visit him, his entertainment was friendly, neat, and bountifull; But his grave deportment and savory discourse surmounted all, being of such influence, that it gave a law to the company and held them (as it were) under a kind of discipline; which that he might somewhat relax and yet not warp from his own principles, he would retire from them to his study, with some grave item, leaving them to enjoy themselves. If they were Ministers or Scholars, he would tarry longer; but so as he would be sure their discourse should be profitable.

And here it cannot be omitted what an admirable gift and grace God had given him in the command and ordering of his speech. For as he was well-stored with all kinds of knowledge; so he was of such sanctified wisdom, that still he would be communicating to others: and that in such a pleasing and delightfull way, that not the least appearance of pride or vain glory could be found in his discourse: no place left for vanity, if he were present; nothing could be heard but piety and morality; no man present but was either pleased, or profited, or charmed. If any other would speak anything savory, he would stand still and hear; yea, of the two, he was more forward to learn than teach; to heare rather than to speak; giving place to any tho' his inferiors by many degrees. Yea, by an art he had, he would so observe the tempers of men, that in discourse with them he would draw forth whatever good was in them, suppressing any vanity by his gravity, and hiding any ignorance by his wisdom and humility. In a word, scarce any man in his time ever exceeded him in the Government of the Tongue : as if God had designed him for a lively and practical Edition of Mr. Perkins's excellent treatise of the Government of the Tongue.* And indeed that Man of God was the man, whom Mr. Bedell did very much propound to himself for imitation.

There is yet farther to be noted, in his domestical course of conversation, his behaviour to the beggars, bedlams, and travellours that use to come to men's doors. These he would not fail to examine, mixing both wholsom instructions and severe reproofs. Nor rested he there; but if they had any passes to travel by, he would be sure to scan them throughly, and finding them false or counterfeit, his way was to send for the Constable, and after correction given according to law, he would make them a new pass, and send them to the place of their last settlement or birth. This made him so well known among that sort of people, that they shun'd the Town for the most part; to the no small quiet and security of him and all his neighbours.

One principal point more is yet behind, and that is his manner of governing his family upon the Lord's day. Being risen himself (most commonly the first in the house), he presently retir'd to his study, and, while he was busied in Prayer and Meditation, his Wife was hastening to get the Children ready, a convenient time before the publick meeting, that all might be in order against his comming down to Prayer in the family. His company being assembled together he would come down among them, but as at all times, so more especially then, with his countenance compos'd to all possible gravity, piety, and solemnity; indeed, the presence of that day, and his deportment together, wrought no small effects both upon children and servants, as to preparation for the service of God, and so truly was he God's Vice-gerent in his family. Before prayer sometime he would give such admonition to his company as he

---

* William Perkins, Fellow of Christ's College, Cambridge, A Direction for the Government of the Tongue, according to God's Word. 8vo. Lond. 1593.—T. W. J.

judged most suitable, and then falling down on his knees he would pray among them, which being done, all repaired together to Church. In the passage from his house to the Church, which was not very far, strict notice was taken of the gestures and behaviour of his children, either by himself or to be sure by his consort, an helper to him to the height in these best things. But especially their words were observ'd. And when once they were come to the place, then all possible reverence and attention were expected both from children and servants ; and of such failings as were committed this godly couple were diligent observers and severe correctors.

Besides his sermons forenoon and afternoon, he used to catechise the youth openly in the face of the congregation, whom he instructed not only to answer in the words of the Catechism, but also to answer such other material questions as might make them understand the principles of Religion. His manner was for an half hour clearly to expound, in order, a certein portion of the Catechism every Lord's-day, so as to go through it once a year. Wherein not only were the younger sort much benefited, but even the elder and most judicious of his auditours found a great measure of satisfaction, and they would profess that they accounted his catechising every whit as profitable as his preaching.

And this leads me, in the next place, to his deportment to the people in his charge, with whom he had a very great authority, not only by reason of his diligent preaching and holy example of life, but especially his constant use of private admonitions and reproofs, which, tho' some stomack'd at, yet they durst not openly despise. The poorest of all he had a tender care over in this respect, whom he used bountifully to relieve every year. The others he entertained at his table once a year all through the whole Parish, with whom he would be very cheary, and yet in so pious and profitable a manner that their minds and souls were no less feasted than their bodies, sin and vanity being allwaies thrust out of doors for wranglers.

Having obtained so great a place in their affections, his due maintenance came in with the more ease to him, and willingness as from them. He held it as a principle of conscience earnestly to preserve the rights of the Church. The edifices which belonged to him as Rector to uphold, he was allwaies carefull to keep in good and sufficient repair. And his care extended herein even to posterity, for he left behind him a Book to his Successours, giving them a clear and exact account what dues to expect from the Parishioners, and some light for clearing of controversies and difficulties about tithing, that might afterward arise. His great exactness herein was the occasion of a long suit between him and William Lucas, Esqr, one of the chiefest of his Parish. The matter was this: Mr. Bedell was given to understand that certein pieces of ground in the possession of Mr. Lucas had formerly belonged to the Rectory of Great Horningshearth, and some then living were able to give pregnant testimony in the business, while no small probabilities were easily gathered by view of the ground itself. Yet for his own fuller satisfaction, by the favour of the Lord of the Mannor, he got liberty to search the Rolls and Records belonging to the Mannor, wherein by his great pains and sagacity he found such light into the business as convinc'd him in his conscience that those grounds by right belong'd to the Church. Whereupon making his claim with all possible respect to Mr. Lucas, expressing his own unwillingness to spend his time in law, or to have any contention with so unequal a match as he, being also his Neighbour and Parishioner, and yet alleadging the tie of conscience urging him to maintain the right of the Church; he receiv'd no other return from Mr. Lucas than in effect a denial of any right of the Church in those lands, and a plain signification of his resolution not to part with them otherwise than by course of law. The suit being commenc'd, besides the charge and expense of time, Mr. Bedell met with grievous vexations, because of the strange delaies and other stratagems of the lawyers. Yet the terms between him and his adversary were fair, as such a long and chargeable suit might permit; the lasting whereof was ten years and upwards. In short the issue was, that after some arbitrations without success, it was concluded by the final award of one man, and the land return'd to the Church, tho' not the same *in specie*, yet the same in quantity, and in a place more convenient for the Minister.

This unhappy occasion, being thus of so long continuance, did necessitate Mr. Bedell to some study of the law, wherein (his own chargeable practice concurring, as also through his great abilities for whatsoever he did undertake,) he became strangely knowing and dexterous for a man of his calling: insomuch as, even during the agitation of his own cause, he was so observed for his abilities, that he was frequently chosen Commissioner, or Arbitrator, in the most difficult controversies that happen'd in the countrey round about; which leads us to consider in what terms he stood with his Neighbours in the Countrey, and especially the Neighbour Ministers.

And here, not to insist upon the frequent applications of several to him for advice, and resolution in doubts and questions in Divinity and other Learning, nor how he was still acquainted with and made party to most Conferences that happened between any of his Neighbours and the Papists, nor to mention what worthy men of the Ministry were his intimate friends and familiars; it shall be sufficient only to insist upon one passage more-than-ordinarily considerable, and that was this:

While he was Rector of Great Horningshearth a Parliament was called, at which, according to the ancient custom, a Convocation of the Clergy also was to attend, to the making up whereof, besides the Bishop and other Dignitaries, two Ministers were to be chosen in the Diocess of Norwich, to represent the Clergy, one for Norfolk, and another for Suffolk. But, as it often falls out, there was much packing and plotting and making of friends by the more ambitious of the Clergy to be chosen for that honour, as they accounted it, insomuch that Mr. Bedell himself was dealt withall by letter, and otherwise, touching the disposal of his voice at the Election. But those indirect proceedings did make such an impression upon his spirit that he wholy declined the meeting appointed for the Election. The ministers being met upon the day, there was great stickling, and much opposition of some against others, till at last Mr. Bedell himself, that was absent, and never made any means for the employment, was the man they pitch'd upon.* The news whereof no sooner came to his ears but it presently affected him with a great deal of grief and dislike, as he spared not to his friends sadly to express to this effect, that he knew he should but loose his time, and sit there and tell the clock, without doing any good, as to what the present exigencies of the Church did most require. And indeed the issue proved his fear too true, which before him Bp. Andrews feared, and prayed against, in his *Concio ad Clerum*, in a Provincial Synod, where he hath these words, Synodum celebrare, non fuit Paulo tum (utinam verò nec nobis nunc) Χρονοτρι-βῆσαι; the holding of a synod was not to St. Paul then (I wish it were not now to us) a wasting of time: he means when St. Paul held the Synod at Miletus. But we have seen sufficient to demonstrate Mr. Bedell's esteem with his Brothers of the Ministry.

And now we must proceed to his removall out of England into Ireland, to be Governour of the University and Colledge of Dublin, from which time till the end of his daies the antient love and friendship between him and Dr Despotine was mainteined, so that their great distance both by land and sea from each other could not hinder a continual entercourse of letters between them; wherein nothing of moment in either Kingdom, whether of publick concernment, or touching their own personal affaires, but still they communicated one to another. And this is therefore here mentioned to

* The date of the election was February 13, 1623. See Memoranda by Rev. W. Cole, in Add. MS. 5832, in British Museum. In Bishop Goodman's Court of King James I. there is, at page 325 of Volume II., a letter to Dr. Samuel Warde, Master of Sidney College, Cambridge, dated from London April 16, 1624, in which Mr. Bedell refers to his attendance in Convocation. The original of this letter is in the Tanner Collection lxxiii. 425, in the Bodleian Library, Oxford.—T. W. J.

advertise the Reader that the main of the ensuing narration, and in many places the very words, are nothing but what Mr. Bedell's own letters to Mr. Despotine have furnished: all other his writings, which might have much help'd on this work, being unhappily lost, together with his library, in that overflowing scourge of the Rebellion of Ireland.*

To returne then to his remove into Ireland; we may observe a special and extraordinary hand of God therein; which Mr. Bedell himself in a letter to his friend the D^r thus expresseth : " My greatest encouragement is, that I have not put my self into this place, but, as I hope, I may truly say I follow God. And, indeed, not only the thing it self, but the juncture of time when it was effected and the instruments helping it on, have much of God observable in them." That a private Countrey Minister so far distant and of so retir'd a life should be sought, for such a publick and eminent employment; That this should be immediately upon the determination of his long suit and recovery of those lands of the Church, to vindicate him from all imputation of self-seeking, and to take him off from all dreggs of anger and dissention, which such a suit might have in the bottom; Finally, that two so eminent men for Learning and Holiness, as those two famous Primates, George Abbot, Archbp. of Canterbury, and James Usher, Archbp. of Armagh, should be the chief instruments of his call to that place; these circumstances cannot be denied to have a special hand of God going along with them, and cannot but testify both the favour of God towards him and his own great abilities. Upon the commendation, therefore, of these two Archbishops, he was chosen by the Fellows of the Colledge, and petitioned for to his Majestie ; who was graciously pleased, upon the testimony of Sr Henry Wotton, to assent to the Fellows' petition. This testimony is given in the following letter from Sir Henry to King Charles I.:—

* In the supplement hereto annexed it will be found that many of the letters from Mr. Bedell to others of his friends have been preserved.—T. W. J.

" May it please yor Matie,
" Having been informed that certain persons have by the good wishes of the Archbp. of Armagh been directed hither, with a most humble petition to your Matie, that you will be pleased to make Mr. Wm. Bedell (now resident upon a small benefice in Suffolk) Governour of your College at Dublin, for the good of that Society; and my self being requir'd to render unto your Majestie some testimony of the said Mr. William Bedell, who was long my chaplain at Venice in the time of my first employment there ; I am bound in all conscience and truth (so far as your Majestie will be pleased to accept my poor judgement,) to affirm of him, that I think hardly a fitter man for that charge could have been propounded unto your Majestie in your whole Kingdom, for singular erudition and piety, conformity to the rites of the Church, and zeal to advance the cause of God ; wherin his travells abroad were not obscure in the time of the excommunication of the Venetians ; For it may please your Majestie to know that this is the man whom Padre Paulo took (I may say) into his very soul : with whom he did communicate the inwardest thoughts of his heart; from whom he professed to have received more knowledge in all divinity, both scholastical and positive, than from any he had ever practiced in his daies, of which all the passages were well known to the late King, your father, of blessed memory.* And so with your Majesties good favour I will end this needless office : For the general fame of his learning, his life, and christian temper, and those religious labours † himself hath

* In a letter (Public Record Office) from Venice dated August 14, 1609, to King James, Sir Henry Wotton says: " My chaplain (whom I am bound to commend unto your Maties goodness for a person of singular lerning and zeale) hathe translated the whole work (King James' ' Apologie ' and ' Premonition ') into this Vulgar (Italian language)."—T. W. J.

† " The Copies of Certain Letters which have passed between Spaine and England in Matter of Religion." Dedicated to the King when Prince of Wales, 1624.

" Interdicti Veneti Historia." A translation into Latin from the Italian of Father Paulo. Dedicated to the King, 1626.—T. W. J.

E

dedicated to your Majestie doe better describe him, than I am able.

"Your Majesties most humble and faithfull servant,
"H. WOTTON."

Mr. Bedell thereupon was made and sworn Provost* of the Colledge of the Holy and Undivided Trinity, near Dublin, in Ireland. This beginning of that part of his life spent in Ireland was (as we see) favoured with the most benign aspect, not only of the best and greatest personages among us, but of God himself, as a sweetning and preparative for the more stormy and troublesome part of his life that was to follow.

During his abode at the Colledge, he was often honoured with the visits and invitations of the greatest persons about the city : As the Archbps. of Armagh, Dublin, and Cashell ; the Lords Clanebois, Angier, and Dowckra ; and in a special manner he had the favour of the Lord Deputy Falkland. His yearly stipend was 100^{li}, to which he had 20^{li} per annum added for preaching a Lecture every fortnight at Christ's Church ; and this was the utmost of his revenew.

As touching his managing of business in the Colledge ; his first care was concerning the Statutes of the House, in which he made some alterations, and some additions to them, and reduced them into a more exact method : But especially he looked more diligently to the strict observance of them, than formerly had been used. In his alteration of the Statutes, it might manifestly appear that he sought the good of the society, and not his own ; and all still with special reference to the good of the Church : Nothing being aimed at either for the addition of maintenance or outward splendor to himself or to the Fellows ; but that every Fellow should study Divinity, and after 7 years' stay should goe out into some employ

---

* Mr. Bedell "was admitted and chosen by the unanimous consent of the Fellowes the XVIth of August, 1627." *Register of the University.*—T.W.J.

in the Church; that the Natives of the Countrey should be exercised in the reading and writing of their own language, that they might be the fitter to convert their countreymen the Irish; that no Acts, Disputation, or Declamation in any other Science or Art, save in Divinity, should at any time be kept in the Chappell ; that the students should allwaies weare their gowns as well in the City as in the Colledge ; that on the Lord's-days, the Fellows, Scholars, and all other the Students should goe together, and accompany the Provost to Church, all in their gowns: Such are some of the heads of those additions which he made to the Statutes. The whole body whereof he wrote out and left in the Colledge. And they bear the name of Bedell's Statutes to this day.

One thing among the rest is not to be forgotten. It·was provided in these Statutes, that allwaies before dinner and supper in the Hall, the Scholars of the House in their turns, every one his week, were to read a Chapter in the Latin Bible, and then to give thanks ; and after meat was brought in, and a little space of time allowed, the Reader was to goe up the Fellows' table (where seldom but the Provost himself was present), and there recite some verse of the Chapter that was read, to give occasion of savory and profitable discourse ; which to be sure, when he was present, was improv'd accordingly.

He was strict in exacting the performance of Divinity Acts as commonplacings and disputations, required by the Statute of the Fellows, wherein himself would still take the first turn; and oftentimes he would dispute at other times with an Argument or two upon the Respondent; which sometimes produced some pretty strong tugging between him and the Moderator (which allwaies was the Divinity Professor, Dr. Hoile) to the great delight and profit of the hearers.

Besides this and such like ordinary work of his place, he us'd, on the Lord's Day, between dinner ended and church, to expound in the Chapell some part of the Catechism ; to which exercise diverse of the most devout persons of the City used to resort. And in this way of settlement his Government in the Colledge proceeded for some time without any manifest disturbance.

But 'twas not long ere some tempestuous winds arose to the no small disquiet of his and the Colledge's peace. Two particulars the Reader may take notice of; one was a schism among the Fellows, arising from a National antipathy. For the Society consisting partly of Brittish, and partly of Irish, it came to pass that there were contradictions and bandyings, one side against another, in all their meetings and consultations: whereby business of publicque concernment was hindred; the House became divided against it self; the Provost was rendred suspected by one side or other, for his moderation and endeavour to keep down this contention; and in short things grew to that height that the Visitors were necessitated to interpose, least the matter should have grown to open scandal. This last refuge, the authority of the Visitors, being join'd with the wisedom and moderation of the Provost, was a means for some time to keep down this fire; but could not extinguish it.*

Another disturbance arose from the Professor, Dr Joshuah Hoile,† a man of great learning, zeal, and piety, but over-hott. The occasion was this: Mr. Bedell, in his Catechiseings and Sermons and at other discourses, used still rather to contract the differences between Protestants and Papists, than to widen them. One thing among the rest he had uttered his judgment in, vizt: the Church of Rome to be a true Church: Which in effect wise men know to mean no more, than that God hath a Church, tho' in the Dominions

---

* A disturbance in the College similar to that here alluded to, appears to have occurred also about the end of the year 1627, while Mr. Bedell was absent in England arranging his affairs there preparatory to his final departure and settlement in Ireland.—T.W.J.

† Dr. Joshua Hoyle became Fellow of Trinity College, Dublin, in 1609. He was Professor of Divinity in the College, and tutor to Sir James Ware. Afterwards, in 1641, he removed to Oxford, where he was Master of University College, and Professor of Divinity in the University. Dr. Joshua Hoyle's name occurs in the list of the Divines who met in the Assembly at Westminster. He died in 1654.—T.W.J.

and under the tyranny of the Pope: and withall he was still wont to distinguish between the Church of Rome and Court of Rome. But this much disrelished with the Professor, who being at that time in his ordinary Divinity Lectures engaged in the confutation of Bellarmine, and being to common-place on a time in his course, chose the text, Revel. xviii. 4, Come out of her my people : Whence he took occasion too plainly to glance at the Provost with somewhat more sharpness (being a hot and zealous man) than could be well digested, without disparagement to his place. But the Provost contented himself only with the satisfaction of a private conference in the Professor's own chamber, immediately after the Sermon; where they debated the business largely together like Scholars, all in Latin, without any witness unless a Sizar, and parted good friends ; and no more was ever after heard of that matter, saving only that the Professor afterward to some of his acquaintance gave the Provost the commendation of a pure Ciceronian, as ever he had discoursed with.

And having been thus employed and exercised awhile in the College not much more than a year from his first settled residence in the place; * God's Providence called him forth into the Government of the Church: wherein he spent the remainder of his life, and wherein we shall find him exceedingly tossed with many and great troubles. His entrance and first advance to this employment was principally by the mediation and procurement of his noble friend and patron Sr Thomas Jermine; who moved the King's Majestie in his behalf and with some difficulty obtained for him the Bishopricks of Killmore and Ardagh, before Mr. Bedell was acquainted in the least with any such designe. The difficulty of effecting this was

* After his admission as Provost, August 16, 1627, Mr. Bedell returned to England and remained there until June, 1628; when, having settled his affairs in England he returned to Dublin with his family and took up his settled residence in the College as Provost. The patent by which he was appointed to the Bishoprics of Kilmore and Ardagh was dated May 29, 1629.—T.W. J.

such, that Sr Thomas was forced to engage for him to his Majestie, as farr as a man might be responseable for another. The cause of this difficulty, perhaps, may appear afterwards. It is not to be omitted how little ambitious he was of any such advancement: for before his acceptance of the Bishopricks he seriously consulted with the Lord Archbp. of Armagh, and crav'd his advice about it: professing himself so indifferent that, if his Grace should judge it more behovefull for the Church that he should still stay at the Colledge, he would then some way decline the Bishopricks. Also to his friend Dr Despotine his expressions concerning this his preferment speak the same : " Thus your friend, who never desir'd or dream'd of this or any other Bishoprick (more than to be Pope of Rome) is to have two Bishopricks at a clap, being insufficient for one." But upon the advice and encouragement of the Ld Primate he accepted the Bishopricks.

And now the next thing was his Consecration, which he was to receive from the most Reverend James Usher, Lord Archbp. of Armagh, to whose Province his Bishopricks did belong. But it happened to be at the time of the Archbishop's triennial Visitation, which was usually managed by the Chancellour, and Register of the Archbishop. And had it only been used to keep up the dignity and preheminence of the Archbishop above the other Bishops of his Province, or for the reformation of such Bishops as were negligent or corrupt in their places, the matter had not been great, but by vertue of this triennial Visitation every Bishop was inhibited from exercising any Jurisdiction, as well the good as the bad, all causes were remov'd from the Bishop's to the Archbishop's Court, and the Sees of Kilmore and Ardagh being now vacant, the Archbishop's Officers were the more active to improve their time, and not willing to be interrupted by the coming in of the new Bishop. Whereupon his Consecration was deferr'd a long time.* But the new Bishop made no hast, resolving in matters of this

* He was consecrated on the 13th of September, 1629.—T.W.J.

nature (as he wrote to his friend the D^r) to follow rather than to lead.

At his Consecration (and so after) he was to enter of necessity .o a more costly garb, both for attire and attendance, than ever .e had used, and this was no small trouble to his humble and heavenly mind. His own wisedom prompted him to some conformity to the Episcopal rank, and his friends were sollicitous lest he should render himself contemptible or lie under sinister censures, by coming too much behind other Bishops in state and gallantry. And, therefore, he took a middle way, rising a little, but differing very much in outward splendor from the rest of his order. He never wore silk, only his girdle, chimier, and tippet were of that material. Never wore bever, castor, or demi-castor, but allwaies felts. He used not to ride up and down the streets of Dublin about his occasions, with his three or four men attending, as was the common usage of the Bishops there, but allwaies walk'd with only one man. And till the time of the Earl of Strafford (for till then 'twas optional) he very seldom used to ride with the State to Church on Sundaies, and when he did it was with as little state as possible. And tho' in this practice he did discontent some, and suffered the gibes of the more Lordly Prelates and their followers, yet he could not be altered. Going to visit a Bishop in plain habit, with shoes made for ease and use (not with high Polonian heels, &c.), " How now, my Lord," (said that Bishop,) " do you weare brogues?" (so the Irish call their shoes) jearing him for his plainness and his known affection to the Irish nation. But he kept his usual composedness, and fell presently upon that Church-business which occasioned his visit, and so spoil'd the jeast by taking no notice of it, and withall gave a sober check to the levity of it.

But we shall now carry the Reader along with our Bishop of Killmore in his plain accoutrements to his Diocess, and take some view of his carriage and entertainment there. And the first thing observable may be his sense of those presents (as horses, fat oxen, brawns) that came then frequently unto him, some from his Officers, and some from his Tennants, and some from Ministers of his Diocess. These were sent so thick that they were a very great disquieting to his mind, for his way was, either to offer money for such as came from farr, and that might be usefull to him for his present necessity, or if that were refused (as allwaies it was, even with indignation as a kind of an affront), then utterly to deny acceptance of any such present. It is hardly credible what discontent arose against him, partly for this refusing of presents, and partly for the plainness of his habit and attendance. Some abstained not from scoffs and scorns, thus seeking to allay their own disappointment and mortification by laying loads on him whom they found inflexible to their corrupt interests.

But notwithstanding all such unkind wellcoms, the Bishop, armed with integrity, patience, and holy zeal for God and the Truth, proceeded with all diligence to acquaint himself of the state of his Diocess, bending his studies wholly and to the utmost of his power that way to reform. And God's Providence concurr'd, for he was no sooner a little settled in his See, but multitudes of complaints daily came in, especially against his Chancellour and those others that under him managed the Jurisdiction. It was the more grievous to the Bishop to meet with such complaints, for that the cause was given by his own officers, and the wrongs done in his own name. And, therefore, with all convenient speed he appoints a Visitation, that so he might see fully and certainly into the state of things.

But at his Visitation, upon some free actings and impartial proceedings of his, for redress of the grievances of some complainants, his Chancellour openly oppos'd him, for going about to alter the course of proceedings observed in his predecessour's time, for intrenching upon the place and office of the Chancellour, as an Innovator, as going about to eradicate all the Professours of the Civil Law, and what not ? And he found some of the Clergy that were not asham'd to abett the Chancellour in this opposition to the Bishop's good intentions for reformation.

It is strange, how high the rage of Satan and men's malice flew against him, at his very first stirring, tho' but gently, for some Reformation. One while they attempted to scare him with the name of a Præmunire, but he too well understood the laws to incurr that danger. Another while they thought to discourage him with giving out that he was a Papist, an Arminian, a Polititian, an Italian, a Neuter. The eies of all men were upon him, the mouths of all open'd against him; he was as a wonder to many, and was forc'd to bear their reproaches and the smitings of their tongues; there was none to stand by him, or scarse to speak a word in his favour. His own nearest friends and relations were no small disheartning to him, as looking upon him and his actings according to the common vote, and help'd rather to break his heart and courage in the cause of God than any way to support him. There was not any worldly gain or advantage in the least to be expected, in case he should have been able to attain his ends, but to be sure he must be at great expences, both of his body, means and time, to the divorcing him from his studies (as he complain'd to his friend the D^r). But none of all these things, nor any worldly considerations, could withold him from using his best endeavour to discharge his conscience in that place God had called him to.

And therefore he begins first with his pretended Chancellour, Mr. Alane Cook, after Dr Cook. For, having received sad complaints against him (the particulars out of respect to the dead shall now be spared), the Bishop held himself obliged to see to the management of the Jurisdiction in his own Diocess, and having met with so hot opposition from Mr. Cooke to his face in open Court, for but beginning to meddle with the rectifying what he judged amiss, he desired to see his Commission or Patent, by which he held the place of Chancellour, signifying farther, that being he was an officer under him, and acting in his name, he must needs therefore call him to account for his actings.

Mr. Cook's Patent being shewn, was found to be only a grant of the Chancellour's place to him from the precedent Bishop, under his hand, and confirmed by the Dean and Chapter.* There were also other just grounds of exception from the incongruence of the syntax, a principal verb being wanting that was to govern a long sentence of about five hundred words. Besides that, the Bishop alleadged that it was against the Canon-law for a Bishop to have a servant (as the Chancellour is) impos'd upon him by his predecessor. These and some other defects in the instrument itself, but especially the exorbitancies of the person, begat a long and chargeable suit between the Bishop and his Chancellour.

The first scene hereof was the Archbishop's Court, and there tho' the Archbishop himself (that renowned Usher) was forward enough to give the Bishop of Kilmore a fair hearing and an equal sentence, yet, alass! he was no more at his own disposal in it than the Bishop of Kilmore could be in causes depending in his Court, the Archbishop being alike tied up by the fullness of [Dr Synge] his Chancellour's power, as the Bishop was by his.

And besides, this was like to be a leading case, that, if determin'd for the Bishop, might have hazzarded to have been an occasion of shortning both the power and the profit of all Chancellours, Registers, &c. and might have proved no small diminution of those honours and preferments which Professours of the Civil law propound to themselves, as the rewards of their study and practice. Thus Mr. Cook labored to represent this case, and thus without much adoe the business presently was resented by the Civilians, so that all as one contributed their uttermost for the mainteining Mr. Cook and worsting of the Bishop, insomuch that when according to the form of those Courts he was to retain a Proctor, none would undertake his cause, 'till one of the meanest they could find was assigned by the Court, and that was in this case as if a man's Adversary should be his Counsel or Attorney,

---

* The patent was not sealed with the Bishop's great seal, though confirmed by the Dean and Chapter. Letter from Bp. Bedell, dated August 7, 1630, to Bishop Laud, in the Public Record Office. See Supplementary Chapter VII.—T. W. J.

tho' how such a man's cause might be likely to thrive any one may judge.

But, notwithstanding this cold comfort, the good Bishop thought himself bound in conscience to do his endeavour for the regulating his Chancellour, and reforming the proceedings in his jurisdiction, and, therefore, trusting his Proctor as little as he could, he applied himself to the management of his own cause in his own person. He missed not a Court-day, tho' the place (being the City of Drogheda) was thirty miles distant from his house. He drew his Answers himself, or whatever else was to be given in in writing, being very throughly seen in the study of the Civil Law. He offer'd himself and earnestly desired to plead and speak in his own cause, when occasion so required, but that would not be allowed. The Bishop alleadged and prov'd that anciently 'twas accounted a shame for a Bishop to have one speak for him: but the Civilians did not like such old fashions; they were resolved that their manner of proceeding should not be altered, the Bishop must speak by his Advocate or Proctor, for whatever else he spake signified nothing: and so still his hopes of prevailing grew daily more desperate.

In these streights he tried some friends in England, from whom he receiv'd only some small verbal encouragement.* The advantage was much every way on the opposite side, yet it was thought the surest way to remove the cause into the Prerogative-Court. And there also much time was spent, and charges ran on, and the same forms of proceeding were repeated again, to no other purpose but only to make the business the more publick, as being now brought to Dublin, and that all the good Civilians might have the better opportunity to join their forces against the Bishop.

Being thus worried among them, and easily perceving what issue he must expect, he expressed himself to his friend the D^r thus: " I have all right on my side, but know not whether I shall find any to

* The copy of Bishop Land's answer to B:shop Bedell's letter of the 7th of August, 1630, is in the Public Record Office. See Supplement.—T. W. J.

do me right." Also he call'd the Law his Purgatory, and his journeys to Dublin his returning into Purgatory ; he complain'd to the D^r of his many troublesom thoughts, and often bemoan'd his own case. The D^r also and his other friends persuaded him to sit still and not to strive against the stream. But the tie of his conscience, and his duty to God in that place, were more than all discouragements, and, therefore, though sure to loose the day, as he wrote to the D^r, he comforted himself with this, *Post tenebras spero lucem, et dabit Deus his quoque finem*, resolving however to be hearty, and to see the uttermost of the business, that he might be able to say, *Liberavi animam meam*.

But before we proceed to relate the final issue of this suit, we shall take breath a while, and observe some other employments of the Bishop's, even while this great cause was depending. For as he laboured to rectify the mis-carriages of his pretended Chancellour and the other Officers in managing the Jurisdiction, so himself was active the mean time to give a better example. And, therefore, most commonly his manner was to keep Courts himself in person. For which purpose, as usually they had set times and places, so whatever weather came he would be sure to be present at the remotest parts of both his diocesses. These journeys took him up sometimes nigh a whole fortnight together: they were very chargeable to him, and sometimes dangerous, by reason of the mountains, and boggy waies, and loughs, and rivers not passable, but by boat ; besides the intemperate rains, that fell allmost all Summer long in those northern parts.

But God not only preserv'd him in these his waies, but encourag'd him, for at the very first beginning of these journeyings to keep Courts he was met a great way from home by the Judges of Assizes, being upon their circuit, as the Bishop was upon his, and though they were of no particular acquaintance with him, yet with very great respect and civilities they congratulated his advancement to the Bishopricks, using this speech unto him : That when his Lordship came to that Diocess it was breathing out the last spirit. The people generally, English, Scottish, Irish, gentle, simple, Protestants, Papists, wellcom'd him wherever he came. He was invited by those of best quality, Knights and Gentlemen, as he travell'd, and sometimes of necessity (the county not affording other conveniency) he accepted such invitations. He would not refuse the courtesies of Papists on these occasions, nor of Papist-Priests, but sometimes hath taken up his lodging even in such men's houses, and very ambitious would they be of entertaining him as their guest. But where the conveniency of Inns was to be had, there he rather would be at his own charges.

It happened once that a meeting of the Bishop and some Ministers was appointed to be holden at a place call'd Mannor Hamilton; and the Bishop having bespoken an Inn, and provision for the entertainment of himself and the Ministers, a noble K^{nt}, Sr Frederick Hamilton, that was Lord of the Town, and dwelt near it, sent to the Bishop to invite him to his house. The Bishop return'd him many thanks, but withall signified that himself and the Ministers had bespoken their entertainment, and were to consult of matters of weight, properly concerning their spiritual function : and, therefore, he desired to be excused for that time; promising that, after their business ended, they would not fail to wait upon him. Sr Frederick not being satisfied with this, being a man of an high spirit, sends again with more importunity, inviting not only the Bishop and his company but all the Ministers; assuring them that they should have freedom and privacy the best his house could afford for their consultations; only requesting earnestly that they would come, adding that he took it as an indignity, that his Lordship and the Ministry should be entertain'd in that countrey any where else than at his house; sending also a threatning messenger to the Host of the house for making provision for them without his advice. The Bishop and Ministers (for some reasons of weight not here to be expressed) judged it not very fitting to yield to the motion of the Knight at that time; though seemingly fair and safe: and, therefore, in all respectfull manner desir'd his pardon; with promise still (for the Bishop's part) to give him a visit 'ere he left the countrey. Accordingly, the next morning, their business being over, the Bishop goes to the Knight's house, with his Register, and a Minister or two, and some servants. And, being come thither, they found the doors all shutt, no person appearing. Having call'd and knock'd severall times, all was still silent. They knock'd and waited again so long, till first shame and then anger possessed all except only the Bishop. His company earnestly advised him to stay no longer. At last some were spied peeping out at windows and laughing. But the Bishop for all this kept his patience, so that, when his company were allmost in a rage, and urgent upon him to be gone, and no longer expose himself and them to scorn, yet still he resolved to stay a while longer, and smilingly told them, 'twas but an humour and would soone be past and over. And accordingly, after allmost half an hour's waiting, Sr Frederick caused the doors to be opened, and himself met and embrac'd the Bp. Some little expostulation there was on both sides, for this carriage of the business; but Sr Frederick, being a gallant-bred man, was so ingenuous as to be mov'd by the known worth, tried wisedom, patience, and humility of the Bishop to lay down this animosity, and to make amends for all by a very noble entertainment of him and his company; and the Bishop was abundantly satisfied in reaping the fruits of his patience.

We return again to his journeying and keeping Courts; whereby as he satisfied his own conscience, so he gave very great satisfaction both to Ministers and People, tho' to his no small charge. And because his law-suit with his Chancellour and other law business would not allwaies in person permit him thus to keep his Courts; he therefore issued out 4 Commissions to 4 Ministers, whom he judg'd most upright and able, authorising them to manage his jurisdiction in his absence. But at this his Chancellour stormed exceedingly; and, though he could not keep the Bishop himself from sitting as Judge when he pleased, yet, by his power and threatnings, he so farr prevailed, as that those Ministers durst not appear in the business, or but very coldly, if at all. Sometimes it happened that the Bishop and Chancellour both met, and sate in Court together; and then the Bishop was sure to meet with opposition and provocation sufficient to have either dismaied or transported him into passion; had not the wisedom, that is from above, both kept and guided him.

One thing that troubled the Chancellour was that, by the Bishop's sitting as Judge in the Courts, he was fain to fall much short in the gain which he was wont to make by his place. For not only his underhand and indirect gains were in a great measure prevented, as wanting now the conveniency of concealment; but also those fees which were ordinarily and punctually exacted by him, the Bishop would still moderate and mitigate, with respect to the poverty of the person and the merits of the cause; preventing hereby in some degree the rigorous exactions of his Chancellour; and (as he expressed it to his friend the D^r) both keeping his own hands clean, and looking to Mr. Cook's fingers also as well as he could.

But the greatest abuse in the exercise of the Ecclesiastical Jurisdiction, and of all other the most grievous to the good Bishop, was the frequent prostitution of that solemn and dreadfull Sentence of Excommunication, which with them (as it were) was become nothing else but an engine to open men's purses; with this the Chancellour, yea and even the very Apparitors, were used to force in their fees and exactions; especially from the Irish, the poorest of all not excepted. The Chancellour, tho' but one man and a meer lay-man, when he saw his time, would decree men excommunicated, and presently the Ministers were commanded to denounce them as such in their Churches, twenty in a parish at once. This command must pass in the Bishop's name, and yet without his consent or so much as knowledge; and being thus denounced, tho' Papists (as comonly they were) whose Religion excommunicates them from our worship and assemblies, the next business was by a Writt, De Excommunicato capiendo, to apprehend them and clap them up in the goale; where sometimes they were famished; or to avoid being taken forc'd to fly to woods and mountains, to turn kerns and live by robbery.

The Bishop with all his might laboured for redress of this : and by moderating the charges of the Court, and other his exemplary tenderness and compassion towards the poor natives, in a great measure prevented it: tho' wholly to reform it (as the laws then stood) it was impossible for one Bishop to doe. But, lest he should hereby seem to favour offenders, he us'd, when any were to be sentenc'd, by instructions and grave admonitions to set their sins before them, with the evil and danger of the same, and to allure them by all meekness and gentleness to repentance; imposing only such moderate fees on them as they might be able to pay in a competent time, without writs or excommunications.

These his proceedings rendred him still more odious to that sort of men, whose maintenance arose out of the Courts; but won him an extraordinary love and respect with the Irish and all that at any time came under the lash of the Court. And his often riding about these occasions was much conducible to his health. For tho' while he lived in England he had been much afflicted with the stone and gravell descending down from the kidneys, yet in Ireland by this continual motion he was in a manner cur'd of his affliction.

The Rever^d Dr Bernard, some time Dean of Kilmore, in his character given of this good Bishop in print,* hath most truly represented him, both as to his keeping Courts and Visitations, as also to all other particulars touch'd by him in that brief account.

Visitations he ever transacted in his own person, and preach'd himself for the most part : and that in a way which was home-searching against sin and pressingly urgent as to matter of practice and reformation; being set off by the extraordinary gravity and heavenliness of his presence and conversation. He never would put up one farthing of the procurations, but spent that money upon the

---

* This was written subsequently to 1659, the date of the publication of Dr. N. Bernard's book, " Certain Discourses, &c."—T. W. J.

Ministers for their enterteinment, and the poor. Also in the keeping his Courts (as Dr Bernard hath truly noted,) he used his Brethren of the Ministry with all possible respect : he made them sit covered on each side of him on the bench; he asked their opinion in any cause that came before him, and would not pass sentence till they had first given it. Neither was the difficulty small to persuade some Ministers to use the liberty he gave them herein. For what through the power of the pretended Chancellour and threatning words given out by him, and through the ignorance of many Ministers in the Ecclesiastical History and ancient Canons, and especially by a long habit of servitude under the Bishop's Officers and Servants, Ministers were in a manner jealous of the Bishop for seeking their deliverance: as the Israelites were of Moses and Aaron for speaking to Pharaoh to let them go; or as one thunder-stricken, who (as the Poet speaks) *Vivit, et est vitæ nescius ipse suæ.*

This good Bishop rested not here, but attempted also the erecting of Diocesan Synods, in imitation of the like practice of primitive Bishops; which he judged himself sufficiently impowered to do, as a Bishop in his own Diocese, both by the word of God and the ancient Canons. And some meetings of the Ministers and conferences were holden by his appointment for this purpose; and some Orders and Canons were agreed upon for Reformation of his Diocese. For this especially he was, however, charged by his pretended Chancellour, and those of the same craft, as an innovator, and as having incurr'd a præmunire, and intrenching upon the King's Prerogative. [*See Supplementary Chapter IX.*]

Such high imputations were frequently and loudly proclaimed against him by his and the Churches adversaries, to deterr him and to stifle his Godly endeavours for Reformation. But, notwithstanding all this, he proceeded as farr as possibly he could, and was prepared and resolved to answer his actions in this behalf at his uttermost perills. But the Ministers, apprehending the dangers likely to ensue upon such an attempt, grew alltogether cold in the business; and the Bishop could not proceed alone to any purpose in this his pious undertaking: whereof complaining to his friend the Dʳ, he useth this speech: It is an universal disease in bodies Ecclesiastical, *Omnes quæ sua sunt quærunt.*

Thus having seen the practice of this Bishop in matter of the Jurisdiction Ecclesiastical, the Reader probably will not think it burthensome to take his judgement also concerning the same, as then it stood in his own words, as they are faithfully transcrib'd out of his letters to Dʳ Despotine: " The corruptions of the Jurisdiction Ecclesiastical are such, as not only not Law, but not so much as Equity is kept; or if law, the new Decretal Law, not the ancient Canons of the Church; not the Canon of Canons, the Holy Scripture." And, in another of his letters to the Dʳ, writing concerning some proceedings by the Lords Justices, then in Ireland, against Friars and Popish Priests and Jesuites, he observes: " The thing most to be wished were some good reformation in Churchmatters : But (he adds) I believe, rather nothing will be done, than any thing much better'd."

Touching some innovations in matter of Ceremony introduc'd into England about anno 1636 (of which the Dʳ had written to him), he return'd this; I am not glad of it ; *Vino qui veteri utuntur, sapientes puto.* And so for his own particular in his own Diocese, he requir'd conformity only unto that, which was then by law established, and no more. [*See Supplementary Chapter IX.*]

The Cathedral Church wanted endowment for the maintenance of Prebends, Treasurer, Chanter, Vicars choral, Vergers, and other Officers and Ornaments belonging to the state and magnificence of a Cathedral. There was only a Dean and Archdeacon; but without any revenue, save only the profits of such Church livings whereof they were Incumbents: and consequently the Chapter in the Diocese of Kilmore was only a Convention of the several Ministers, so many of them as could come together upon occasion; any benefic'd man having his place and vote in the Chapter.

And hence we may fitly pass to acquaint the Reader how his manner was, and what rules he observed, in the Ordination of Ministers and Collation of Livings. For which purpose 3 things must be noted : one, that the most of the livings in that Dioccsse (and in a manner all) were the Bishop's, as rightfull and undoubted Patron; and the whole power of disposing them, when any fell, was in him; another thing was, that 'twas then the custom in Ireland for one Minister to enjoy 3, 4, 5, or more livings, as they were able by friends or other waies to obtain them; Yea, not only many Rectories, but many Viccarages were there possessed by one man; and, which yet may seem more strange, many Clarkships. One man, some servant or kinsman to the Bishop, and no poor man neither, might be Clark to 3 or 4 Parishes. Such was the state of the Church when Bishop Bedell came first to the Diocese; a third thing to be noted is, that most of the people in every Parish were Popish and Irish. In several Parishes there was not one Brittish or Protestant, save the Minister's family; and sometimes not all his family so neither.

Our Bishop to stay the fuller grouth of these disorders took this course. First, he ceased not to admonish those Ministers that had pluralities to be resident upon some one or other of their livings, and to provide sufficient Curates in the rest, and, as he could, he improved his authority to urge them hereunto. But this came far short of effecting that reformation that was needfull, and, therefore, he used a more effectual remedy, as God gave opportunity, and that was, as any livings became void, never to bestow above one on one man, and to require an oath of every one to be perpetually and personally resident upon his living. By this means, tho' some were highly displeased (the hopes of their gains being thus taken away), yet the number of Ministers was made something the more proportionable to the work.

And whereas they generally accounted those livings, where all or most of the people were Papists, to be *sine curâ*, saving only to take care to sell tithes, our Bishop in time brought them to another belief, and would tell them, Tho' the people would not hear them preach, yet 'twas very fit they should see their good conversation, and therefore by no means would he allow non-residency or pluralities.

And to make yet a farther provision for the effectual discharge of the Ministers' work, he was very carefull that, if possible, Ministers might be placed (where the people were most Irish) who had skill in the Irish tongue, in prosecution of that Statute in the College of Dublin, wherein it was provided that Scholars of the Irish nation, for their encouragement and better fitting themselves for the conversion of their own countrey-men, should be exercised in the reading of the Scriptures in the Irish language, for which exercise every such Irish Scholar had a yearly stipend of 3^{li}, beside his Scholarship. The Bishop very zealously prosecuted this pious designe in placing of Ministers, and if such men were offered to him, or himself could find out such as were able to converse with the natives and perform Divine Offices to them in their own language, he would rather preferr them to such livings than others of greater learning and abilities that wanted the language. And to them that would cavil or object against this his practice, as less propitious to learning and Englishmen, he would produce that saying of the Apostle, 1 Cor. xiv. 19, Yet in the Church I had rather speak five words with my understanding, that *by my voice* I might teach others also, than ten thousand words in an *unknown* tongue. And he would plainly tell the Ministers, such forward men as used to ride and run for a benefice, that tho' they had St. Paul's gifts, yet he could not see how they would be able to doe any good unless they had the language of the people.

One main objection was made against these his proceedings upon a politick or State-reason. For by laws in force in Ireland the Irish were requir'd to learn the English language, and use English fashions, which law this practice of the Bishop seemed directly to cross. But his answer was, That those people had souls which ought not to be neglected till they would learn English. And therefore, not being mov'd by any such objections, he persisted in his course which he had begun, and applied himself for example-sake to the study of Irish, wherein as to reading and writing he had attain'd a good perfection. [*See Supplementary Chapter X.*]

And as in preferring men to livings, so in conferring Holy Orders he was very carefull. He used allwaies, with the assistance of the Archdeacon and two or three other Ministers, to examine openly in the Church such as were to be ordeined. He had a very sweet and brotherly way of proceeding in his examinations, and would press that point (among the rest) Whether the Examinant did think himself call'd of God and moved by the Holy Ghost to take that calling upon him. At the Ordination allwaies he preach'd and administred the Communion himself, one of the other Ministers assisting in the distributing of the cup. The Letters of Orders, as also the Instrument for Institution and Induction, he allwaies wrote and sealed with his own hand, not suffering one farthing to be paid by any Minister, either to himself or any servant of his, that he might shun all appearance of simony, which himself rendred as the reason of his doing. And thus sending forth labourers as fit as he could into the Lord's Vineyard, he did endeavour, what lay in him, that every parish in the Diocese might have a Minister able to doe something towards the Conversion of Souls.

It must not here be concealed that the success was not so answerable to his good intentions; for being bent upon it, to place none but such as had the language where most of the people were Irish, he was fain to preferr many Irish-men, who had been Popish, even Priests and Friars, and who, either by some injury or disgrace from those of their religion, or through poverty and desire of preferment (being once acquainted with the Bishop's way and principles), were moved to desire conference with him, and so by degrees becoming converts, and carrying themselves at first fairly, they were by the Bishop preferr'd to places as they fell void, meerly out of his zeal for the conversion of the Irish. But some of these men prov'd scandalous, returning again to their vomit, not by revolting to Popery, but by breaking out into dissoluteness of life, to the great dishonour of God, disgrace of the Ministry, and grief of the Bishop. Yet these evils he never so far resented (how odiously soever aggravated) as to alter that good principle, that the Minister ought to be able to speak to his flock in a tongue that they could understand. And not only his own conscience, but all men (even his adversaries) bore him witness, that no secular or sinister end induced him to take this course, but meerly to discharge his conscience the best he could.

Before we leave this subject, one rare and remarkable passage may fitly be remembred. The Bishop, being a great opposite to plurality, had this objected (either by others or his own conscience or both): That himself gave the same bad example in holding two Bishopricks. And, therefore, his heart was a long time set upon it, to use all lawfull means to quit one. In order whereunto he dealt very earnestly with a Reverend and Learned man, Dr John Richardson, to accept of the Bishoprick of Ardagh, which he offer'd to resigne; engaging to use all his interest in such friends as he had in England about the Court, to procure him the grant thereof from his Majestie. Dr Richardson had allready the best Church living in that Diocese; which was some means to farther the Bishop of Kilmore's designe, tho' the Bishoprick it self was of no tempting value.

Bishop Bedell, consulting with his friend Dr Despotine concerning this matter, was much dissuaded by him as also by all other his friends, who were made acquainted with this his purpose. His own words in his letter to Dr Despotine to satisfy him in the thing were these: " That the example of holding two Bishopricks was not Canonical; but justifying the holding of many benefices by one person; that 'twas an unreasonable thing of him to seek to reform heapers of benefices, being himself faulty in having two Bishopricks: that he was sensible of his own disability to discharge the duty of a Bishop to two Churches, yea, even to one; that this Bishoprick, as to the revenues thereof, had been most horribly injured, and therefore requir'd some abler man, both for purse and friends, to recover the rights of the Church; and such he knew Dr Richardson to be, as having a good estate and no charge of children, and a man deserving a far better Bishoprick." And whereas 'twas objected by the D^r that by parting with one of his Bishopricks he should shorten his means: his answer was, that still he should have enough to live on, and leave his children more than was left him; and *Domini est terra, et plenitudo ejus.* Thus armed against all arguments of flesh and bloud, and finding Dr Richardson not altogether averse from the motion; Bishop Bedell never ceased, till the business was effected to his great joy and content; wherein he invited his friend Dr Despotine in a letter to rejoice with him.*

And now, this great rubb being remov'd, he went on more confidently to reform those too common and rooted maladies of the Clergy then and there, plurality of benefices and non-residency: which were grown to that height in Ireland, that some would take the liberty, tho' possessors of several livings, to reside at none of them all; some men had livings in several Dioceses; some still lay at the catch to pick holes in the titles of other Ministers, so as, under some pretence or other, to make their benefices lapse to the King, and then they would get the broad seal, and thus, in spight of any Bishops, possess themselves of what livings they had a mind to.† If a Bishop should refuse to give Institution, or a Mandate for Induction, in any such case the intruder needed no more but to goe to the Prerogative Court, and for his money he might have both. Bishop Bedell, in his Diocese, was not a little infested with this kind of men, and omitted not to oppose them with all his might. And hereupon he drew on himself a great deal of trouble

* Bishop Bedell's resignation of the See of Ardagh is dated the 28th of February, 1632-3. See Copy of the Instrument in Supplementary Chapter VII.—T. W. J.

† Mr. Murtagh King, Vicar of Templeport, who made the Irish translation of the Old Testament, under the auspices of Bishop Bedell, was thus treated. See Supplement, Chapter X.—T. W. J.

and charge from some of the Ministry. And what by his pretended Chancellour encouraging, and the iniquity of the times conniving at, or (which is worse) encouraging such offenders, he could prevail but little, but was fain to goe by the loss in all, save only in what is more worth than all, the peace and comfort of a good conscience.

It would be too long to relate his troubles, occasion'd by some necessary secular affaires, such as his just endeavours to vindicate the rights of his Churches. That of Ardagh was scarce worth 100^{li} per annum when he first came to be Bishop, the revenue being so grossly embezel'd that he had not left him in that Diocese where to set his foot; the very site of the Bishop's Mansion-house had been leased away, and it cost a long and chargeable suit e're he could recover it. The troubles and suits that lay upon him in right of that Bishoprick, he used to say, were an Abyssus, or bottomless gulf.

He had also enough and more of the same in his Diocese of Kilmore, being forc'd to sue for some of his Mensal Lands, leased away quite contrary to law, and was held out of his right by the potency and the subtiltie of some enemies he had to doe withall, in most plain cases, for many years together. One very unkind suit there happened between him and his predecessour's widow, about lands leased to her by her husband, at a very mean rent, and for a longer time than by law they ought, and to the manifest injury of the Church, and yet hardly was the business ended till just upon the breaking out of the rebellion, and even then he was fain in a manner even to buy his right.

It was the usual course of his Predecessours, the Bishops of Kilmore and Ardagh, to gratify their wives, children, kindred and servants, by granting them long leases of the lands of their Bishopricks, to the manifest injury of the Church; and the Deans and Chapters, for favour and affection, were procured to confirm such unlawfull acts, whereby the succeeding Bishops were reduc'd to a very small allowance, and the lands in long process of time in danger of alienation from the church, an abuse not seldom incident to most Church lands, but strenuously oppos'd, and in some manner rectified and prevented, by our good Bishop, who never was guilty of doing any such unconscionable act in all his time.

Thus have we seen what incessant and setled troubles, like a constant storm, did still weatherbeat our Bishop; that grand suit also with his Chancellour continuing all this while over. And besides all other matters we shall now see how God was pleased yet farther to exercise him with trialls of another nature, wherein the Higher Powers fell foul upon him. Two instances only of this nature may here be presented to the Reader, [of which one occurred about the beginning of his Episcopate, and the other towards the end.—T. W. J.]

The first was this. The Protestants of the County of Cavan, in his Diocese, both Clergy and Laity, found themselves very much aggrieved by certain heavy impositions, the manner as well as the thing it self being grievous to them. For whereas Agents * had been sent to his Majestie from the Protestants of this County and the whole Province of Ulster to desire ease of the burthen of an Army, then lying upon them very heavy : these Agents, when they came to Court, joined and consented with other Agents at the same time emploied by the Papists, that the summ of six score thousand pounds should be raised and paid within a set time out of the whole Kingdom, and this money, thus strangely impos'd, was in some places forc'd in by those very soldiers which they had desired to be eased of.† And in the County of Cavan a violent Papist, then Under-

* The agents were Sir Andrew Stewart and Sir Arthur Forbes, Knts. and Baronets.—T.W.J.

† The directions from the Lords Justices and Council for levying the contributions here referred to were dated the 12th of February 1632-3. See the copy of the Petition annexed to Bishop Bedell's letter of the 5th of November, 1633, to the Lord Deputy Wentworth, printed in Strafford's Letters and Dispatches, vol. i. pp. 146-151, folio, London, 1739. See also William Prynne's Breviate of the Life of William Laud, Archbishop of Canterbury;—Necessary Introduction to the Archbishop of Canterbury, his Tryall, disçovering the Practises used to usher Popery into our Realme, pp. 113, folio, London, 1644.—T. W. J.

CAMD. SOC. H

Sheriff, and that used much injustice and partiality against the Protestants, was made a chief actor herein. Whereupon, they (being very considerable in that County and Province, both for number and quality,) join'd together to complain and seek more redress, which they agreed first to doe by way of a Letter to the Lords Justices that then were the Chief Governours of Ireland. Their letter they had drawn up and concluded upon, only some of them mov'd to have the Bishop's advice about it.* Upon his sight of their letter, which was too full of height and discontent, the Bishop acquainted some Knights and Gentlemen that were active in it, that he dislik'd that manner of proceeding, and somwhat he had to doe by his best persuasions to allay their spirits. Yet their respect to him was such that they desir'd him to draw up somthing himself, in order to the acquainting the State with their grievances. The Bishop accordingly draws up an humble petition, in which they only desire that their paiment of such imposed contributions might not be prejudicial to them, their posterity and successors for time to come, and that their Lordships would forbear any farther imposition of any such burthen upon them untill they should present their humble remonstrances to his Majestie. This Petition the Bishop of Kilmore, with two other Bishops, and many Knights and Gentlemen subscrib'd, and it was presented to the Lords Justices that then were, the Lord Viscount Loftus, Lord Chancellor of Ireland, and Richard Lord Boyl, Earl of Cork.†

But, notwithstanding this moderating of the business by the Bishop of Kilmore, he was specially complained of to the King for setting his hand to this Petition and so opposing his Majesties service. He was accused also to the Archbishop of Canterbury for the same. And the Lord Wentworth, then design'd Chief Governour of Ireland (a man of great severity), was likewise inform'd and prepossessed against him.

* This was on the day after Lent Assizes, 1633. —T. W. J.
† Lord Wentworth, who had been appointed Lord Deputy, did not arrive in Ireland and "take the sword" until July 1633.

First the Archbishop falls upon him in a sharp letter.* Next the Lord Wentworth, saying that such men that should oppose the King's service were unworthy to be Bishops; and farther, the Bishop of Kilmore's name being in among others for a Commissioner in a business, he caused his name to be blotted out. The Bishop to assert his innocency takes up his defensive weapon, his pen (in the use whereof he was inferior but to few); and first to the Lord Archbishop, and then to the Lord Wentworth, in large letters of his he partly excused and partly justified his action. In that to the Lord Wentworth,† in defence of himself he expresseth his humble thoughts thus to his Lordship: " That the way ought not to be foreclosed to Subjects to have recourse (in humble and dutifull sort) to his Majesties goodness, to declare their grievances; this serving to evaporate their discontents, a good mean to keep them from festring inwardly." It was a good while after the Lord Wentworth his landing in Ireland, before the Bishop would goe to Dublin to wait upon him, as all or most of the other Bishops had done: and the reason was, because he had declar'd so much displeasure against him, as we have heard. And some of his friends questioning with him, why he deferr'd so long to present himself to the Lord Deputy, he answered with that of Solomon, " If the Spirit of the Ruler rise up against thee, leave not thy place." He rather chose to make his way by mollifying letters and by patience; and so in time, by God's blessing, this storm ceased: which as soon as the Bishop understood, he took occasion to visit the Lord Deputy

---

* Dated the 14th of October, 1633, in which he said: "I was, under God, the man that put your name to his Majesty for preferment, and, therefore, must needs in part suffer for any thing that shall be deemed a miscarriage in you. I never saw your Lordship to my knowledge, nor did I ever know you but by a little tract of yours against Wadsworth; and were it but for that alone, I should be very sorry you should do any thing in your place unlike it, for that is very full of judgment and temper." See Strafford's Letters and Dispatches, *ut supra*. Archbishop Laud here passes over in silence the share which Sir Thomas Jermyn had in Bedell's preferment. See above, p. 29.—T. W. J.

† Dated Kilmore, the day of our deliverance from the Popish Plot, 1633.

at Dublin, and was treated with due respect by himself and his favorites, and for a while seem'd to stand *rectus in Curiâ;* till another occasion happen'd.

And this leads us to that other instance, wherein the Higher Powers frowned upon him; and that was in the case of the Bishop of Killalagh, Archibald Adaire. The case was this: A certain Scottish Minister, that fled out of Scotland upon occasion of the tumults there about Episcopacy and the Common Prayer Book,* coming into Ireland, made his case known to those in power, and in such a way as rendred the proceedings of his countrey-men (especially the Covenanters) very odious. Whereupon, being regarded as a man driven out of his countrey, destitute of maintenance, and zealous of Episcopacy, he was soon preferr'd to a living, which happen'd to be in the Bishop of Killalagh his Diocese: and going thither to possess his living, there happened some differences between him and the Bishop, tho' both of the Scottish nation. Whether the rise of their difference was, that the Bishop thought it his right to have the bestowing of the living, and this Minister to be obtruded wrongfully upon him; or that this Minister carried not himself dutifully and submissively to the Bishop; or whether the matter was, that the Bishop did not sufficiently approve his flight out of Scotland into Ireland, as perhaps having more perfect intelligence concerning matters there, and not taking the man's own word only: whatever the matter was, (which, perhaps, some yet living do more distinctly know, than can here be related,) in summ, being both men of high spirits, the contention grew very hot between them; and, words arising, the Bishop let fall some speeches that sounded too favorably towards the Covenanters in Scotland; withall sharply rebuking the Minister for accusing his own Nation, and, like an unclean bird, defiling his own nest. The Minister thus entertein'd by the Bishop, with the first opportunity complained of him, either immediately to the Lord Deputy Wentworth or to some that soon carried it to his ear; and that with such success, that the

* In the year 1639.—T. W. J.

Bishop was soon after summon'd into the High Commission Court, then newly erected in Ireland, there to be proceeded against and to answer his words.

The business upon hearing was judged so scandalous (especially in a Bishop) that the Court came soon to sentence. The Judges of this Court were the Lord Lieutenant, the Lord Chancellour, the Archbishops and diverse Bishops, and other men of chiefest quality in the Kingdom, and among others the Bishop of Kilmore. When the day for sentence came, there was no small appearance; the Court was full, as well of Commissioners as of auditors and spectators; and after the usual manner every Commissioner in a set speech deliver'd his judgment in the present case, beginning at the last, and so on to the first. There were many that spake before it came to the Bishop of Kilmore; and tho' some were more favourable or not so severe as others, yet for the generality the Judgement of the Court was very heavy, decreeing no less than deprivation against the Bishop of Killalagh, besides an heavy fine to be set on his head. When our Bishop of Kilmore came to deliver his sentence, he insisted much on the tenderness and favour that still in antient times were wont to be used in case of the accusation of any Bishop; the Scripture it self requiring no less. And he learnedly and largely discussed the present case; but so, as his judgement differ'd much from the most of them that had spoken. And tho' he blam'd and aggrávated the faults of the Bishop with solid gravity and without sharpness; yet he stood much for the most favourable censure that might be possible, as most requisite and convenient in the present case; concluding with submission of this his Judgement to the rest of that Honourable Court.

This carriage of the business was no way pleasing; as crossing, in a manner, the very designe divulg'd before the day of Sentence; which was, to make this Bishop an example for all to take warning by. But the Bishop of Kilmore had the testimony of his own conscience for him, and such solid grounds delivered in his speech as none would take in hand to overthrow. He had no manner of intimacy with the Bishop that was censured, nor indeed was capable of any; both because of the distance of their habitations (the one in Connaught, the other in Ulster), and because of the National difference, the one a Scot, the other an Englishman; which for the most part desire to have as little to do the one with the other, as may be. Neither had the Bishop of Kilmore any party to make, nor any ready made to his hand to back him, but stood single in this matter: and so was sufficiently check'd and chidden for his pains, as a willful and singular man, to differ from the whole Judgement of so honourable a Court. But the Bishop of Killalagh, that was censured, he indeed professed a great deal of respect to the Bishop of Kilmore from that time forth; still calling him his Patron : but that was a small matter to be laid in the ballance against the displeasure of the chiefest in the Kingdom. But our Bishop being a plain man, and not ambitious of any thing but to promote God's glory and to keep the peace of his conscience, was the better qualified to bear that burthen of men's displeasure, though grievous enough to be born.*

* Sir George Radcliffe, the intimate friend of the Earl of Strafford (in a letter preserved in the Public Record Office, dated the 3rd of March, 1639-40), gives a report to his Lordship who was in England at the time, of the proceedings of the High Commission Court on passing sentence: " The cause being hearde," says Sir George, " ye sentence was y^t the Bp. should be degraded by his metropolitane with his Provintiall Clergy, by Comission under ye great Seale; with a fine of 1000 ^{li}, imprisonment and costs. The Judges declared some of his wordes, if they had bene found by a Jury, to have been high treason. The Bp. of Corke was very sharpe against ye offence, yet leaft ye pearson to expect ye Kings mercy wth censure or fine as conceiving him cracked in his Braine. The Bp. of Kilmore exercised his wit (as boyes doe in Schoole declamations, endeavouring to maintaine a paradox), for he commended or excused him in all the particular charges layed against ye def^t. All ye rest agreed unanimously."

In pursuance of the sentence, Bishop Adair was deprived on the 18th of May, 1640; but the King, considering the Bishop to have been too hardly dealt with, appointed him Bishop of Waterford and Lismore on the 13th of July, 1641, and on the 7th of June, 1642, wrote to the Lords Justices and Lord Chancellor in Bishop Adair's favour, commanding them to expunge and vacate the sentence of deprivation passed against him by the High Commission Court.—T. W. J.

It is time now to give some account of the final issue of that tedious and chargeable suit between the Bishop and his Chancellour : wherein he resolved to see the uttermost, notwithstanding the unanimous engagement of all the Civilians against him, and those many great discouragements he met withall. Finding himself not fairly dealt with in the Prerogative Court, he came to the last refuge, an Appeal to the King;* whereby all proceedings were stopp'd, till the King's pleasure was known. And after some time (according to the usual manner in such cases), a Commission issued out under the King's broad seal, nominating a certein number of men of the chiefest rank, beginning with the Lord Deputy himself, and so on to Privy Councellours, Judges, Archbishops, Bishops, Doctors of both Laws, &c. and appointing those, or a certein number of them, to hear and determine the cause depending. The Bishop had some hope at first this way to have obteined his purpose; which was only to have liberty to appoint his own Chancellour himself; or else to correct the exorbitances of his pretended and obtruded Chancellour.

The expectations of all men were intent upon the final issue of this cause. Some of his Judges spoke favourably, as by name Sr George Shirley, Lord Chief Justice of the King's-bench, who was heard to say, that he thought it hard if a Shepherd might not have liberty to drive a wolf away from his fold. But others were as much the other way, openly declaring their judgements against the Bishop, before ever the Delegates came to sit. Whereupon at the first sitting he put in his exceptions against one or two, allwaies saving the reverence due to their persons, and the reasons of his exceptions were judged valid, so that those he excepted against were set by. Thus after a full hearing, wherein the Lord Chancellour Loftus was chief Judge, and seldom absent from the Court, the matter *in summo* came to this final sentence :—That Mr. Alane

* See a letter to Archbishop Laud (in the Public Record Office), dated Dublin, May 24, 1639; and one to Dr. Samuel Warde of Cambridge (in the Bodleian Library) dated May 30, 1639.—T. W. J.

Cook (after Dr. Cook) should still hold his place of Chancellour to the Bishop of Kilmore, and that the Bishop should pay him the sum of 100ˡⁱ for his costs and charges during the suit. The Bishop was quite out of hope or rather sure to loose the day long before the cause came to this end, and was told as much by one of his Judges, Lancelot Lord Arch-Bishop of Dublin,* a very loving friend of his, who was able to discern as much, by what he heard and knew of the minds of the rest of his Delegates.

The Bishop of Kilmore had now done what lay in him according to the understanding God had given him, he spared no lawful cost nor pains to redress what was amiss in managing the Jurisdiction Ecclesiastical, and, therefore, though he lost the day, yet he kept his conscience. That which troubled him most was to be deserted (as he was) by the rest of his Brethren, the Bishops, who, had they join'd in this cause, so nearly concerning them, and the well-governing and reforming of the Church, as the Civilians did in mainteining their worldly interest, some better issue might have followed. The Bishop of Kilmore applied to himself that saying of the Apostle, 2 Tim. iv. 16, *No man stood with me, but all men forsook me; I pray God that it may not be laid to their charge.*

Mr. Alane Cook, tho' now victor, yet used his victory with a great deal of ingenuity and moderation. For he never urged the Bishop to pay the 100ˡⁱ costs that was imposed upon him by order of the Court's Delegates, nor did he at all grow insolent upon his success, but rather more moderate and mild than ever before, and to avoid any farther differences between the Bishop and himself, he put off his place to the Register, Mr. Richard Ash, a man that entirely lov'd the Bishop, and would be guided and directed by him in the execution of the place, so that after this the Bishop had somewhat a calmer time than before, but it was not long, for after some two years the Nation's peace and his Life expired, of which more hereafter.

* Dr. Bulkeley.

It will not be amiss now to present to the world the more free and retired thoughts of the Bishop touching these his troubles, and touching his own condition in his Episcopal function, as they are set down by himself in his familiar letters to Dr Despotine. It hath been hinted heretofore how intimate the friendship was between these two. For as in joy and grief, in mutual freedom and openness, in help and counsel, so even in reprehension they were faithfull each to other. The Doctor did not stick often to blame him, for employing his time and abilities no better than in suits and wrangling business. The Bishop's defence for himself was in these very words: " God doth know how unwilling I spend my time and pains and means in such sordid employments. But there is no remedy, unless I would resigne my Bishopricks, which I could be very willing to do. On the other side, I consider that I never desir'd this place, and being call'd to it by God, I must not choose mine own work, but do that little good I can, and leave the rest to God." And in another letter, giving an account to the Doctor why he would resigne one of his Bishopricks, he writes thus: " For my part I wish I were rid, not of one only but of both, rather than spend my life in lawing, and riding up and down, especially with so little furtherance from some who might (I will not say ought to) have afforded more favour or equity at least, than I have hitherto found." And again, speaking of the resignation of the Bishoprick of Ardagh, his own words are : " God doth know I would be more willingly rid of it than eat my dinner when I am hungry, having found nothing since I came into this calling but troubles and suits and wranglings." And, again, he expresseth himself thus: " I might be an happy man if I were rid of my Jurisdiction, and all the profits of both my Bishopricks, reserving meat and drink and cloathing." Such were the thoughts and expressions of this good Bishop touching his calling, and the troubles that attended him therein.

The Bishop had some friends in England of some place and power about the Court. The most real were the Earl of Holland

and Sr Thomas Jermin, Vice-chamberlain to the King. Doctor Despotine still communicated the affairs of the Bishop with Sr Thomas, and the Bishop himself wrote frequently to him. Sir Thomas's love and respect to him were such that he laboured to remove him into some Bishoprick in England, which purpose and endeavour of his the Doctor comming to understand, could not hold for joy, but must needs hint it in his letters to Bishop Bedell. His friends at Court thought this an honourable way to take him off his troubles, and render themselves capable of enjoying him, which at so great a distance they could not do. But it was not thought fit by the more potent at Court to have him over into England. The Doctor certified the Bishop both who and why, and nextly the Reader shall understand Bishop Bedell's own sense of this business.

Before he was advanc'd to the Bishopricks, there was some mediation by letters from Sr Thomas Jermin to the Lord Deputy Falkland, to confer the Deanery of Christchurch in Dublin upon him, the present Dean, Dr Barlow, being upon his advance to the Arch-bishoprick of Tuam, and the Lord Deputy openly profess'd his purpose to do it. But when it came to the point, the imputation of Puritanism by some at Court lost him the Deanery, and had like to have put him by the Bishopricks also. And herein his own expectation was fulfilled; " My Lord Deputy (saith he in a letter to the Doctor,) professeth his purpose to confer the Deanery upon me, and signified to me lately that he had receiv'd from Sr Thomas Jermin very effectual letters in my commendation. I know not what will be, but, in conclusion, I think, nothing."

After he was Bishop, there were several endeavours by his friends to have him remov'd into England, of which himself writes thus : " Now for that which toucheth me and my removal, God doth know I desire it not : may I desire rather that it may not be : not but that the love of my countrey moves me, and the society of your self and other my friends, but because, if I be fit for any thing, I conceive I may do God and his Majestie better service here than I can in

England; here, where my deafness and other defects are better cover'd with difference of languages, and my different course in some things pertaining to Jurisdiction is justified by the exorbitant courses that have been holden by my opposites. There I should draw the hatred of all men upon me, and yet do no good." Again, mentioning his suits with his Chancellour and others for the rights of his Church, he thus expresseth himself: " God knows how unwilling I am to spend my better time upon them: but there is no remedy. As for that remedy you write of, mention'd by Sr Thomas Jermin, it is worse than the disease. I have not failed, nor yet shall fail to suggest to those that are in place, what I think perteins to the safety of the common ship, wherein we all sail: but I am glad the opinion of one * too vehement, or any thing else, may bar me from that employment." And in another letter again, thus: " As for the thoughts of removing into England, let it never come to the mind of any of my friends; God hath brought me hither, and I have begun to lay some foundations here; which, if God will, I shall endeavour to build upon: *Hic requies mea in sæculum.*"

Some would scarsely account a life of so many labours and so many troubles to be *Requies*, a Rest: but yet this good Bishop did, as a good Christian should do; he did acquiesce in what portion God had laid out for him: and yet for the rest of his life still behind to be related, we shall find him as little at rest (according to the common notion of the word) as before. For besides what is allready set down, two very great labours lay both together upon him for diverse years together before his death, of different natures, but both tending to the same end, which were these: The building of all the Churches in his Diocese; and the translating the old Testament into the Irish tongue.

As for the building the Churches, the Reader must know; That when this work was first taken in hand, there were not 5 Churches in his whole Diocese, but were all ruin'd, so as scarsely the walls

---

* Archbishop Laud ?—T. W. J.

were left standing in some places. The reason was, that the land had been much harass'd with war, and the people were but few and poor in those Northern parts, and all too backward, both English and Irish, to such good works as building of Churches. But God stirred up the Spirit of his Majestie, to give Commissions by his Vice-gerents in Ireland for the setting forward of this pious work. And among other men of principal quality, the Bishop was the first and chief Commissioner. This occasioned him many hard journeys, first to view the several Churches, then to meetings of the Commissioners at several times and places for the assessing of every Parish, and taking accounts when the work was done. And as his labour, so his charges were very great by reason of this business, and, which was worst of all, he found very corrupt dealing. Moneys collected were wasted or spent, or some way converted to men's private uses, and the work neglected: with all which difficulties he so struggled and encountred, that before his death all the Churches were repair'd and fit for the people to meet in for God's service, had the people been as willing to meet in them.

That other labour of his comes next to be considered, and that was the translation of the Old Testament into the Irish tongue. The Bishop judg'd the Scriptures as essential to the Church as the building of Stone-walls, and that it more properly belonged to his care and function to open the fountains and clear the channells of those waters of comfort for Christ's sheep. He expected no Commission from man for this undertaking, but acted by vertue of Christ's Commission. Nor did the mean and slight esteem which some had of his designe herein a whit remove him from prosecuting the same with all his might. He had the example of a Reverend Prelate of that Kingdom, William Daniel, sometime Arch-bishop of Tuam, who caused the New Testament and Common-prayer-book to be translated into Irish and printed, out of his zeal for the salvation of the people. And the Bishop of Kilmore thought it a good work to add the Old Testament also.

For this purpose he enquir'd out the ablest men he could to employ about the work; and among diverse that he made trial of, two especially he employed, Mr. Murtagh King and Mr. James Nangle. Both these men, when first the Bishop came acquainted with them, were Papists: But being Irish men, and more knowing than the ordinary sort, they were so ingenuous and well-affected to their own Nation and Language as to afford their help to this work. Mr. King was the chief translator; and the other was the reviewer and correcter. They had their entertainment at the Bishop's house, as long and as often as any comparing and reviewing work was in hand, wherein the Bishop allwaies made one: and through the skill he had attain'd in the Irish language, he contributed not a little to the work. Besides these Translators he had a servant, an Irishman, that could write exactly well; and he writ out fair, sheet by sheet, as they translated and corrected.

It pleased God while this work was in hand to incline the hearts of both the Translators to the embracing of the Reformed Religion:* God's Spirit, and those Scriptures, and the Bishop's gentle and able way of reasoning, and answering their objections, all concurring together to the changing of their judgements. And so in conclusion the work was finished, and fair written ready for the press, a little before that dismal time of trouble, rebuke, and blasphemy, wherein God call'd his faithfull Servant to himself.

Thus we have seen not a perfect, but true relation of the troublesome life of this good Bishop. What remains, is to take a view of his end, which was every way suitable to the former progress of his life; and, as to outward sufferings, surmounting whatsoever had before befallen him. And herein we may observe (as in multitudes of other the like examples, both former and later), that God's way

---

* Mr. Murtagh King, according to another account (Supplementary Chapter X.), is stated to have been converted some time in the preceding reign. Bishop Bedell ordained Mr. Murtagh King Deacon on the 23rd of September, 1632, and Priest on the 22nd of September, 1633, and collated him to the vicarage of Templeport on the 29th.—T. W. J.

with the choicest of his servants, in this life is, to exercise and train them for heaven by the most eminent trialls and afflictions; even as the glorious Captain of our Salvation was made perfect through sufferings. God will have the ablest and choicest Christians to be the compleatest Sufferers. A lesson legible in Capital Letters all along the series of God's Providence; yet learn'd by heart by very few. But God be blessed, our good Bishop will appear to have studied it to some purpose.

And here the Reader must be entreated to understand a little the quality of the Countrey,* where the Bishop's seat was, and what neighbours he liv'd among. His house was situate in the County of Cavan, in the Province of Ulster, in Ireland; in a countrey consisting alltogether of hills very steep and high; the valleys between being most commonly boggs and loughs: the countrey was then meetly well planted with English; but scatteringly here and there, which facilitated their ruine. The only considerable Town in the whole County was Belterbert, which yet was but as one of our ordinary Market-towns here in England;† having only but one Church in it. This town was 7 miles distant from the Bishop's house. The town of Cavan it self, being the County Town, was nearer, about two miles distant from Kilmore; but not so big by one-half as Belterbert. Excepting these two towns there was nothing considerable in the county. Kilmore it self was but a meer countrey village, of good large bounds, but so thinly inhabited that no where in the whole Parish was any street or part of a street to be found. There was a competent number of English; but the Irish were more than five times their number, and all of them obstinate Papists. The Bishop's house join'd close to the Church, being built upon

---

* In Additional MS. No. 4436 in the British Museum, there is at page 314 "A description of Lough Erne," written about the year 1740, by the then Vicar of "Killasher," in which an interesting account of the region referred to in the text is given. For reference to this I am indebted to a correspondent in ¡Notes and Queries, signing himself C. S. K.—T. W. J.

† This expression shows that the writer lived in England.—T. W. J.

one of the highest hills in the countrey; not near any neighbour of any quality by a mile.

In this posture, alltogether unfit both for offence and defence, in a manner solitary and naked, and exposed to any insolencies, our Bishop, being then at home, was on a suddain environ'd and involv'd with that horrible and ever-lamentable Rebellion. It was in several respects an astonishing accident, not admitting any consultation or attempt for opposition against it. There was not the least suspicion in the English of any such thing; nor could they at first conceive or believe the depth of the wickedness; no, not when they had in part felt the bitter effect thereof. And that place was so far distant from Dublin, that no intelligence could be had: God had cover'd them with a cloud in that day of his anger.

There wanted not some forerunning tokens of this calamity, but they were not heeded: as the manifest height and fullness of sin in all ranks and sorts of men; pride, gluttony, uncleanness, deceipt, oppression, extortion, and a supine neglect of Religion and the Worship of God and of the eternal concernments of precious souls; such were general: but more particular and relating especially to those parts wer these:

A strange multitude of ratts, in a manner overrunning the houses and so bold as to come in view in the day-time, and to gather the crumbs and bones under the table; which was a thing so much the more remarkable because that, till a little before the Rebellion for many years space, seldom any rat was to be seen in the countrey. And the elder Irishwomen would say often and openly, that these rats were a signe of war. Another very strange thing was seen about a mile from Kilmore, not far from the house of Edmund O'Rely, the chief Gentleman of that name, and the chief Actor in spoiling and killing the English, and this not long neither before the Rebellion. In a plat of ground by the high way, a strange number of insects or worms of the length of a man's finger, and of a strange fashion, were observed for some weekes, and many went to see them. They lay for the most part within the ground, which they had turn'd up and fill'd with their cells and caverns; so that the whole surface of the ground where they encamp'd was wholy bare of any green thing to be seen.

A third, the most remarkable token, was given by a mad man, and therefore the less heeded. This distracted man was a very accute scholar, that had crack'd his brain with too much study, and, being also very poor, partly out of necessity, and partly out of his running fancy, pass'd up and down from one gentleman's house to another, and so got his livelyhood. Among other places of his resort, the Bishop's house and Ministers' houses had their turns, tho' the man was for nation Irish, and for Religion Popish. It seems by that which follows that he had been in company where discourses had passed concerning that their horrid plot against the English. His manner was to speak in Latin when he came among scholars, and wherever he could light upon pen and ink he would be scribling upon paper or book, what came next to hand. But both in his speaking and writing the shatterdness of his brain did appear, for his words and sentences were for the most part inconsistent with one another. Being entertein'd at a Minister's house not long before the Rebellion first brake out, he was observed to be extreamly sad, contrary to his usual manner, which was rather a merry kind of madness. In that Minister's house, walking up and down, and sighing, he diverse times was heard to utter these words, *Where is King Charles now?* This sentence he had up several times, with some other odd whimsies between. Besides this he had gotten an old Almanack, which he had all scribled over on the one side, and among other broken sentences there was this written, *We doubt not of France and Spain in this action.* These expressions were taken notice of, but, comming from a distracted man, for present were thought to signify nothing, till being put together and commented upon by the rebellion in bloudy characters, they were found and felt to be very significant. The things that belonged to their peace were then hid from their eyes, and it was the holy will of God that that cup should not pass away.

Yet the Bishop had very strange respect in such a time as that was; for all the countrey round about and in a manner the whole county was dispeopled of the English, before ever any violence was used either to his house or his person. The manner of his behaviour, and the occurrences that he encountred withall in that sad time, the Reader may please to take as followeth.

There was one and the same day set for the first rising of the Irish all over the nation, which was Saturday, the 23d of October, 1641. But yet even in Ulster it self, the North part of Ireland, where the Rebells were most forward and fierce in that bloudy action, they did not proceed in all places with the same fury. In the County of Cavan they carried their business at first with a kind of hesitation; here and there some particular houses of the English were spoiled, and that was all. The chief of the Irish Gentlemen there being of the name of the O'Relys, rather sought to persuade the English by fair words and promises to depart the countrey, than to fall upon them at first by plain force. The chief of those O'Relys not dwelling far from the Bishop, came frequently to visit him at his house; especially Philip McMullmore O'Rely. And tho' the daily report of cruelties acted about in the countrey came so thick, that the business they were in hand with could not be hidden any longer; yet these O'Relys still gave comfortable words to the Bishop; and for a week or fortnight's space did not so much as take away any of his cattel. But before the first fortnight was expired, there began to come a great confluence of poor stripped English people to the Bishop's house for some shelter; like Job's Messengers bringing one sad report after another without intermission. They heard, that the Bishop was yet permitted the enjoyment of his house and goods, and the place was near to fly unto, and thither they were glad to retire.

The Bishop most freely entertein'd all that came, and fill'd all his out-houses with those Guests, as many as could sit one by another. Those that he knew to be of better quality, tho' as then levelled with the meanest, he receiv'd into his dwelling house: and thus for a little while those poor distress'd creatures were refreshed there. But the Irish had an evil eye at this goodness and charity of the Bishop, and used all their skill to hinder his entertcinment of the poor strip'd English : as first, by forewarning him not any longer to entertein those enemies, and to spend provision upon them. This message the chief of the O'Rellys sent to the Bishop ; and when that prevailed not, he came himself and told him the same ; threatning to take another course unless he would forbear. The Bishop's answer was, that he could not in charity but pitty and relieve those poor distress'd Christians ; and withall earnestly besought him to use his power for the restraining the rage of the multitude against them. But this prevailed so little, as that rather it did exasperate that cruel man the more. And, therefore, though some other of the Irish Gentlemen (as Luke Dillon, Esq., and Philip McMulmore O'Relly) labour'd to mitigate and soften his mind toward the Bishop; yet, being chief of them all, and Lord of that Countrey (after the Irish account), he would go on his own way: and after many threatning speeches to the Bishop (which he still meekly answered with some pious and religious returns), this tempter departed from him for a season.

But in the night time he sent men to the Bishop's out-houses where those poor English lay, who stripp'd them over again of what little covering they had gotten and frighted them with their drawn skeans* to drive them away from thence. And lamentable it was to hear the shrieks and outcries of those desolate comfortless people, who had no remedy but to fly where they could in a dark cold night from the rage of these persecutors. And some of them, rather than by their stay to bring any mischeif to the Bishop, chose to commit themselves to God's Providence and so wander away allmost naked, God knows whither. Others, shifting out of the way for the present, when they could with most privacy would return to their old shelter; and, besides such, there came daily other new Guests: all

* The name of the daggers used by the Irish and also by the Scotch Highlanders. —T. W. J.

which, while the Bishop had wherewithall, were daily provided for.
But Edmund O'Relly would no longer bear this expense of provision, which he said must be for the Mainteinance of the Souldiers. And, therefore, in short space a course was taken that the Bishop's cattell, some by night and some by day, were driven all off his ground. They began with the Oxen and Cows; next they seized upon the Horses both abroad and in the Stable; and lastly they took away the Sheep out of the court-yard. All this in a stealing filching way, mostly by night, as if they would seem not altogether to own their enterprize: but afterward it was well known, that the cattel were convey'd to Edmund O'Relly's land and there kept.

The Bishop for all this still relieved many poore stripped people in his out-houses: but it was a most grievous and daily burthen to his heart, (as needs it must to any Christian,) that he was forc'd to hear the cries, and see the cruel sufferings of those poor and naked people daily under his walls and windows: the common Rascality of the Irish still daily gathering together about the house, as ravens about a carcass, and growing more and more insolent, especially those few among them who had gotten any kind of arms.

One time amongst the rest, when a company of Irish, of whom some few had musquets, were rifling and tearing among those all most naked people; the cry was so great and dolefull, that the good Bishop would needs go out himself to their rescue. Those about him judg'd it very hazardous and labour'd to disswade him. But notwithstanding all their persuasions he would go out, taking three others in his company all unarmed; only the Bishop himself had a good long staff in his hand, handsomly carv'd and coloured, which an Irish Gentleman had sent him as a present some years before. As soon as they perceived the Bishop, they left harassing the poor English and fled about a stone's cast: and then two or three of the Musqueteers made a stand, and presented their musquetts right against the Bishop's breast. But the Bishop still went on, and clapping his hand upon his breast, bid them shoot there rather than offer violence to those miserable people. And God was pleas'd hereupon so to awe them, that they dismounted their musquetts and went away.

From henceforth the Bishop was more closely besieged (or rather taken) in his own house; nothing without-doors being now left, nor any freedom or safety to him or any with him within, but at the courtesy of the Irish; which (in comparison to what others met withall) was very much. For they suffer'd the Bishop thus to continue, and in some measure to enjoy himself from the first beginning of the Rebellion October 23d, till near upon Christmas following. And tho' he was prohibited from protecting or relieving any without the doors of his dwelling house; yet those that were within the Ark with him, were all this while free from violence through God's gracious and Allmighty protection: whose Holy name be therefore prais'd and magnified for ever.

The Reader shall next be acquainted with some passages, that occurred while the Bishop thus continued in his own house. As first, that even then and there (the house joining close to the Church) they had the comfort of God's publick and solemn worship on the Lord's days : the Bishop and two or three other Ministers performing the duties of that day in reading the Scriptures, publick Praiers, and the preaching of the Word without any considerable interruption. Then farther, they had the comfort of private prayers and conference between the Bishop and some Ministers, and others of the better sort of the English, that had taken Sanctuary in the Bishop's house. The present streights were excellent means to stir them up, and to dispose them to a more serious and heavenly managing of those duties: neither could they want the comfort of singing Psalms and Praises unto God, even in this their sad captivity. In all which holy exercises the good Bishop led them on, and by his truly heroick and chearfull deportment in this his Christian Academy, or School of Affliction, was no small encouragement to their sad hearts.

But as there were these encouragements ; so withall there wanted not discouragements able to break a well-establish'd heart. For the Bishops well-settelled and resolved mind was doubly assail'd all this while. First by the Irish: who tho' they did forbear him, as we have seen, yet laboured and desir'd very earnestly to have him go out of the Countrey. And as they profess'd much freindship to him so they often told him of his unsafety and danger in that place and condition, wherein he then stood; and offer'd him (if he pleased) to see him and his company safely guarded and convey'd to Dublin, or what other place he should choose.

This they often and earnestly offer'd; but the Bishop told them, he could not, nor would, of his own choice, desert his place and calling, that God had set him in : but if by force they would put him out, he would then cast himself upon God's Providence. And another thing was also in the way to hinder his embracing such a motion ; namely, the sad experience of many who, having accepted of Guards and Convoys from the Irish, were in their passage betraied and stripped, and sometimes murther'd outright by those that undertook to guard them.

But however others far'd, those English that were with the Bishop in his house had a confident persuasion that if he would have accepted a convoy for Dublin, he might have pass'd safe, and so have been a means of bringing them safely off also. And accordingly they all did in a manner continually lie at him to take a guard of the Irish and begon. Among others, his own Children helped (not a litle) to break his Christian courage; but all was in vain : he was allwaies ready to answer such as did solicite him, with some savory and pious apothegme or other: as, that it was a shame for a Bishop to be affraid of death; that it was a great weakness to be impatient in times of suffering : to which purpose he brought in a saying, related by an ancient writer, as represented in a vision from God unto him; *Pati non vultis ; exire non vultis ; quid faciam vobis ?* In English thus : you are unwilling to suffer ; you are unwilling to die ; what shall I do unto you ? And farther he would alledge, that for his own part he was ancient, and, if God so pleased, willing and desirous rather to die there than in another place. And to his children he said, that if they would go they should have his leave and furtherance and blessing: but for his own part, he was resolv'd not to stir till he was forc'd from his place.

When they saw his resolution thus settled they ceased; and most of them that were thus shelter'd with him took their opportunities (the best they could) some at one time, and some at another, and departed to Dublin. But the difficulties and dangers, the frights and insolencies they suffered, and the strange and miraculous waies of escape, which God made out for them, each man in a different manner, would make a tragical history: yet not alltogether so; forasmuch as they all escaped with their lives, *per tot discrimina rerum*; and, like St. Paul's fellow-passengers, some on boards and some on broken pieces of the ship, were all at last safely landed at Dublin.

Some weeks and allmost months thus passing, and the fury of the Rebellion being somewhat cooled, and nothing being now left to be taken as pillage or plunder from the English, nor in a manner any of the English Nation left in the countrey, the Irish began to think how they might secure what they had thus possessed themselves of. The only work they had to do, was to take some course with the Bishop of Kilmore who was all this while at their mercy, and to reduce two Castles that stood out upon their own defence. These castles were defended by their owners, two Scottish Knights,* that were of the Brittish, that had fled for refuge into them (with their neighbours and tenants).

As for the Bishop, tho' all his Cattell were taken from him, yet his corn (whereof he had a great quantity) and all his Substance within doors still remained. This booty the Irish had a long time expected; only, having as yet spared the Bishop, they would not proceed to the rifling of his house or seizing of his person without some seeming-urgent provocation thereunto. And for want of a better, they laid hold on this. Those Scottish Knights that stood

* Sir Francis Hamilton of Castle Keilagh; and Sir James Craig of Castle Croghan.—T. W. J.

upon their defence, as is above related, had several times made out small parties to bring in provision, which, how small soever, were a very great terror to the Irish. And at one time above all the rest, a party going out happen'd upon some persons of such quality among the Irish, as they thought it might be some advantage to themselves to take them as Prisoners. These Castles of the Scottish Knights had a long time stoutly defended themselves, and as dreadfully vex'd the Irish with but a very small company of men. But of all other indignities, this of taking prisoners did most trouble them; and the rather because one of the Prisoners was a chief man of the O'Rellys. But being a people of a base courage, unable to help themselves by any warlik exploit, they fell upon the unarmed Bishop and took this occasion to seize upon his house and goods.

There was also another thing that put on the designe; and that was the urgent importunity of the Popish Bishop or Anti-Bishop of Kilmore. For the Reader must know, it was the common condicion of all Ireland in those daies to have in every Diocese two Bishops, and in each Parish two Priests, the one Popish, the other Protestant. The Popish Bishop claimed his House and his Church, unjustly detein'd from him by one, in their account, an Heretick.

Therefore Edmund O'Relly, the chief man of that stock or family and Lord of the Countrey, comes to the Bishop's house, not as formerly in a peaceable manner, but with countenance, company, and language more compos'd to terror and revenge. He searched the house for arms, and seiz'd upon those few that were; he threatned and upbraided the Bishop for what the Scotts had done in frighting the countrey and taking prisoners; and told him that both Scotts and English should know that the Irish could take prisoners as well as they: and without many words the said Edm. O'Relly himself laid his hand on the Bishop's shoulder, saying, I arrest you in the King's name; you are my Prisoner. The Bishop with a chearfull countenance answer'd him to this effect: That he did not know wherein he had offended the King's Majestie, neither could he believe he had the King's Authority for what he then did; but however, that he should yield to the power then in his hand, withall putting him in mind that there was a God who would judge righteously.

But O'Relly not standing to word it with his Prisoner, call'd for an account of what was in the house; especially the plate, which was presently brought forth. It was not much; the chief was plate belonging to the Church which the Bishop, at his own cost, had caused to be made not long before and dedicated to the Church; a larg Flagon, a Chalice, and a Patin with this inscription, ECCLE-SIÆ KILMORENSIS. This the Bishop told O'Relly was the Churches and not his; and, therefore, desired it might not be converted to any other use, but be committed to his Brother (as he call'd him) meaning the Popish Bishop: who also had been inquisitive not only after the plate, but all the rest of the Bishop's goods, which he counted his part of the spoil and more properly belonging to himself. The Church-plate O'Relly durst not deny him, wherein Bishop Bedell's desire was fullfilled; and as for the rest of the goods, there was a contest between the Popish Bishop and O'Relly: but they made a shift to agree in the parting, as well as the taking. The greatest thing that stuck with our good Bishop was his Library. Yet some little satisfaction he had by thinking it should come into the hands of Scholars; for O'Relly told him, such things should be left to the Bishop.

Bishop Bedell being thus arrested by Edmund O'Relly, had only one night's lodging more in his own house. For the next morning O'Relly with very much verbal kindness and civility acquainted him that 'twas resolv'd he must be secur'd in a Castle not far off, in the midst of a great lough, above canon-shot from any shore, called Loughwater Castle: and as for his moneys, he told him they would leave him that to live on. As for his children, they might remain somewhere in the countrey. The Bishop had two Sonns and their Wives, partners and spectators with him in all these troubles; and it was to them a very hard thing to be parted from the company of their Father, whether in life or death: and therefore the Bishop made it his request, that they might go along with him to the Castle; and with much ado it was at last granted.

When the time was come that the Bishop and his company were to be sent to the Castle, the Bishop's own horses being taken away long before, O'Relly was so civil as to furnish them all with horses; and so with a small guard conveighed them to the water-side, and thence by boat wafted them over to the Castle, standing in the midst of a great Lough or Lake. In the passage, the Bishop behav'd himself with a strange measure of chearfullness, telling his sons, whom he saw somwhat dejected, that he bless'd God for that day wherein he was pleased to honour him so far, as to call him to suffer somthing for his name: and said farther, he thanked God that he found himself as chearfull and joifull as ever he was upon his marriage-day: but alass! there were none so furnish'd for such a trial, as to answer the Bishop with the like Christian fortitude, either in heart or voice: yet it was no small comfort to all the company to have such a Champion.

Being come into the Castle they were accommodated well. The Governour Mr. Owen O'Relly, formerly a tenant to the Bishop and a very civil and honest Gentleman, used the Bishop with all possible courtesie. The place it self was very commodious for room and lodging; and there was also good company, Mr. Arthur Cullum and Mr. William Castleton,* fellow prisoners with the Bishop. Neither wanted there any provision; for by the care of the Governour they were furnish'd with sufficient for their money. They had free liberty to exercise their Religion together in a chamber for themselves; with very strict charge from the Governour that none should interrupt them. And it was no small privilege, that there they were free from the insolencies of the common people: in this only being in the condition of prisoners, that some of them for a time were forc'd to wear iron bolts; which honour the Bishop was very ambitious of, and desir'd that he might excuse all the rest or else bear them company in this suffering; but it was denied.

* Or Castledyne, according to Mr. Clogie.—T. W. J.

In this posture, our good Bishop and his fellow-prisoners kept their Christmass, not in feasting, but in Prayer, Doctrine, Exhortation, and Godly Conference. Besides the private comfort of which Holy Exercises, God was pleased to send in some comfortable news by a strange way concerning the publick, which was thus. The English in those parts (those few that were left), by reason of the great distance from Dublin, were kept from all intelligence but what the Irish pleas'd to communicate; and that was only such as might terrify them, and render their condition hopeless of any succour or relief whatever. All their discourses in the audience of the English were still of the successes of their Army: as of that sad defeat of the 500 men, the first that took the field for the English cause and were intended for the strengthning of Droghedagh; of their firm union together by reason of the conjunction of the Lords of the Pale with the rest of the Rebells, and especially the siege of Droghedagh and even of the taking of the city: which they so confidently affirm'd, that they named the very day, and in their reports divided the spoil, as the Mother of Sisera: This was the chear the poor English had to keep Christmas.

But it happen'd that in the Castle where the Bishop was prisoner, one night a soldier newly-come from Droghedagh was entertein'd by some of the guards, who kept their court in the lowest rooms. In the night late some of the guard question'd the souldier what news there was from Droghedagh. One of the English prisoners that understood Irish, being just over their heads, laid his ear to a clift in the plancher, and listned to their discourse. The souldier told them plainly that the siege was broken up, and shew'd them his own hands and arms all scratch'd and rent with thorns and briars, while he was in a hasty retreat from an assault they had made upon the City. He told them also that the bulletts pour'd down as thick from the walls as if one should take a fire-pan full of coals and pour them down upon the hearth, which he acted before them, sitting all together at the fire. And for his own part he said he would be hang'd before he would go forth again upon such a piece of service. He that listned soon communicated this good news to his fellow-prisoners, whereby it pleased God to revive their spirits not a little, but they were fain with all diligence to keep the matter to themselves.

After Christmas, without the Bishop's desire or good-liking, had it been in his choice, his removal from the Castle was effected thus. Some special friends of the Bishop, Luke Dillon, Esqr., Philip McMullmore O'Relly, Mr. Dennis Sheridon, did intercede for his enlargement with Edmund O'Relly, that then had the chief command of the countrey, who, tho' willing to have that Castle, their chief magazine, clear'd of the English prisoners, yet liked it well so to be sought to for their enlargement. Nor was that all, but another solemnity must be observ'd also. For he requir'd an exchange of those that the Scottish Knights had taken prisoners, that they might be set at liberty in lieu of the Bishop and his company. And accordingly persons were sent to treat with the Scotts, whose respect to the Bishop mov'd them to consent to an exchange, which the Bishop could not deny, knowing it to be the desire of those in whose power he was then.

All being agreed, and the time concluded upon, the Bishop and his children were set at liberty, but such a liberty as was more dangerous than the former imprisonment. As for his own house, that was in possession of Edmund O'Relly and the Popish Bishop, and thither they would not suffer him to return. So that now he that was wont to give entertainment to others had no place to hide his head, but at others' courtesy. He had his choice of two places, both not much above a mile distant from his house. One was the house of Luke Dillon, Esqr., brother to the then Earl of Roscommon, who very importunately invited him to abide with him till they might have a safe conduct to Dublin. The other was the house of Mr. Dennis Sheridon, an Irish man, and of a family, tho' inferior to the O'Rellys, yet numerous and potent in the countrey. This man had been educated from his childhood in the Protestant Religion, in the house of a very Reverend and Godly Divine, Mr. Hill, sometime Dean of Kilmore, by whom he was so well principled that he allwaies stood firm to the Protestant Religion. The Bishop of Kilmore took allwaies a special notice and liking of him, and for his good conversation and skill in the Irish language he promoted him to the Ministry, and conferr'd on him a Church-living; * where the inhabitants being all Irish, an Englishman had been unable in any sort to discharge that duty incumbent upon a Minister to such a people.

This man, tho' a Protestant and a Minister, yet being Irish, and of a name and family powerfull in that countrey, was exempted from that violence which then Protestants sadly suffer'd from the Irish. To his house the Bishop made choice rather to retire; which indeed was a common asylum or sanctuary to as many distress'd English as it could contein. Here the Bishop had the most loving and best accommodacions that the house could afford. And all the chief of the name, Sheridons, out of their love to their kinsman and the Bishop now sojourning with him, did often express and promise their utmost endeavours, to the hazard of their lives, to secure them and the house from any violence whatever.

While the Bishop liv'd here, being not above a mile from his own house, he had a desire to hearken after his Library which he had left there; and, if it might be, to have the use of some books and papers of his own. Wherein by Mr. Sheridon his means he had his desire. For he, having some familiar acquaintance with the Popish Bishop, had liberty to go where the books were, and so procur'd for our Bishop his Desk, and some books and papers at several times, as he saw his best opportunity. And among the rest (as Dr. Bernard in his character of Bishop Bedell hath published) the Bishop's MS. Hebrew Bible was by the care of this Mr. Sheridon preserv'd, and brought away out of the Irish's hands ;. and is now, according to the

---

* The Vicarage of Killasser. *See* Supplementary Chapter XVI.—T. W. J.

Bishop's last Will and Testament, in the Library of Emmanuel College in Cambridge.*

As for the rest of his books, some of them were taken away by Friars and Priests, that had frequent access to their Bishop while he there continued. The rest were little regarded by the Irish; and as soon as any alarum of the approach of English forces could reach that countrey, the Irish, after their usual manner, fled to the mountains and woods ; not troubling themselves with such luggage as books, but leaving them behind for booty to the English souldiers. And thus what *enemies* left, *friends* took away ; so miserable a comforter is war, that those that should have reliev'd the forlorn and desperate affairs of the English did but add to their affliction and oppression. The Bishop's books went every way but the right; and certain of his Sermons were preach'd in Dublin, and heard there by some of Bishop Bedell's near relations, that had formerly heard them from his own mouth : some even of the Episcopal Order were not innocent in this case; and, 'tis more than probable, are still beholding to Bishop Bedell's *papers*, that never would own his righteous cause when alive and upon the stage.

But to return to the Bishop. He continued some weeks in the house of Mr. Sheridon in some good measure of health; and during that time his manner was to pray in the family himself every day, as he formerly us'd to do in his own ; and the Lord's daies he spent with the company that was there, in prayer and preaching of the Word, both forenoon and afternoon, as long as health permitted. For the manner of this Bishop was never to make use of a Chaplain (tho' he had still one or other in his house), either to pray in his family or to give thanks at his table; unless in case of some young man, that intended the Ministry, whose gifts he had a desire to take some trial of. And as for preaching he seldom omitted a Lord's day, while he enjoy'd his place, and was at home, without doing

* There is no mention here of the saving of the MS. of the Irish translation of the Old Testament also by Denis Sheridan.—T. W. J.

some part or all the works of that day. In this course he held on till the last, when his *Diocese was reduced to but one family.*

And now the time drew near which God had destinated to put an end to his Labours; the manner whereof was thus. In the house of Mr. Sheridon (being very full of English who shelter'd themselves there) it pleas'd God, that a grievous sickness fell among them. It was a violent and continued feaver, commonly call'd by the name of the *Irish-ague.** It usually distracted the patient more or less. It was very infectious, generally passing through a family where once it seiz'd. To ancient people most commonly 'twas mortal, and that in little space. Those of younger years that escaped were sure to be brought very low, and to be a long time ere they could recover their strength. Most of the English in the house were sorely visited with this ague, and some ended their daies; having this comfort, that they were not suffer'd to fall into the hands of men but were taken away by the immediate hand of a Mercifull God.

Among others, the Bishop's wife's son † by a former husband was taken sick of this ague, and being not so well accommodated as he could have desir'd, (if the place and present condition of things could have afforded better,) the Bishop was the more sollicitous about him and would be too often at his bed. By this means it pleas'd God, that himself also was taken with this pestilential and deadly ague; which in a few daies took away his appetite and by consequence his strength; so as he was scarsely able to go or stand, but was necessitated to take to his bed. But yet before evening he would constrain himself to rise and pray with the family; till at last the force of the disease so far prevailed that being in Prayer his speech failed him, and he was not able to articulate his words. And

---

* From the description here given it is to be inferred that the fever was malignant typhus, which prevailed in Ireland in 1641 and subsequent years. It had nothing in common with *ague* or *intermittent fever*, which is extremely rare in Ireland and not contagious. *See* Supplementary Chapter XII. for further observations on the nature of Bishop Bedell's last illness.—T. W. J.

† Mr. Edward Mawe.

before this he complain'd, that he could neither command his mind nor get his tongue, either to conceive or express what he intended and desir'd.

When he was become thus weak, among others that came to visit him, one of more principal note, that bore a great affection to him, and yet a zealous Papist, may deserve especially to be mention'd. It was Philip McMullmore O'Relly, Brother to him that imprison'd the Bishop. This Gentleman from the very first spake openly against the rebellion and whoever were contrivers of it, and in his ordinary discourses would curse them bitterly. He being come to see the Bishop, after some few words (which he hardly could utter for tears) he besought the Bishop if he wanted money or any other necessaries, to make use of any thing that he was able to furnish him withall. To which the Bishop, rising up out of his chair, made return thanking him for his great civility, desiring God to requite him for the same and to restore peace to the Nation: though hardly able to stand, he yet beyond expectation thus expressed himself without any faultring in his speech, which he had not done for a great while before. After this he seldom spake and but brokenly. Being sometimes asked, How he did; his answer was still, *Well;* nor did there appear by any excessive heat or groaning or other sign that he felt any great pain. Being himself not able to speak, others often went to prayer by his bed's side: and he, by the elevation of his eyes and affectionate pronouncing the word *Amen,* when he never else was heard to speak, testified his concurrence in that duty.

Drawing now near his dissolution, when his breathing was turn'd into panting, his sons craving his blessing, he expres'd himself thus: *God bless you and bring you to Eternal Life.* When they had receiv'd his blessing and saw him hastening away, they brake forth into tears and fell a weeping over him; not thinking ever to have heard him speak more. But on a suddain looking up, even when death was allready in his eyes, he spake unto them thus: *Be of good chear ; Be of good chear : whether we live or die we are the Lord's.* And these were his last words.

Thus this good Bishop ended his daies:—A man eminent for Godliness, Integrity, Humility, Learning, Laboriousness in his Calling, Zeal for the Reformation of the Church, and above all Eminent in trials and sufferings. When he was dead, the Popish Bishop at first would not suffer him to be buried in the Churchyard of Kilmore, because he was (as he accounted) an Heretick. But O'Relly and the chief of the Irish Gentlemen overul'd the Bishop in that, and liberty was given to bury him where himself had appointed in his last Will and Testament.

So great an enemy he was to worldly pomp and vanity that his very grave and burial may be a Monument hereof to posterity, concerning which he appoints thus : " For this corruptible flesh I appoint that it be committed to the ground without any funeral pomp in the Church-yard of Kilmore, at the south corner thereof, in the same grave or hard by the corps of my dear Wife Leah and my Son John ; about whose coffins and mine, I do appoint that there shall be a wall of stone raised up from the bottom and the ground raised up to the levell of the rest of the walke by the wall on the west side of the Church-yard, and one or more large Grave-stones laid over, with this inscription : GUILIELMI QUONDAM KILMORENSIS EPISCOPI DEPOSITUM." He allwaies bore a reverend respect to the place of God's publick worship, and upon all occasions was wont to testify his dislike of burying dead bodies within those walls ; both as savouring of pride in death and a vain affectation of worldly pomp; and also as a kind of prophanation of that place, destinated to a more Spiritual and Holy use. For himself, he took a sure course to avoid it; choosing the remotest corner of the Church-yard to be the burying place for him and his. Where according to his own appointment his corps was interr'd.

Onely in one thing his will was not fulfill'd, because the Irish would have their wills; and out of their affection to him would needs accompany him to his grave not without some kind of pomp.

The manner was thus: when the day appointed for his burial was come, the Irish in a considerable number resorted to the house; especially those of the Sheridons, being of the same name with the Minister in whose house he died; and some of the principal of them would needs be the Bearers. When the company had passed something above half-way to the Church, Edmund O'Relly, that had imprison'd him and dispossess'd him of all (being then resident in the Bishop's house joining close to the Church), came forth to meet the corps, being accompanied with Mullmore O'Relly his son, then Sheriff of the County, and some other Gentlemen, and attended with a party of Musquetteers and a drum. The comming of this company in this warlike manner was thought at first to be intended to hindei and oppose the burial of the Bishop's corps; but when they met the Beare, it prov'd no such thing. For O'Relly and those with him applied themselves in most courteous and condoling language to the Bishop's sons; speaking respectfully and honorably of the dead, and comfortably to the living: and so commanding their drum to beat, as the manner is when a souldier is buried, and placing the Musquetteers before the Corps, they thus conveighed the Bishop to his Grave. And being come thither, the Sheriff told the Bishop's sons that they might use what Prayers or what Form of Burial they pleased; none should interrupt them. And, when all was done, he commanded the Musquetteers to give a volley of shot, and so the company departed.

To close up this Narrative of the Life and Death of the Bishop of Kilmore, and, as it were, to set his seal to it, let the Reader take notice of the Sculpture or Engraving of his seal; conteining in it, as it were, a prophetical synopsis of the whole course of his Life. It was his own device, and engraven first by his own hand upon the haft of his knife, before he could foresee what lot God had laid out for him. The hint that he took for his conceit, as by the inscription may be gather'd, was out of the Scripture, Isay i. 25, *And I will turn my hand upon thee, and purely purge away thy dross, and take away all thy tin.* The last sentence of this verse in the Hebrew goes thus, וְאָסִירָה כָּל־בְּדִילָיִךְ In conformity to this Scripture with allusion to his own name, *Bedell* (or, as 'twas anciently Bedyl), the device was this: A crucible or Fining-pot standing in flame with this Superscription, *הָסֵר מִנִּי כָּל־בְּדִילִי* Purge from me all my Tin*: turning what the Prophet sets down as a promise to Sion, into a Petition to the Lord for himself to take away all his Tin from him. After he was made a Bishop, he caused this in a larger figure to be set upon his Episcopal Seal: possibly not thinking then, much less imagining in his younger years, that God would have answered his Petition so punctually according to the literal sense, as by experience he after felt. But 'tis the Lord's usual manner in answering the Prayers of his people, to do it in waies least imagined by them, but most tending to the advancement of his own Glory and their Spiritual advantage; as may be plainly observ'd in his dealings with this his Faithfull Servant. Blessed for ever be his Holy Name. Amen.

* *Haser minni col bedili.* On the seal the Hebrew superscription is without points. In the Public Record Office, there are several letters from Bishop Bedell to Archbishop Laud, with this seal attached. From one of them, I made the drawing for the annexed wood-cut.—T. W. J.

SUPPLEMENTARY CHAPTERS,

GENEALOGICAL AND HISTORICAL,

COMPILED FROM ORIGINAL SOURCES,

BY

THE REPRESENTATIVE OF THE BISHOP'S MOTHER'S FAMILY OF ELLISTON,

THOMAS WHARTON JONES, F.R.S.

CHAPTER I.

BIRTH AND PARENTAGE.

In some of the biographies of Bishop Bedell it is assumed as a fact that the Bedells of Black Notley were of the same family as the Bedells of Writtle, and a pedigree of the latter is quoted from Morant's History and Antiquities of the County of Essex as the pedigree of Bishop Bedell's family. There is, however, nothing in Morant's account of the Bedells of Writtle, nor in the entry of the family in the Heralds' Visitation Books for Essex, to show that there was any near relationship between them and the Bedells of Black Notley. The latter, however, may have been, and most probably were, originally of the same stock as the Bedells of Writtle, but the separation of the two branches must have taken place prior to 1550, the date from about which the Bedells of Black Notley are to be here traced as a distinct family.*

Thomas Bedyll of Black Notley in the County of Essex, Yoman, in his will, dated September 16, 1550 (and proved in the Commissary Court of the Bishop of London for parts of Essex), directs his body to be buried in Black Notley church, and mentions his wife Johan, his daughters Alice, Custans, Johan, and Margery,

---

* Bedell is sometimes pronounced with the accent on the last syllable, but in Essex it is pronounced with the accent on the first. That this has been the usual mode of pronunciation is shown by the frequency with which we meet the name spelt Bedle or Beadle. As to the etymology of the name, it is likely enough to have been derived from the office of a Bedell or Beadle, though it has been supposed to have had a local origin. I have seen the name variously written Bethell. This, therefore, suggests the idea that if not identical with Bethell, the name may still have had a similar ancient British derivation, and thus have been originally Ap Edell or the like, and converted into Bedell by striking off the A of the "Ap," and converting the p into b, just as *Bethell* has been formed out of *Ap Ithell*

and his sons John the elder, Thomas, James, and John * the younger.

The will of a Johanne Bedell of Hatfield Peverell, co. Essex, widow, was proved in the Commissary Court of the Bishop of London for parts of Essex in 1576. It is dated April the 7th, 1573, and the first witness to it is "John Bedell of Black Notley." She mentions the children of three daughters, Brokes, Wyseman, and Rix or Cricks. This testatrix was probably Johan, the widow of Thomas Bedyll of Black Notley.

I have not ascertained anything concerning the sons Thomas, James, and John the younger.

It is the line of John the elder, the father of Bishop Bedell, which is to be traced here.

Bishop Bedell's mother's maiden name was Aliston, or as it is written in the text Elliston, which was another mode of spelling the name. She was sister of Mathew Aliston or Elliston of Castle Hedingham, co. Essex, the Mathew Elliston senior of the entry of the family at the Heralds' Visitation of Essex for 1634. In the original Book of Entries (C. 21) at the College of Arms, the name had been first written with an A, but an E had afterwards been written over the A.†

* It was not uncommon in the age of the Tudors to give the same Christian name to two of the children of a family.

† See " The Pedigree of Alliston or Elliston of Essex and Kent, &c." in the HERALD AND GENEALOGIST, vol. v. 1868. According to Domesday Book certain lands in Black Notley were, in the time of Edward the Confessor, held by a freeman named Alestan. This Alestan possessed lands in several other parishes of Essex, but was deprived of them all at the Conquest, except a portion in Notley and Stambourne. I do not know whether it was this same Alestan or another, who was a Thane, and had large possessions in Norfolk. The name Alestan is obviously the Saxon original of our Aleston, Aliston, or Alyston, with or without a double l, and with or without a final e. As in the case of the Saxon Athelstan or Ethelstan, and the German Adelstein or Edelstein, the initial letter was written indifferently A or E, sometimes, also, Ae. Alestan, or Elestan, indeed appears to be merely a contracted form of Athelstan, Aethelstan, or Ethelstan; for example, " Elystan " or "Ethelystan " Glodridd, the name of the Welsh Prince who was godson of Athelstan the Saxon.

BIRTH AND PARENTAGE.

John Bedell was buried at Black Notley on the 1st of August, 1600 (P. R.*). His will, dated December 10, 1597, the 40th of Queen Elizabeth, was proved at Braintree, in the Commissary Court of the Bishop of London for parts of Essex, on the 2nd of September, 1600. In it he directs his body to be buried in Black Notley church. He mentions his wife Elizabeth, his son John the elder, his second son William, his third son John the younger,† his eldest daughter Grace, and his two younger daughters Elizabeth-Joane and Rachel. He named his son John the elder executor, and his wife Elizabeth executrix. His " well beloved freende, his brother-in-law Mathew Alistone of Castle Hedingham," his cosin John Bedell of Fayrsted, his cosin Hawtrey of Langford, and his son William, he appointed overseers of his will.

Mrs. Elizabeth Bedell survived her husband nearly twenty-three years. She was buried at Black Notley on the 28th of March, 1624,‡ and her will, dated March 14, 1623-4, was proved at Braintree, in the Commissary Court of the Bishop of London for parts of Essex, on the 15th of October following. In it, she directs her body to be buried in the parish church of Black Notley in the same tomb or as near as may be to her dear husband John Bedell deceased. This shows that her husband's direction in his will that he should be buried in Black Notley church had been carried into effect.

The testatrix mentions her eldest son John, her second son William, to whom she leaves her Bible, her daughter Walford (Grace), her daughter Jervis (Elizabeth), and her third daughter Rachel

---

* I have myself traced the records of the Bedell Family in the Parish Register of Black Notley, and have, in addition, been favoured with communications on the subject from the Rector, the Rev. T. Overton, B.D. to whom for his obliging courtesy my best thanks are due.

† This is another example of repetition of the same Christian name in one family.

‡ In the Parish Register her burial is entered under 1623, though properly the year was as above mentioned.

without naming her, to show whether she was married or not, though Rachel was then married, as will be seen below. Mrs. Bedell makes small bequests in money to all her grandchildren without specifying them in particular, further than that she leaves more to her daughter Jervis's children than to her other grandchildren. She leaves a ring to each of her two daughters-in-law, that is, Marable, the wife of her eldest son John, and Leah, the wife of her second son William, then Rector of Horningshearth, co. Suffolk. Her eldest son, to whom she gives her silver bowle, &c., is named executor and residuary legatee.

The family of John and Elizabeth Bedell, it is said in the text, originally consisted of three sons and four daughters. The three sons, but only three of the daughters, we have seen, were living at the time their father made his will. The three daughters were still living, as just indicated, in March 1623-4, the date of their mother's will; but the son John the younger is not mentioned.

The Parish Register of Black Notley begins in the year 1570; and the first baptism in the Bedell family recorded in it is the following:—

"John Bedle, the son of John Bedle, was baptized the xxiij. day of October, 1570."

This was John Bedell the elder, above-mentioned as one of the executors of his father's will and sole executor of his mother's will; but whether he was actually the eldest son or only eldest surviving son is doubtful. The burial of a James Bedle, the son of John Bedle, is recorded under the date of September 12, 1572 (P. R.). Though there is nothing to show what was the age of this James Bedell, he is put down as the eldest son of John and Elizabeth Bedell under notice, in one of numerous marginal MS. notes regarding the Bedell family in a copy of Burnet's Life of Bishop Bedell, edition 1685, now in the possession of a gentleman in the county of Monaghan, in Ireland; for extracts from which notes I am indebted to the courtesy of the Rev. Dr. Reeves, of Tynan, near Armagh.

The book in question belonged to, and has in the handwriting of the owner the superscription, " Thomas Bedell, in Charles Square, Hoxton, 1721." He was a Merchant and appears to have considered himself the next heir-male of Bishop Bedell's family, after the death of the Bishop's grandson Ambrose (s. p.), as we shall see more particularly below.

This Thomas Bedell, however, evidently knew nothing certain of the parentage of the James Bedell of the entry in the burial register of Black Notley above-mentioned. But if the James Bedell in question was really a son of John and Elizabeth Bedell, that couple must have had originally four sons instead of three as stated in the text.

The daughter who died young was Jone, whose baptism is recorded under the date of August 11, 1583. (P. R.)

To recur to John Bedell the elder, who was baptized on the 23rd of October, 1570. The following extract from the Parish Register of Black Notley appears to be the record of his marriage :—

"John Bedle and Marable Burtel,* widow, were married 25th April, 1613."

There does not appear to have been any issue of this marriage. No child of John Bedell, at least, survived him. In the Parish Register of Black Notley, the burial of " Marable the wife of John Bedle " is recorded April 13, 1630. In a list of freeholders in the county of Essex, *circa* 1633 (Harleian MS. 2240, in the British Museum), the following occurs :—

" NOTLEY NIGRA. Johes Beadell, gen. junr."

It is just possible that this was a son; who had afterwards died. Bishop Bedell in his will dated February 15, 1640-1, leaves his brother John a ring, but makes no mention of any child of his, though he leaves small legacies to the children of his three sisters.

---

* The parchment is here so wrinkled, and the writing so defaced and indistinct, that it is not certain whether Burtel or Bulteel be the correct reading of the name.

That John Bedell was living in 1643, appears from a letter * written by the Rev. William Bedell, the eldest son of the Bishop, to Dr. Samul Warde, his father's friend and his own godfather, from Whipstead, under the date of June 12, 1643, in which he says, that he rested in Essex *in his father's brother's house* after his long and dangerous journey out of Ireland. The following is probably the closing record of the elder brother of Bishop Bedell :—

" 1653. John Beadell, buried October 18." (Black Notley P. R.)

William Bedell, second son, the future Bishop of Kilmore, and special subject of our history, will come under notice below.

John Bedell the younger was the third son living in 1597, the date of his father's will. The following is the entry of his baptism in the P. R. of Black Notley:—

" John Bedle, son of John Bedle, was baptized viii January 1578."

This John the younger, not being mentioned in his mother's will, had, it is to be presumed, died before March, 1623-4.

Grace Bedell, the eldest daughter, was baptized at Black Notley on the 3rd of September, 1576. (P. R.) She is mentioned in her father's will (1597) as unmarried ; but in her mother's will (1623-4) she is spoken of as Mrs. Walford. She was the first of the four witnesses to her mother's will. Her brother the Bishop in his will says: " Item, I give to Edwin Walford and each of his sisters Phœbe and Elizabeth to everie of them ten pounds. Item, I give to John Walford five pounds." Edwin, Phœbe, and Elizabeth Walford were no doubt the children of Mrs. Grace Walford. Whether John Walford was her husband or another son, I have not been able to determine.†

* For this letter see Chapter XIX.
† In Black Notley church there is an inscription recording a benefaction to the parish, as follows :—

"Mary, daughter of Edwin Walford, of this parish, gent. married first to Humphrey Neudeck, of London, Physician, and afterwards to Capt. Thomas Kitching, dying 16th of December, 1722, left to the poor of this parish £10 a year for ever."

BIRTH AND PARENTAGE.

Elizabeth Bedell, the second daughter, was baptized at Black Notley on the 10th of June, 1581. (P. R.) She is mentioned in her father's will (under the name of Elizabeth Joane) as unmarried, but her mother, in her will, speaks of her as her daughter Jervis. Her brother the Bishop in his will mentions her children thus: " Item, I give to Mary Jervice ten pounds, and to William Jervice five pounds."

Rachel Bedell, the fourth, but third surviving, daughter, was baptized at Black Notley on the 24th of September, 1586 (P. R.), and was married at Black Notley to Thomas Willis on the 12th of November, 1618. (P. R.) It has been above stated that she is mentioned in both her father's and mother's wills. In her brother the Bishop's will, five pounds are left to each of " the two sonnes of my sister Willys."

To recur to William Bedell, the second son of John and Elizabeth Bedell: In the Parish Register of Black Notley there is the following entry :—

" 1571.
" William Bedle, the son of John Bedle, was baptized the xiiij day of January, 1571."

To this there has been appended the marginal note : " Ep^{us} de Kilmor in Hibernia."

In all the published biographies of Bishop Bedell, the year of his birth is put down as 1570. This mistake no doubt originated by confounding William's baptism with that of his elder brother John, who was really born in 1570, as appears from the entry in the Parish Register of Black Notley above quoted. According to the mode of numbering the months of the year in present use, William Bedell was baptized on the 14th of January, 1572, having been born probably in the preceding month, viz. December, 1571. In his letter to the Roman Catholic Bishop Swiney, declining that Prelate's offer to come and take up his abode with him, as a protection against the rebels, dated November 11, 1641, Bishop Bedell himself approximately mentions his age when he says he is "*jam* *pene Septuagenarius.*"* The entry in the Parish Register of Black Notley, above quoted, shows that the Bishop at the time he wrote this wanted only about six weeks of seventy.

In the MS. of the text it was stated that William Bedell was born on Michaelmas Day, but I corrected the mistake, as there can be no doubt that it was his elder brother John who was born on that day, seeing that he was baptized on the 23rd of October; William had most likely been born at Christmas time, possibly on Christmas Day. Therefore the quaint remark, which I have struck out, about William's birthday presaging him an antagonist against the Devil and his Angells, on the supposition that it was Michaelmas Day, is inapplicable. If the day of William Bedell's birth presaged anything of his future career, it presaged that he would be a messenger of peace and goodwill whithersoever he went, and an intrepid soldier of the Cross of Christ. Having been led by the providence of God to Ireland, it was in that kingdom he executed his holy and beneficent commission.

CHAPTER II.

EDUCATION AND ENTRANCE INTO HOLY ORDERS.—COLLEGE CONTEMPORARIES.

William Bedell and his brother John had no great distance to walk to school at Braintree from Black Notley Hall-Farm, close by the Church, where they lived. The dislike of John for school, mentioned in the text, seems to have been the counterpart of that so quaintly related of his father, though John was more indulgently treated than his father was. William, at the same time that he had no small share of his father's determination and firmness, took more

* Clogie's memoir printed from the MS. No. 6400 in the Harleian Collection, British Museum, and edited by Mr. W. Walker Wilkins: London, 1862. Bedell's words are: "Episcopo jam pene Septuagenario, Christi causa, nulla mors acerba esse potest, nulla non oppetenda." P. 189.

after his mother, who from the glimpse we have of her in the text, and in her will, appears to have been, like her brother Mathew Elliston or Aliston, and his family,* a person of superior mental endowments.

Before he had completed the thirteenth year of his age William Bedell was sent to Cambridge, where he was admitted Pensioner of Emmanuel College, on the 1st of November, 1584, and, on the 12th of March following, matriculated scholar, being the 19th on the list from the foundation, including the four first scholars named in the Charter. In 1588 he graduated B.A. and in 1592 M.A. In 1593 he was elected Fellow of his College, being 14th on the list from the foundation, including the three first fellows named by the founder, Sir Walter Mildmay.†

On the 10th of January, 1596-7, being then twenty-five years of age, Bedell was ordained Priest, and in 1599 he took the degree of B.D.

From its foundation, Emmanuel College was distinguished for the devotional earnestness of its members, so that it acquired a reputation for Puritanism.

In the text (page 4) it is stated that Mr. Bedell's first essay in practical Divinity was the discharge of the office of Catechist in the College; and in a MS. note in the copy of Bishop Burnet's Life of Bedell, 1692,‡ in the British Museum, it is said that whilst still at the University, he, "in conjunction with Mr. Abdius Ashton of

* The Ellistons or Alistons were Puritans or of a Puritanical turn (that is, holders of matters doctrinal against mere ritualism). For indications of the part—religious and political—taken by the sons of John Aliston of Black Notley, the second son of Mathew the brother of Mrs. Bedell, during the Commonwealth and at the Restoration, see Whitelock's Memorials, p. 226; Calamy's Continuation of the Life and Times of Richard Baxter, under Stanford Rivers in Essex, and under Horsmonden and Sandhurst in Kent; the Rev. T. W. Davids's Annals of Evangelical Noncomformity in Essex; the Rev. Bryan Dale's Annals of Coggeshall.

† Coles' MSS. in the British Museum, 5851.

‡ This volume formerly belonged to Dr. Thomas Birch, and contains, besides this note, written by Mr. Lewes of Margate, also some MS. notes by Dr. Birch himself.

St. John's, Mr. Thomas Gataker of Sydney Sussex College, previously of St. John's, and some others, set on foot a design of preaching in places in the neighbourhood of Cambridge, where there were no pastors able to teach and lead the people in the ways of truth, peace, and life." This, which was probably encouraged by that "famous and worthie Minister of Christ, Master William Perkins," looks like an anticipation of the movement from which Methodism sprang, made at Oxford more than a century later by the Brothers Wesley, James Hervey, author of the "Meditations," George Whitfield, and some others.

To complete the history of this part of Mr. Bedell's life, it is necessary here to say a few words of his friends and contemporaries at Cambridge.

The Master of Emmanuel College during Bedell's time was Dr. Lawrence Chaderton, one of the divines to whose care the preparation of the authorised version of the Bible was entrusted by James I. In reference to his training under so excellent a master, Bedell, in a letter to Archbishop Ussher, observes, " The arts of dutiful obedience, and just ruling also, in part I did for seventeen years endeavour to learn under that good father Dr. Chaderton, in a well-tempered Society." Dr. Lawrence Chaderton was Fellow of Christ's College, and presided as Master over Emmanuel from its foundation in 1584 until 1622, when he resigned. He died in 1640, at the age of 103.

Samuel Warde, the intimate friend and correspondent of Bedell, and godfather of his eldest son William, was first entered at Christ's College, Cambridge, and thence was elected, in 1603, Fellow of Emmanuel College, being 12th on the list after Mr. Bedell. On January the 5th, 1609, Warde was appointed to the Mastership of Sidney Sussex College. In 1620 he was made Vice-Chancellor of the University, and in 1621 Lady Margaret's Professor of Divinity. Besides these University appointments, he had several preferments in the Church. Though of a Puritanical turn, he was, on the breaking out of the Civil War, for the King against the Parliament. In consequence of this, Dr. Warde was deprived of his Mastership and Professorship, and imprisoned, first in his own College, and subsequently in St. John's. Dr. Seth Ward, Fellow of Sidney College, and afterwards Bishop of Salisbury, was not a relation of Dr. Samuel Warde, but had been, as a student of Sidney College, patronized by him, and in his adversity proved himself an attached and faithful friend.*

Dr. Samuel Warde died on the 7th of September, 1643, and was buried on the 8th, according to an extract from the Parish Register of All Saints, Cambridge, in Cole's MSS. in the British Museum. His will, dated September 3, 1643, was proved at Oxford, November 25, 1644. He directed that he should be buried in Sidney College Chapel, and, among other bequests, he gave to Sidney College the gold medal which was presented to him by the State of the Low Countries, on returning from his attendance at the Synod of Dort. This medal bears a representation of the Members of the Synod in Session round a table in the *Kloveniers Doelen* Inn. Besides his wife and step-daughter, whom he named executrices, he mentions in his will brothers and other relatives, and it is satisfactory to infer therefrom, and from his bequests, that he did not die in so friendless and impoverished a state as is represented by his biographers.

James Waddesworth, a fellow-student of Bedell at Emmanuel College, graduated M.A. in 1593, and B.D. in 1600. In the latter year he was preferred to the two rectories of Cotton and Thornham Magna, in Suffolk,† as a double-beneficed man. He was also chaplain in ordinary to Dr. Redman, Bishop of Norwich. In 1605, he went to Spain as chaplain to Sir Charles Cornwallis, the English

* Dr. Seth Ward, in his preface to a volume containing some of the works of Dr. Samuel Warde, which he published in 1658, pronounces an eulogium on him, which breathes all the affection and devotion of a son.

† Davy's MS. Collections for Suffolk, in the British Museum, under the heads of Cotton and Thornham, Hartismere Hundred.

Ambassador. He had not been long in that country, when, having formed an acquaintance with some English Jesuits at Valladolid, he began to argue confidently with them against Popery, but, in the end, was himself perverted. On this, Waddesworth left the Ambassador's house, under the pretext of paying a visit to the University of Salamanca, and did not return. In letters to the Earl of Salisbury, dated from Valladolid, August 18 and September 8 and 15, 1605, Sir Charles Cornwallis expresses great grief at the " unhonest and unmannerlie revolt of his chaplaine," and feels himself " unhappie to have brought with him one so imperfect as to become occasion of such a scandal."* In another letter, Sir Charles mentions that the son of Lord Wotton † had been " *drawne by* Walpoole *the Jesuit to die a Papist.*"

After his perversion, Dr. Waddesworth remained in Spain, receiving a pension of 40 or 50 ducats a month from the King. Towards the end of his life he was employed to teach English to the Infanta Donna Maria, in anticipation of her projected marriage to Charles, Prince of Wales. In a letter to the Duke of Buckingham, dated Madrid, November 11, 1623, Waddesworth says: " I am sure the Infanta proceeds very cheerfully to learn English." And, speaking of himself, observes : " Good my Lord, I do (and ever have done) avow and profess myself a loyal subject and yet a Catholic."‡ A few days after writing this, Dr. Waddesworth died from consumption, it would appear, or, as his son called it, " cough in the lungs."

From the book written by Waddesworth's son James, entitled : " The English-Spanish Pilgrime," published by authority in London in 1630, it appears that Mrs. Waddesworth with her four children, who had been left in England when her husband went to Spain,

* Sir Ralph Winwood's Memorials of Affairs of State in the Reigns of Queen Elizabeth and King James I. vol. ii. pp. 109, 131, 136; fol. London, 1725.

† And nephew of Sir Henry Wotton. In his letter from Valladolid, Sir Charles Cornwallis refers to the expense he had been at in relieving young Wotton's pecuniary difficulties. (Winwood's Memorials, vol. ii. p. 151.)

‡ The Court of King James the First, by Dr. Godfrey Goodman, Bishop of Gloucester. Edited by John S. Brewer, M.A. Queen's College, Oxford, from the MSS. in the Bodleian Library. Vol. ii. p. 319.

was allured in 1609 into Flanders and thence to Spain. The son James, the author of the book just referred to, born in 1604, received his education at Seville and St. Omer's. After Dr. Waddesworth's death, the pension from the King of Spain was continued on his widow and family. The son James was nominated to a captaincy in the Spanish service in Flanders, but, renouncing popery, and being "converted into his true mother's bosome, the Church of England," came over to this country and published the work above mentioned.

In a strangely-written note at page 319, vol. ii., of Goodman's Court of King James the First, *ut supra*, this son James is confounded with his father, or rather the two are rolled into one monster, with the demerits of both attributed to him. The James Waddesworth said to have been living in 1655 was of course the son, the author of the " English Spanish Pilgrime," and, if there be any truth in the allegations of the note, he had turned out a most disreputable person.

Mr. Bedell was much grieved at Mr. Waddesworth's change of religion, and corresponded with him on the subject. After Waddesworth's death Bedell published the correspondence. It is referred to in the text (page 10) and will be noticed more particularly below. Here only may be quoted what Isaak Walton (Life of Sir Henry Wotton) has remarked of the tone of the correspondence:—" In these letters," says he, " there seems to be a controversie, not of Religion only, but who should answer each other with most love and meekness."

Joseph Hall was a fellow student of Bedell and Waddesworth at Emmanuel College, of which he became a Fellow, being 8th on the list after Bedell. He graduated M.A. in 1596, B.D. in 1603, and D.D. in 1610. He was at first Minister of Waltham Holy Cross in Essex (a donative benefice). In a letter to Bedell dated from that place May 15, 1615, Hall says that he was about to go to France as chaplain to the English Embassy there. In 1617 he was made Dean of Worcester. In 1618 he was one of the ministers deputed by King James to the synod of Dort. The gold medal, which, like Dr. Samuel Warde, Dr. Joseph Hall received on this occasion, is represented in his portrait,* suspended over his breast, and is said to be now in the possession of Emmanuel College, Cambridge. In 1627 Dr. Hall was made Bishop of Exeter, and in 1641 was translated to the Bishopric of Norwich. On the recommendation of Archbishop Laud, Bishop Hall composed his treatise of " Episcopacie by Divine Right asserted," which he published in 1640, 4to., and dedicated to King Charles I. It is said that the work was remodelled by Laud according to his own views and sentiments.

When the civil war broke out, Dr. Hall was removed from his bishopric by the Parliament, and subjected to much harsh treatment. The writing entitled "Hard Measure," and dated May 29, 1647, which he published, is a review of the proceedings of the Long Parliament against the Church and of the sufferings of the Bishops and Clergy.

Bishop Hall died at Higham near Norwich on the 8th of September, 1656, in the 82nd year of his age.

Hall, as well as Bedell, addressed Waddesworth on his change of religion, but it was to denounce him as an apostate. Waddesworth returned the letter to Hall through Bedell, to whom he wrote on the subject, saying:—

"Worthy Sir, I was exceeding glad to perceive by your kind, modest, and discreet letters, that you are still permanent in your own good nature, and constant in your love to me; not like Mr. Joseph Hall, neither bitterly reviling nor flourishing impertinently. Unto whom I pray you return his scoffing railing letter with these few marginal notes. When your reply unto my plain and few reasons come, I will, for your sake, read them over; and return you some such short rejoinder as it shall please Almighty God to enable me."

* The Rev. John Jones' Life and Times of Joseph Hall, Bishop of Norwich, 1826.

Another contemporary of Bedell at Emmanuel College was his own Cousin Joseph Aliston, who was however six years his junior. Joseph Aliston was the fourth son of Mathew Aliston of Castle Hedingham, co. Essex, the brother of Bedell's mother. He was admitted of Emmanuel College in 1595, graduated M.A. in 1602, and B.D. in 1609. In the last-named year he became Fellow of his college, and in 1614 was presented to the Rectory of South Runcton, in the county of Norfolk.

In the Tanner MS. lxxiv. 8, in the Bodleian Library, there is a writing dated Paris, April 9, 1612, by Dr. Joseph Aliston, addressed to Dr. Samuel Warde, on the "Idolatry of the Roman Catholic Church; the public Solemnization of the double match between France and Spain; and on Synods and Ministers of the Reformed Church." This writing is signed with Aliston's initials, of which the annexed is a fac-simile:—

and is accompanied by a short note to Dr. Warde from Mr. Thomas Lorkin.

Dr. Joseph Aliston died in 1631. By his will proved in P. C. C. July 19, 1631, he gave injunctions to his wife to send his two sons when old enough to a good "Free School," and afterwards to Emmanuel College, Cambridge, and to maintain them there for eight years. Besides portions, he left each of his three daughters an *English Bible.*

William Sancroft, born at Withersdale in Suffolk, graduated M.A. 1604, B.D. 1611, D.D. 1629. He was fourth on the list of Fellows after Joseph Aliston, and in 1628, August 2, was elected Master of Emmanuel College, on the death of Dr. John Preston, the successor of Dr. Chaderton. In a letter, dated Kilmore, Feb. 2,

1633-4, to Dr. Samuel Warde,* Bishop Bedell begs to be remembered to Dr. Chaderton and Dr. Sancroft, the only two besides Dr. Samuel Warde he had knowledge of while he lived at Cambridge—that is, the only two then at Cambridge.

Dr. Sancroft died at Bury St. Edmund's in 1637.

The Dr. William Sancroft who was afterwards Archbishop of Canterbury was nephew of the preceding. Of Emmanuel College, he graduated M.A. 1641, became Fellow 1642, graduated B.D. 1648, and D.D. 1653. He was elected Master of Emmanuel College, August 14, 1662, in room of Dr. William Dillingham. Dr. Sancroft was successively Dean of York, Dean of St. Paul's, and Archbishop of Canterbury. He was one of the Seven Prelates put on their trial by King James II.; but, after the Revolution of 1688, refusing to take the oaths to William and Mary, he was deprived. He now retired to Fressingfield his native parish, where he died and was buried in 1693.

Archbishop Sancroft, as shown in the preface, contemplated at one time the publication of the Life and Works of Bishop Bedell. For this purpose he obtained the MS. of the text here printed from Capt. Ambrose Bedell, and from Mr. Clogie a copy of his narrative. The Archbishop probably relinquished his intention on the appearance of Burnet's "Life."

CHAPTER III.

RESIDENCE IN VENICE.—SIR HENRY WOTTON.—FATHER PAULO.

On the 23rd of January, 1601-2, Mr. Bedell was licensed as a preacher in the Diocese of Norwich, having been appointed successor to the Rev. George Estye (author of an Exposition of the Creed and Ten Commandments) at St. Mary's, Bury St. Edmund's.

* Tanner MS. lxxi. 189, Bodleian Library.

After being five years resident at this place he received an invitation to go to Venice in the capacity of chaplain to the English Embassy there. Sir Henry Wotton the ambassador had been, in June 1604, accredited by King James to the Serene Republic for the purpose of supporting the Signiory in heart and courage against the Pope (Leo XI.) and that which they more feared—the power of Spain by which he was backed.

In May 1605, Camillo Borghese was elected Pope, in succession to Leo XI., and took the title of Paulo V. In about four months after, a quarrel with the Republic of Venice broke out, on account of various grievances which it was alleged the Church suffered at the hands of the Venetians; the crowning grievance being that the Signiory resisted the demand of the Court of Rome to deliver up to its authority two Ecclesiastics who had been committed to prison by the Civil Power in Venice for flagrant crimes. The dispute at last culminated in the Interdict which the Pope issued against Venice on the 17th of April, 1606. Nothing daunted, however, the Signiory ordered that no regard should be paid to the excommunication, and gave notice by a proclamation, dated April 28, 1606, " That whosoever hath received from Rome any copie of a Papal Interdict published there, as well against the law of God as against the honour of this Commonwealth, shall presently render it unto the Councill of X, uppon payne of death."*
At the same time the Jesuits, Theatines, and Capuchins, because they stood up as violent partisans of the Pope against the Republic, were expelled from the country.

Isaak Walton in his Life of Sir Henry Wotton says, that Sir Henry, on being appointed to the Venetian Embassy, " left England nobly accompanied through France to Venice by gentlemen of the best families and breeding that this Nation afforded; they were too

---

* Besides this, which is quoted from a letter of Sir Henry Wotton, there is, among the Venetian State Papers in the Public Record Office, a printed reply of the Council of Ten to the Pope's Interdict.

many to name, but these two for following reasons may not be omitted, Sir Albertus Morton, his nephew, who went his secretary, and William Bedell, a man of choice learning and sanctified wisdom, who went his chaplain." That Bedell accompanied Sir Henry Wotton to Venice in 1604 is however a mistake, which has been repeated in the published biographies of Bedell; and appeared even in the text, but by an alteration of three or four words I have corrected it. The fact is that Mr. Bedell only joined Sir Henry Wotton at Venice in 1607, in succession to the Rev. Nathaniel Fletcher (son of Dr. Richard Fletcher, who was Bishop of London from 1594 till his death in 1596), who had returned to England in the latter end of September 1606.*

That this was really the time when Bedell first went to Venice appears from several documents, which, as they illustrate our subject in various ways, I shall here set down in abstract: 1°. In a postscript to a letter (Venetian State Papers in the Public Record Office) dated Venice the 23rd of February 1606-7, to the Earl of Salisbury, Sir Henry Wotton begs his " Lordship's passport and incouragement for one Mr. Beadle whom I shall be very glad to have with me in the place of Chapelan, because I heare very singular commendation of his good gifts and discreet behaviour. It may therefore please y^r Lo^p (when he shall take the boldnesse to present himself before you) to sett forward also this piece of God's service."† 2°. Among the Tanner MSS. in the Bodleian Library at Oxford, there is a letter from Mr. Bedell to Dr. Samuel Warde, referring to preparations for his journey to Venice, and begging Dr. Warde to inquire of Mr. Fletcher, Sir Henry Wotton's previous chaplain, by what route he returned from Venice.‡ 3°. In

* See a note in the handwriting of Dr. Birch on a fly-leaf of the copy of Burnet's Life of Bishop Bedell, 1692, in the British Museum.

† See also the MS. note in Burnet's Life of Bedell 1692, in the British Museum, just referred to.

‡ It does not appear what answer Bedell received to this inquiry; nor by what route Bedell travelled to Venice, beyond the remark in the text that his passage

the letter which Bedell wrote to Mr. Adam Newton, lay Dean of Durham, and Preceptor of Henry Prince of Wales, dated Venice, " New year's day in our own stile 1607," being January 1, 1608, there is an indication of the date of his arrival in Venice, thus :—Bedell writes as if it was his first letter to Mr. Newton from Venice, and that he had been already some months in that city. He states that peace between Rome and Venice was concluded a few days before his arrival, by the revocation, on the 21st of April, 1607, of the interdict * which the Pope had fulminated against Venice on the 17th of April 1606. Then again Bedell states that the attempt to assassinate Father Paulo was not long after the first interview he had with him. The attempt to assassinate Paulo was made on the 5th of October, 1607, and, as Bedell's first interview with the Father did not take place until after Bedell had been already some time resident in Venice, we may conclude that the date of Bedell's arrival in that city was early in the summer of 1607.

The letter last quoted from is one of a correspondence between Mr. Bedell when in Venice and Mr. Adam Newton.† This correspondence has been published under the following title : " Some original letters of Bishop Bedell concerning the steps taken toward a Reformation of religion at Venice, upon occasion of the quarrel

over the Alps was especially difficult. *Apropos* of this it may here be stated that Sir Henry Wotton, in a letter (Sir Ralph Winwood's Memorials, *ut supra*, vol. ii.) dated July 19, 1604 (from Dover on his way to Venice), mentions that the route he was going to take was first to Boulogne then to Amiens, and so through Lorraine to Strasburg and thence by Augsburg. In returning to England in 1610 Sir Henry, we shall see, came by Lombardy and France, taking Paris in his way.

* Among the Venetian State Papers in the Public Record Office, there are two or three copies of the printed circular, dated April 21, 1607, which the Senate sent to the Archbishops and Bishops of the Republic, announcing the conclusion of peace with the Pope.

† Newton was a native of Scotland, and was made Dean of Durham in 1606 by King James, which dignity, though not in Orders, he held till 1620, when he resigned it, and was made a Baronet. Newton married Dorothy, daughter of Sir

between that State and the Pope Paul V. Dublin, 1742, edited by E. Hudson." The letters were printed from copies which had been supplied by Bedell to Archbishop Ussher.* The originals of the two principal letters, as received from Venice by Mr. Adam Newton, are contained in Volume 90 of the Lansdowne MSS., Articles 54 and 66, in the British Museum. A copy of Bedell's signature, traced from Letter II. which was written in the beginning of the year 1608-9, is here given:

William Bedell

In a letter from Venice to Dr. Samuel Warde, " dated St. Stephen's Day, in your account," 1607, Bedell, referring to the attempt made to assassinate Father Paulo, says, " I hope this accident will awake him (Paulo) a little more, and put some more spirit in him, which is his only want. Remember me to my cousin " (Alistone).

Though Mr. Bedell did not arrive in Venice until a few days after the revocation of the Papal interdict on the 21st of April, 1607, it is evident, from Sir Henry Wotton's letter to the Earl of Salisbury above quoted, that he was appointed to the Chaplaincy some considerable time before that date, viz. when the interdict against Venice was still in full force. When therefore Gilbert Burnet, in his Life of Bedell, says that " Bedell's reputation was so great and so well established, both in the University and in Suffolk,

---

John Puckering, Lord Keeper of the Great Seal in the time of Queen Elizabeth, and dying in 1629, was succeeded by his son William, who died unmarried, and was succeeded by his brother Henry, who assumed the name of Puckering on inheriting the estates of his uncle. Sir Henry Puckering died January 22, 1700, aged 83, when the title became extinct.

* These MS. copies are preserved in the Library of Trinity College, Dublin. There are copies also in the Bodleian Library. (Tanner MSS.)

that at the time of the interdict he was recommended as the fittest man to go Chaplain (to the Embassy at Venice) in so critical a conjuncture," he is quite correct. But following his informant Clogie in his mistake about the date of the interdict, and the time of Bedell's going to Venice, he laid himself open to the attack of Dr. George Hickes,* who, without himself possessing any particular knowledge of the matter, took exception to Burnet's narrative altogether, and threw discredit on his eulogium † of Bedell, merely because of an error in his dates. Burnet ought certainly to have taken better care to inform himself of the historical facts of the date of Sir Henry Wotton's Embassy to Venice, and of the Venetian interdict. But he can scarcely be blamed for confounding, as Isaak Walton and Alexander Clogie did before him, the time when Bedell went to Venice with that when Sir Henry Wotton himself proceeded on his mission.

From the knowledge of the facts such as he possessed Dr. Hickes ought to have seen, 1°, that Bedell had been recommended for the Chaplaincy at Venice in so critical a conjuncture as the interdict, and 2°, that there was some reason or other for recommending him. That reason, as above quoted from Sir Henry Wotton's letter, is the reason given by Burnet. Burnet negligently repeated what he had been told, but Dr. Hickes, affecting to argue from premises, nevertheless shuts his eyes to the obvious conclusion.

Though by the time Bedell arrived in Venice the dispute with

* Discourses occasioned by the funeral sermon of Bishop Burnet upon Archbishop Tillotson. London, 1695. 4to. Dr. George Hickes had been Dean of Worcester, but was deprived for refusing to take the oaths to William and Mary. He was one of the two non-jurors selected by King James from the list sent him by Dr. Sancroft (the deprived Archbishop of Canterbury) to St. Germain's, to be made Bishops, in order to keep up the Episcopal succession among the adherents of the King by Divine Right. Dr. George Hickes was accordingly consecrated titular Bishop of Thetford by Sancroft.

† It is something amusing, if not to be regretted, that Dr. Hickes, and even others after him, of High Church tendencies, should, out of animosity to Burnet, have endeavoured to depreciate Bedell, for surely there was nothing whatever in common between Bedell and Burnet.

CAMD. SOC. P

Rome had been compromised, the relations between the two governments continued to be far from amicable, and a secession of the Venetians from the Roman Catholic Church was still the hope of some and the dread of others. Isaak Walton, in his Life of Wotton, says, that it was at one time reported abroad that the Venetians were all turned Protestants, which was believed by many, for it was observed that the English Ambassador was often in conference with the Senate, and his Chaplain Mr. Bedell more often with Father Paulo.

Father Paulo, of the Order of the Servites, who played so important a part in the transactions of that period between Venice and Rome, was one of the most learned men of his time. Bedell says, in his letter to Mr. Adam Newton, dated January 1, 1607-8, that he " is holden for a myracle in all maner of knowledge divine and humane." Withal, as Sir Henry Wotton said of him, " He was one of the humblest things that could be seen within the bounds of humanity, the very pattern of that precept, ' Quanto doctior, tanto submissior.' " Though theology, morals, and politics constituted the subjects of his special department, Paulo is said to have been not only attached to physical science and anxious to promote its progress, but to have been himself an active investigator and discoverer. Baptista Porta acknowledged himself debtor to Paulo for much information; Galileo called him " Father and Master," and Fabricius Abaquapendente, the teacher of William Harvey, was his friend; nay, according to his biographer Griselini,* Paulo anticipated the discoveries in physiology, magnetism, and algebra, which are associated with the names of later celebrities in those sciences.

Griselini (in his preliminary address to the reader, p. xv.) says that " F. Paolo fu sommo Filosofo e sublime Matematico per destinazione della natura, e Giureconsulto soltanto per un caso fortuito

* Memorie Anedote spettanti alla vita ed agli studj del sommo Filosofo e Giureconsulto F. Paolo Servita, Raccolte ed ordinate da Francesco Griselini, Veneziano, della celebre Accademia dell' Istituto delle Scienze di Bologna. Ed. 2ª. In Losana, 1760. 8vo.

ed accidentale." It is no doubt true that Father Paulo manifested a capacity by nature to become pre-eminent in philosophy and science, but it is to be remembered that, how great soever the mind's capacity may be, knowledge in philosophy and science is not intuitive, but that it is only by prolonged investigation that man can find out what nature *does* and *suffers*. In putting forth the exaggerated claims just mentioned in behalf of Father Paulo, therefore, Griselini did little honour to his memory, whereas he misrepresents the real character of the man when he tries to ignore the well-known fact of Paulo's opposition to the errors of Popery, and that leaning of his to the Reformed Faith, which procured for him at Rome the epithet of "Mezzo Luterano." Sir Henry Wotton, writing to the Earl of Salisbury from Venice on the 13th of September, 1607, says that he sends his Lordship a very true picture of Maestro Paulo, the Servite, taken at his request. " It may be some pleasure unto his Matie," observes Sir Henry, " to beholde a sound Protestant as yet in the habit of a fryar, which I affirme unto youre Lo^p, not out of that vanitie (which maketh Jesuites register every great witt in their cataloge) but upon assurance thereof given me by my Chaplain, who hath sounded him in the principal poynts of our religion. By him (Mr. Bedell) I deale with him (Paulo) for lesse observation in diverse things of importance, and they spend upon agreement together every week almost one half day. He (Paulo) " continues Sir Henry, " seemeth as in countenance so in spirit liker to Philip Melancthon then Luther, and peradventure a fitter instrument to overthrow the falsehood by degrees then on a sodayne."

In a subsequent letter, dated Venice, December 21, 1607, Sir Henry Wotton tells the Earl of Salisbury that the picture just referred to was lost on the way, and in sending another picture of Padre Paulo Sir Henry remarks of it that " his Matie shall now, through the miscarriage of the former, receive one with the late addition of his scarrs."*

* The scars left by the wounds inflicted on Father Paulo by the assassins.

Father Paulo was born in Venice, August 14, 1552, and was baptized Peter, but he assumed the name of Paulo on entering the order of the Servites, November 24, 1566. He renewed his profession May 10, 1572, and was ordained priest at the age of twenty-five. Francis Sarpi, the father, was a person of an unsteady disposition, and did little for his family; but his wife Isabella, *née* Morelli, the mother, was a woman of great merit. Paulo seems to have inherited his moral and intellectual endowments from her, whilst to the kindness and care of her brother, Fra Ambrosio Morelli, he owed his early education. Under Father Giammaria Capella, of the Order of the Servites, he studied philosophy and divinity.

Father Paulo's position as " Chiefe Counsellour of the Signory of Venice in Affaires Ecclesiasticall " gave him high rank and influence. Associated with him were six other Theologians, viz.— Pietr' Antonio Ribetti, Archdeacon and Vicar-General of Venice; F. Bernhardo Giordano, Minor Observantine; F. Michel' Agnelo, Minor Observantine; F. Marc' Antonio Capello, Minor Conventual; F. Camillo Agustiniano; F. Fulgentio, of the Order of the Servites. These seven divines composed the protest against the validity of the Papal Interdict, entitled:—" Trattato dell Interdetto della Santità di Papa Paulo V. Nel quale si demostra, che egli non é legitimamente publicato, et che per molte ragioni non sono obligati gli Ecclesiastici all' essecutione di esso ne possono senza peccato Osservarlo. Venice, 1606," 4to. Of this a Latin translation, entitled " Tractatus de Interdicto S. Pauli V. Papæ," was published at Venice in 1610, 8vo.*

" Maestro Paulo and his schollar Fulgentio, Servites, both of great learning, piety, humility, discretion, integrity of life, and, which is especially to be considered as to our purpose, in great account with all sorts and deservedly," Bedell tells us, " desired

---

* This tractate, it is to be remarked, is a different work from the "History of the Interdict," by Father Paulo himself, which was first published in Italian in 1624, at Venice, after Paulo's death, and a translation of which into Latin by Bedell was published in 1626, as will be noticed below in Chapter V.

much the reformation of the Church, in a word, the substance of religion;" and entertained hopes that this might be accomplished if, as was expected, the Venetian Government had broken entirely with the Pope. Peace, however, having been brought about, as above-mentioned, this hope was for the time dashed, though not destroyed. A dread that Father Paulo might yet carry out his plans for a Reformation led the Papal party, it was said, to encourage the attempt that was made to assassinate him. On the evening of the 5th of October 1607, when on his way home from St. Mark's to his monastery, the Father was attacked by bravoes before and behind who inflicted on him three stiletto wounds, two in the neck and one in the face. The last entered by the right ear and passed out between the nose and the right cheek. The stiletto was found sticking in this wound.

Besides physicians and surgeons of the city of Venice, Fabricius Abaquapendente and Adrian Spigelius (names still known to the medical student), the eminent Professors of Padua, were summoned by the Senate to attend on the wounded Father, and received injunctions not to quit their patient until they were assured he was out of danger. Paulo, knowing whence the blow came, bitterly remarked to Abaquapendente, on being shown the stiletto which had been withdrawn from the wound in his face, that it was the style or pen with which the " Curia Romana " writes its arguments. This attempt on Father Paulo's life was considered a case of " Majestas læsa," as by a decree of the senate, passed some time before, the Father was declared to be under public protection.

On Father Paulo's recovery the Republic created Abaquapendente a Chevalier, and presented him with a rich gold chain and medal in recognition of his services.

During Paulo's confinement, Mr. Bedell, it is said, was one of the few permitted to visit him.

In the copy of Burnet's Life of Bedell, edition 1685, in the British Museum, there are some MS. notes by Dr. Richard Farmer.*

* Master of Emmanuel College, Cambridge, from 1775 to his death in 1797, aged 63.

In one of them it is stated that " Sir H. Wotton hath service and sermons in his house after the Protestant manner, which I think was never before permitted in Venice, that solid divine and worthy scholar Mr. William Bedell being his preacher." In non-accordance with the remark here made, that service after the Protestant manner was never before permitted in Venice, I found, among the Venetian State Papers for 1606, in the Public Record Office, a writing by Sir Henry Wotton, in which it is said that ambassadors may have what chaplains they please, it being criminal only when they practise against the safety of the State.

Bedell had resided in Venice some months, when Sir Henry Wotton communicated to him plans for a Reformation of Religion in Italy, which had been in agitation. It had been proposed, in conjunction with Father Paulo, to increase the number of those who had received any light of Gospel truth, and to formalise and unite into a congregation some part at least of that great number, including many patrician families, which in Venice stood already alienated in heart and tongue from Rome. In Daru's Histoire de la Republique de Venise (Tome iv. p. 237, note, 4th edition, Paris, 1853), we read : " At one time, remarked Father Paulo to Mr. J. B. Linckh, an agent of the Elector Palatine, we did not regard the English as Christians. But, since they have kept an ambassador here, we have quite another opinion of their religion." We also read that " Signor Pessenti, an advocate, told Linckh that there was in Venice a secret Society of more than one thousand persons disposed to secede from Rome, and that this number was increasing, three hundred patrician families being among them ; that this society was directed by Paulo and Fulgentio the Servites. Linckh, having asked the English Ambassador if this was true, received a confirmation of it, and was conducted by him to visit Paulo and Fulgentio."

" The chiefe meanes," says Bedell, " y^t was to be used heere," in carrying out the proposed plans, " was the intended comming of Mr. Jhon Diodati " to Venice. This gentleman was a native of

Geneva, but of Italian extraction (his parents having been Protestant refugees from Lucca), and author of the well-known Protestant translation of the Bible into Italian. Diodati arrived in Venice in September, 1608, "in companie of a gentleman of Geneva, his cousin, and another, his nephew, both young men, and a French gentleman sent from Monsieur Plessis,[*] from Samurr, called Monsieur De Luques."

Consequent on Diodati's arrival, there were meetings and conferences on the subject in hand, in which Father Paulo took an active part. There already existed in Italian "a short summe of ye Scriptures, stamped in Venice in the yeare 1567 with ye licence of the Inquisition, wch embraced all necessary and fundamentall pointes of Faith, wthout any ye least touch of Popish corruption." Besides this, Bedell had prepared for the use of the congregation an Italian translation of the English Liturgy.

After much consultation, however, it was judged that the time was not yet ripe for action in the matter, by pronouncing finally for a rupture with the Church of Rome. " Nevertheless," says Bedell, " Fulgentio intends this Lent to preach Christ Jesus. There passeth," he continues, " at most no day wherein we" (he and Fulgentio the Servite) " are not an hour or two together, and under p^{r}tence of reading English to him (as indeede this last summer I made some entrance therein to him and M^{ro} Paulo, and giving some rules of o^r language,[†] we read over the Actes of the Aplēs together,) under this coulour we read and conferre about the whole course of ye Gospells on wch he is to preach every day this Lent." In a letter dated Venice, March 20, 1609-10, Sir Henry Wotton says that Fulgentio the Servite preacheth here daily, except Saturdays, at the church of

---

[*] Du Plessis-Mornay, the Pope of the Huguenots, as he was styled, and one of the purest and grandest characters of his time.

[†] These rules appear to have constituted what has been called the English Grammar which Bedell wrote for the use of Paulo and Fulgentio, (*supra*, p. 4.) Dr. Nicholas Bernard tells us that he had seen a copy of it in Bedell's own hand.

San Lorenzo, sermons wholly orthodox and full of zeal and courage to large audiences, comprising numbers of senators and gentlemen.

Besides Fulgentio the Servite, pupil, friend, and biographer of Father Paulo, there was in Venice, at the time under notice, another Fulgentio, a Franciscan, who, during the interdict, preached against the Pope and the Jesuits, though, as Sir Henry Wotton observes, more against their manners than doctrine. After the peace with Rome, this Fulgentio was silenced, but was pensioned by the State, and received for his own Order of St. Francis a grant of the House of the expelled Jesuits. Not content with this, however, our worthy Franciscan revolted to Rome. Bedell used to have conferences with him, in which he appeared to be still strongly opposed to Popery, when " it was sodenly noised y^t he (Fulgentio) was departed." At this Bedell confesses himself wholly confounded, and, at the same time, vexed, especially as Fulgentio's sermons made a great impression on the multitude, " being very vehement and invective against ye vices of ye Roman Court."

This Fulgentio, the Franciscan, it is said, was much favoured in Rome at first, but soon after was burnt to ashes in the Field of Flora.* In reference to the charge against Fulgentio at Rome, Sir Henry Wotton, in a letter to the Earl of Salisbury, dated Venice, April 23, 1610, says: " The Pope hath accused Fulgentio the Franciscan (whom he drewe from hence long since under safe conduct) of a practise grounded uppon our King's Embass^r to conveighe him thence to our Kinge, which he pretendeth to have been healed [held] betweene him and the sayed Embass^r, by letters, and by the intermission of a pilgrime. And this I conceave to be the maynest cause of his imprisonment theare, a thing meerely surmised and coyned in that shopp of lies. True it is, indeede, that since his

---

* Sir Dudley Carleton (successor of Sir Henry Wotton), in a letter from Venice to Sir Ralph Winwood, mentions the incident of a Fulgentio being burnt for a heretick, but confounds him, as has been done by others since, with Fulgentio the Servite. The latter was then living in Venice, and lived to attend Father Paulo on his death-bed in 1623, and afterwards to write his life.

being theare he (Fulgentio) wrote a letter unto the Chaplaine of our King's Embass^r (Mr. Bedell), expressing some discontentment, which was never communicated with any of the world, nor any further prosecuted on oure part for some doubts we had in it."

In reference, again, to Fulgentio's execution, Sir Henry Wotton, writing to the Earl of Salisbury, October 29, 1610, says, " In the process of Fra Fulgentio, the Franciscan lately executed at Rome, was openly readd in the Church of St. Peter's, for one of the maynest articles that he had heald correspondence and practise with his Matie, thorough the English Ambassad^r at Venice, about conveighing of him thense to London. This having been related unto me first by letter, but more authentically by one that was present at the publication of the process ; I repeated it heere of late at one of my audiences in College,* telling them that though I could not restore that poore soule his lyfe, yet I was bounde in honor and conscience, and in the feeling of humanitie, to discharge him of all that which had pompousely been inserted in his process touching his Matie and me the unworthiest of his servants—which I affirm on my salvation to be as fayned and as false as I believed all the rest to be of the Roman Court. Which asseveration, when it was afterwards related *verbatim* in senat, youre Lo^p cannot imagin what a general assent theare was of those that cryed, ' Per Dio l' è vero !' "

Fulgentio the Franciscan was not the only one who revolted to Rome among those who were active against the Pope during the interdict. One, if not more, of the seven Theologians who wrote the " Trattato del Interdetto " did so. Monsignor Pietr' Antonio Ribetti followed Fulgentio the Franciscan (being induced thereto by the Patriarch on his return from Rome to be confirmed), and as Sir Henry Wotton says, was put to public penance and abjuration of the book. Sir Dudley Carleton in a letter from Venice to Sir Ralph Winwood, alleges that Marc' Antonio Capello also fled to Rome. An attempt was made to inveigle even Father Paulo himself to that

* The College was the place in Venice whither Ambassadors resorted.

city. But, in reply to the Pope's invitation to come and receive his blessing, Father Paulo observed that " his Holiness might bless him from Rome voluntarily, as easily as he did curse him from thence; though for his part he found his conscience stand in no need of the proffered blessing ! "

The places in the list of the seven theologians, left vacant by the defections mentioned, were filled up by stauncher men.

At the time the conferences respecting a reformation of religion above-described were going on, an incident occurred in Venice which, as it caused some talk at the time, deserves mention here, more especially as the account of it given by Burnet in his Life of Bedell has been subjected to stricture. Bedell in his correspondence with Waddesworth (p. 77, London, 1624) observes : " As for the *Protestants making the Pope Antichrist*, I know that it is a point that inrageth much at Rome. * * * What can the Protestants doe with the matter ? I will take the liberty here to relate to you what I saw while I was in Venice, the rather because it is not impertinent to our present purpose. And though, perhaps, you may have heard somewhat of it, yet the particulars are, I suppose, unknowne in those parts.* And yet it doth more import they were knowne there then otherwhere, being occasioned by a subject of the Crowne, though of a name and family whereto it is not *much* beholding."†

" In the year 1608," continues Bedell, " F. Thomas Maria Ca-

* Spain.

† Allusion is here made to the enmity of Pope Paul IV. (John Peter Caraffa), and other members of his family, to the King-Emperor Charles the Fifth. The Caraffas were Neapolitans, and, as such, were at that time subjects of the Spanish Crown, and, in common with their countrymen, had suffered from the oppression of the Spanish yoke. But as a family they had special grievances of their own against the King of Spain, which John Peter was not disposed to forget on his elevation to the Papal throne, even if the Spanish Royal-Imperial party had not brought them vividly back to the new Pontiff's remembrance by their endeavours to prevent his election.

John Peter Caraffa was elevated to the Popedom in 1555, and in 1556 the Emperor Charles V. abdicated.

raffa, of the Order of Fryers-Preachers, Reader of Philosophy in Naples, printed a thousand *Theses* in Philosophy and Divinity to be disputed thrice, once at Rome in the Church of St. Marie super Minervam, twice in St. Dominick's at Naples. * * * These were all included in the (pictorial) form of a tower, and dedicated with an Epistle to the present Pope Paulus V. * * * On the top of this tower was this representation curiously and largely cut : An altar, &c. * * * In the middest for the altar-piece was the Pope's picture. * * * Underneath the picture of the Pope on the foreside of the altar was this inscription : ' Paulo V. Vice-Deo, Christianæ Reip. Monarchæ Invictissimo, et Pontificiæ Omnipotentiæ Conservatori Acerrimo.' "

" The copies of these *Theses* were sent as novelles from Rome; and did the more amuse men at Venice, because of the controversie that State had with the Pope a little before, and the seeing their Duke's *Corno* (cap of State) hanged up, among his trophies, under all Princes' Crowns. But most of all, the new title VICE-DEO, and the addition of OMNIPOTENCIE gave matter of wonder. The next day it was noised about the citie that this was the picture of *Antichrist*,
$$\overset{5\;50}{\text{Pav l o}} \overset{5}{\text{V.}} \overset{5\;1\;100\;500}{\text{V i c c Deo}}$$
for that the inscription Pav l o V. V i c c Deo contained exactly in the numeral letters the number of the Beast in the Revelation 666."

Bedell in his second letter from Venice to Mr. Adam Newton in the beginning of the year 1608-9 relates the anecdote, and tells him that a " Retraict " of Caraffa's diagram with the inscription was sent at the time to King James by Sir Henry Wotton. In the same letter he informs Mr. Newton that it was he himself who first detected the coincidence as to the number of the Beast. Bedell's words, after mentioning the inscription, Pavlo V. Vice-Deo, are, " ye numerall letters whereof (as I remember I showed to Fulgentio) containe ye iust number of the Beast, 666."*

By the blundering inaccuracy of Clogie and the negligence of

* Lansdowne MS. xc. 66, in the British Museum ; also some original letters of Bishop Bedell, &c. *ut supra*, pages 69 and 77.

Burnet, who received his materials from Clogie, it is stated in Burnet's Life of Bishop Bedell that it was during the existence of the Interdict that this incident occurred, that Caraffa was a Jesuit instead of a Dominican or Friar Preacher, and that he actually came to Venice himself, whereas copies of his Theses only were sent from Rome to Venice. These mistakes were laid hold of by Dr. Hickes (op. cit. p. 89) to disparage Burnet, and thereby to throw a doubt on his attribution of the discovery to Bedell, of the coincidence of the numbers represented by the numeral letters in the words Pavlo V. Vice-Deo, giving when summed up the total of 666, thus:—

$$V = 5$$
$$L = 50$$
$$V = 5$$
$$V = 5$$
$$I = 1$$
$$C = 100$$
$$D = 500$$
$$\overline{666}$$

The story of the presentation of King James's Book to the Senate of Venice, again, is in its circumstances inaccurately related by Clogie and repeated by Burnet. The facts were these:

Sir Henry Wotton in a letter (Public Record Office) to the Earl of Salisbury dated from Venice July 3, 1609, style of the place, said:—" The *Pope* * hath renewed his complaynt personally to the now Venetian Resident with him about Bibles (*printed in Italian*) introduced into Venice by *the King of England's Ambassador*, and it pleased the Prince at the tyme of the advise in the Senat, after speaking earnestly in commendation of the King of England and against " the Jesuites and such nourselings of the Roman Court," who sought to slander his name, " to expresse some good will to

* The words here printed in Italics are written in cypher in the original.

the *King of England's Ambassador* uppon this occasion." This no doubt was the utterance of the Doge referred to in Clogie's version of the story which appeared, as alleged, to Father Paulo and his theological colleagues, with many others, to indicate a disposition in favour of a reformation in religion. But whether Father Paulo and his colleagues really acted on such a supposition in the manner Clogie relates, and entreated Mr. Bedell to beg Sir Henry Wotton to lose no time in making the presentation to the Senate of the copy of the Latin Translation of King James's Book, which had been specially prepared for the purpose, there is no document to show.

It may possibly have been that Father Paulo and his colleagues, aware of the intrigues that the Papal Nuncio was carrying on to obtain the permission which was subsequently granted for the Inquisition to suppress the publication of the King's Book in Venice when it should arrive there, thought that the design might be thwarted by a timely presentation of it and the King's letter to the Doge.

This Book of King James comprised a reprint of " An Apologie for the Oath of Allegience " which His Majesty had published anonymously in answer to the Bull of Pope Paul V., issued in 1606, forbidding English Papists to take the Oath of Allegiance, with a Preamble, now first published, entitled " A Premonition to all most mightie Monarches, Kings, free Princes, and States of Christendome." The Latin translation was entitled " Apologia pro juramento fidelitatis."

Whether urged by Mr. Bedell (as Clogie alleges), or not, to present the Book earlier, Sir Henry Wotton presented it and His Majesty's letter on St. James's day (being Saturday July 25) 1609, the anniversary of " his Majesty's happy Coronation." In a letter (Public Record Office) dated Venice the last of July 1609, to the Earl of Salisbury, Sir Henry says:—". The King's letter was publiquely read by one of the Secretaries, and the Prince having kissed bothe that and the booke with a very cheereful and ingenuouse countenance," answered in a gracious and complimentary strain.

In a letter to King James himself (Public Record Office) dated

August 14, 1609, Sir Henry Wotton,* after referring to the censure of his Majesty's Book which had been sent by the Pope to Venice with the intention to forebarr the Senate from receiving it, says:—
"In the mean while for anticipation of tyme (which was never deerer) my Chaplain † (whom I am bound to commend unto your Maties goodness for a person of singular lerning and zeale) hathe translated the whole work into this vulgar, conferring the progress of his labour weekly, twice or thrice, with Padre Paulo and Fulgentio, who both much rejoice that your Matie hath interserted therein an admirable summarie of your own faythe,‡ which the world may now see to have been most impudently slandered, as likewise the magnanimitie and moderation of your Royal Government."

Whether the translation of the King's Book into Italian by Bedell here referred to was ever printed does not appear. As will be seen, it was the Latin translation which was forbidden by name (viz. *Apologia pro juramento fidelitatis*) to be sold in the booksellers' shops in Venice.

Three weeks before the arrival of his Majesty's book in Venice, the Pope had through the Secretary of the Venetian Embassy at Rome (the Ambassador himself being at the time ill of gout) expressly commanded the Venetian Senate not to accept it. Extracts from the book comprising King James's Articles of Faith were adduced as justifying his Holiness's command. The Papal Nuncio iterated the like office in Venice, and said that the Pope intended to excommunicate the book, which he afterwards did.

* Sir Henry Wotton's letters to King James himself among the Venetian State Papers in the Public Record Office, are signed :—" OTTAVIO BALDI." This was the name under which Sir Henry Wotton was first introduced to the notice of King James, when, before James's accession to the throne of England, he presented himself to his Majesty in Stirling Castle (having travelled from Italy to Scotland by way of Norway for greater privacy), as an Italian envoy from the Grand Duke of Tuscany, to warn him against Popish emissaries who sought his life. See Isaak Walton's Life of Sir Henry Wotton.

† This word was written in cypher.

‡ This was rather a sanguine and overstrained view, on the part of Sir Henry Wotton, of the approval by Father Paulo of King James's Articles of Faith. See note *, *infra*, p. 120.

Notwithstanding all this, the Doge in the name of the Senate graciously accepted the book, as above-mentioned.

On presenting the book Sir Henry Wotton explained that his Majesty King James's object in writing it was to vindicate himself from slanders that had been propagated against him, and that his Majesty, merely wishing to " respect the common right of Princes, *senza alcun altro fine qui dentro*," * it was not his purpose to innovate on the religious opinions of others—that he left to the good pleasure of God.†

" A Republic is a kind of Government where one may loose all the goodwill in a morning which he hath hardly gotten in five years." Thus thought Sir Henry Wotton again (as, in words, he had shortly before remarked to the Earl of Salisbury), when, in another letter (Public Record Office), dated the 28th of August 1609, it became his duty to communicate to his Lordship the following information : " Since the acceptation of his Maties Booke heere in that kinde maner (which I have formerly advertised), theare hath order been given to all the booksellers of this towne out of the Office of the Inquisition to consigne immediately to the General Inquisitor all the copies that have or shall come to theire hands of a booke intituled : Apologia pro juramento fidelitatis. On being informed of this, Sir Henry goes on to say that he was at first inclined to disbelieve it; but on further inquiry he found that it was true. He ascertained that, during the absence of the Doge from illness, and without the participation of the Senate, the Papal Nuncio in an underhand way at the College procured a consent from the ' preconsultors ' there, that the Inquisition might forbid the book to be on sale in the bookbinders' shops in Venice; though with this reservation, that his Majesty's name was not to be mentioned, the title of the book only to be quoted, and that no penalty was to be attached to a transgression of the order on the part of any bookbinder. In-

* This is a Venetian phrase, Sir Henry Wotton remarks, in a marginal note, signifying, *in the present purpose*, or *in the matter in hand*.

† Despatch from Venice in the Public Record Office.

dignant at such a procedure, Sir Henry adds that he had demanded an audience for the following day, viz. August the 29th. Sir Henry Wotton writing again (Letter in Public Record Office), on the 8th of September 1609, says that he had had an audience and expressed his surprise that a *Friar* should be permitted to prohibit the publication in Venice of his Majesty's Book, which the Senate had so short a time before received graciously. The "Savio della Settimana" answered for the Doge, who was still unwell, that the matter should be brought before the Senate. But, twelve days having elapsed without his receiving an answer, Sir Henry Wotton demanded another audience, in which he complained that the forbidding of the King's Book to be sold in the shops in Venice did negative the grace of the Senate's acceptation of it, and demanded the personal chastisement of the Inquisitor. Next day Sir Henry was invited to the College, and had an answer read to him to the following effect: That the Senate could not revoke the mandate without a rupture with the Roman faith, as the book contained points contrary to their religion.* At the same time they denied that the mandate implied an actual prohibition, as there was no penalty attached to the transgression of it.†

Sir Henry Wotton, still not satisfied, had a third audience, when the Doge himself was present, and expressed himself so strongly as to draw from the Doge the remark that he had spoken out with "troppo calore," though, added the Prince, with sententious gravity, "quel che è fatto è fatto."

---

* Griselini (*ut supra*) quotes a letter from Father Paulo on this subject to James Lecasserio, written at the end of the year 1609, in which the Father remarks, that, "if the oath proposed to Catholics by the King of England had come to us bare and unmixed with the controversies of the time, it would have been approved of by the more judicious, but, as the King has entered so much into theological questions, were we to approve his articles, we should be supposed to receive all the doctrine."

† The penalty, had there been one, in such a case, would have probably been a fine, and ten years at the galleys, or, in case the condemned was not able to row, imprisonment for life.

The secret story of the underhand negotiations at the College, above referred to, by which the Papal Nuncio procured a consent that the Inquisition might prohibit King James's book from being on sale in the bookbinders' shops in Venice, as gathered from Sir Henry Wotton's letters, was this: The abbot of S. Maria of Vangadezza, in the Comaldulo, a young man "of so loose a lyfe," says Sir Henry Wotton, "as for that matter he might have been a Cardinal," having died, a question arose as to the right of presentation to this very rich abbacy, between the Pope and the State of Venice. At last, after much contention, on which account the Abbey came to be called the "Litigious Abbey," Signore Priuli, a Venetian of great influence, negotiated a bargain with the Papal Nuncio, by which the Pope, on the one hand, agreed to the appointment of one of his (Priuli's) sons to the abbacy, and Priuli, on the other, procured the sanction of the Senate to the prohibition of King James's book by the Inquisition.

It is, however, to be observed that the Senate denied any bargain with the Pope about the Abbey.

In consequence of their *imbroglio* with Sir Henry Wotton, the Senate appointed the Chevalier Contarini as Ambassador extraordinary to proceed to England on the subject; but in the meantime wrote to their ordinary resident in London desiring him to see King James and explain matters to him. The Venetian resident accordingly had an audience of the King, an account of which is given in the following letter (Public Record Office), in his Majesty's own handwriting: "My littel beagle, I have bene this nighte surprysed by the venetian ambassadoure quho for all my hunting hathe not spaired to hunte me out heir, to be shorte his chiefe earande was to tell me of a greate fraye in venice betwixte my ambassadoure thaire & that staite anent a prohibition that the inquisition of venice hathe sett foorthe against the publishing of my booke thaire, he hathe complained that my ambassadoure takis this so hoatlie as passeth, in a worde he hathe bestowid an houris vehement oration upon me for this purpose, my ansoure was, that I coulde never dreame, that ather the state of venice wolde ever give me any iuste cause of offence, or yett that ever my ambassadoure thaire wolde do thaime any evill office, but as to give him any particulaire ansoure I tolde him I muste firste heare from my owin ambassadoure, for he knew well anewgh that everie prince or state muste have a greate truste in thaire owin ministers, I only wryte this unto you nou, that incace this pantalone come unto you ye maye give him the lyke deferring ansoure, albeit if I shoulde tell you my conscience, if all this mannis tale be trewe, my ambassadoure hathe usid this maitter with a littel more fervent zeale then temperate wisdome, I now hoape to heare from you the assurance that youre sonne is well, & so fair well,

JAMES R."*

In answer to the representations of the Senate through the ordinary Venetian resident in London, mentioned in his letter just quoted, King James sent an autograph letter dated October 3, 1609, to the Doge, acknowledging the polite reception of his Majesty's book by him, and smoothing away the asperities of Sir Henry Wotton's complaints.† The reception of this letter by the Doge and Senate is thus described by Sir Henry Wotton in a letter (Public Record Office) to the Earl of Salisbury, dated from Venice, December 4, 1609 : "The world cannot expresse unto your Lo^p with what cheerfullnesse, and with what eager attention the letter was heard by them all, nor with what ingenuitie and tendernesse of

---

* To this letter there is neither date nor address, but it is endorsed " His M^r to me, 12 Sept^r, 1609," and occurs among letters addressed to the Earl of Salisbury on the subject.

† The story of the presentation of the King's Book by Sir Henry Wotton to the Senate on St. James's Day, as related in a letter from Sir Thomas Edmonds to Sir Ralf Winwood, dated London, October 4, 1609 (Winwood's Memorials, *ut supra*, pp. 77, 78, vol. iii.), is in substantial agreement with the account now given from the original documents.

countenance this good Duke composed himself to speak," which he did, after acknowledging his Majesty's former good offices to the Republic, to the effect that " they had receaved His Majesty's Booke, and so would preserve it amongst theire deerest monuments."

By decree of the Senate it was ordered that the Book should be received as a Royal gift, though not to be published, that it was to be consigned to the Grand Chancellor, to be by him kept locked up in a chest and not to be shewn to any one, nor removed from the chest nor anything whatever done with it, unless by decree of the Senate.*

By the blundering and inaccuracy of Clogie, the incident of the presentation of King James's Book to the Senate of Venice is represented to have occurred during the Interdict, at a time, therefore, when the " Premonition " had not yet been published, and when of course no Papal Nuncio would be resident in Venice. Burnet not only reproduces the story in the inaccurate form in which Clogie communicated it to him, without having taken the pains, as he ought to have done, to see that it tallied in respect to time with the then well-known dates of the Venetian Interdict and of the publication of King James's " Premonition," but most unjustifiably censures Sir Henry Wotton for an alleged procrastination in presenting the Book, at the same time improving on Clogie's arrogant and absurd remarks. On the other hand Griselini,† the Roman Catholic biographer of Father Paulo, greedily seized upon the anachronisms of Burnet, as exposed by Dr. Hickes,‡ (who himself drew what little information he had on the subject from Mr. Fulman,) to impugn altogether the accuracy of the account of the transactions in Venice towards a Reformation of Religion, in which Paulo and Bedell took a leading part.

---

* Andreæ Maurocceni (Morosini, in Italian) Senatoris Historia Veneta ab anno M.D.XX.I. usque ad annum M.D.CXV. In quinque partes tributa. Folio, Lib. xviii. p. 690. Venetiis, 1623.

† Opere citato, p. 134.   ‡ Opere citato.

The time now approached when Mr. Bedell was to leave Venice. In a letter (Tanner Collection, Bodleian Library, lxxv. 354) dated July 23, 1610, to Dr. Samuel Warde, he says that his return to England will be in November next, and speaks of his cousin Aliston (Fellow of Emmanuel College) as desiring to succeed him in the chaplaincy to the Embassy at Venice, but Bedell rather dissuades from the project, and hopes for something better for his cousin. In the same letter Bedell, in reply to some proposition made to him by Dr. Warde as to obtaining preferment on his return to England, observes:—" Touching the plan you mention I doe not understand the quality of it and therefore can say nothing. I desire rather a quiet retyred life than to live in Princes' Courts, with losse of tyme and liberty of enjoying not only other things but even a man's own selfe."

Before his return to England Bedell visited Constantinople, as appears from Waddesworth's letter to him, dated " Sevill in Spaine, April 1, 1615."* But of this visit I have not discovered any account.

CHAPTER IV.

Return to England from Venice—Dr. Despotine.

Sir Henry Wotton in a letter to the Earl of Salisbury, dated Venice, December 10, 1610, says that he had resigned his charge as Ambassador to his successor Sir Dudley Carleton †, and describes his farewell audience with the Senate, and Sir Dudley's reception by the same.

On Sunday December the 26th, being St. Stephen's day, 1610, " stile of the place," Sir Henry Wotton writing from Padua, where he arrived on Friday the 17th of December, to the Earl of Salis-

* The copies of certain Letters between Spain and England, &c.
† Venetian State Papers, in Public Record Office.

bury, mentions that he found his Lordship's son the Lord Cranbourne there ill of ague, and announces that he was about to depart for England next day, Monday the 27th, by way of Lombardy and France.*

Sir Thomas Edmonds in a letter to Sir Ralph Winwood from Paris, 7th of February 1610, O.S. (January 26, N.S.) says that Sir Henry Wotton had been in that city for a week past, and intended to spend three or four days longer there.†

Sir Henry Wotton, having arrived in Paris about the 19th of January, had thus been about three weeks on his way from Padua to Paris.

The Rev. John Sanford, writing to Sir Thomas Edmonds, March 6 (February 24, N.S.?) 1610-11, informs him that Sir Henry Wotton had lately arrived in Court.‡ ·

Mr. George Calvert, writing also to Sir Thomas Edmonds March 10 (February 26, N.S.?) 1610-11, says that he (Mr. G. C.) arrived in England at Hythe in Kent on Saturday last late at night, and that he reached Charing Cross on Sunday. He then observes that " Sir Henry Wotton arrived here some three or four days before me."§

No doubt Mr. Bedell would accompany Sir Henry Wotton in his journey from Venice. We may therefore conclude that he was safely lodged in the house of Mr. Nunne (p. 13) by the end of February or beginning of March 1610-11, after an absence from Bury St. Edmund's of rather more than three years and a half.

Mr. Bedell was, as stated in the text (pp. 10-13), accompanied from Venice by Dr. Jasper Despotine, whom by his influence he established in medical practice at Bury St. Edmund's. In the

* Venetian State Papers, in Public Record Office.
† Sir R. Winwood's Memorials, *ut supra*, vol. iii. p. 179.
‡ The Court and Times of James I. By the Author of Maria Dorothea, &c., vol. i. p. 105; 1848.
§ Eodem Opere, vol. i. p. 111.

Parish Register of Horningshearth there is, under the date of August 10th 1619,* a record of the marriage of Dr. Despotine with Susan Brand, and in the Register of St. Mary's, Bury St. Edmund's, we find under the years 1620, 1622, and 1624, records of the baptism of three daughters of Dr. Jasper Despotine and his wife Susan—Catherine, Isabell, and Anne.†

Burnet in his Life of Bishop Bedell, repeating the statement of his informant Clogie, says that Dr. Despotine, one of Bedell's Italian converts, came over to England with him and was by Bedell brought to St. Edmundsbury. Dr. Hickes (op. cit. p. 32) takes exception to this statement, saying: " It was in the year 1610 that Mr. Bedell returned with Sir Henry Wotton into England, and the bringing Despotine should in all Reason and Decency have been ascribed to the Ambassador rather than to his Chaplain." But this is a mere quibble, for the fact is both had a share in bringing Despotine to England. The account given in the text as well as here shows what was Mr. Bedell's share. On the other hand, Despotine most likely came with Bedell in the Ambassador's suite, and thus Sir Henry Wotton had the share to which he himself refers in the following letters:—Sir Henry Wotton, writing to Sir Edmund Bacon from his lodging in King's Street, April 2, 1611, to introduce a friend to Sir Edmund along with Dr. Despotine, says of the latter that he " is a man well practised in his own faculty, and very Philosophical and sound in his Discourses. By birth a Venetian, which though it be not *Urbs ignobilis* (as St. Paul said of his own Mother City) yet, in his second Birth, the more excellent; I mean his Illumination in God's saving Truth, which was the only cause of his remove. And I was glad to be the Conductor of him where his Conscience may be free, though his Condition otherwise (till he

---

* Mr. Bedell was at this time Rector of Horningshearth. For the verification of this entry I am indebted to the Rev. S. D. Brownjohn, of Horninger.

† The entries of these Baptisms I found copied in Davy's MS. Collections fo Suffolk, Thingoe Hundred (Br. Mus.), but for their verification I am indebted to the Rev. John Richardson, of St. Mary's.

shall be known) will be poor."* In another letter, written to his friend Mr. Nicholas Pey, more than twenty years after the preceding, Sir Henry Wotton says, " More than a voluntary motion doth now convey me towards Suffolk, especially that I may confer with an excellent Physician at B(ury), whom I brought myself from Venice."† Sir Henry appears to have been suffering from liver complaint, contracted in Venice, and which he supposed Dr. Despotine, from his medical experience of the " Inclinations " of that region, would be the best able to treat. There is no date to this letter, but it was probably written in 1632, which is the date of a letter of Despotine's in one of the Tanner MSS. in the Bodleian Library, in which he speaks of seeing Sir Henry Wotton professionally, on the recommendation of Sir Theodore Mayerne, the King's Physician.

Bedell writing to Dr. Samuel Warde under the date of April 5, 1622,‡ begs him to consult Mr. Legat, the printer at Cambridge, about printing and publishing a work by Dr. Despotine, entitled " De Magnitudine Morbi Disputatio: In quâ propositâ Sanitatis naturâ et naturali perfectione in quâ primum Deus hominem creaverat, &c. : Opus Philosophis quidem jucundum,—Theologis utile,— Medicis vero apprime necessarium." In a subsequent letter Bedell begs Warde to proceed no further in the matter of the proposals about the printing and publishing the book for the present. I have not ascertained whether the book was ever published.

After Mr. Bedell went to Ireland, he kept up a correspondence with Dr. Despotine, and it was, as stated in the text (p. 24), from his letters to the Doctor that much of what is recorded there of Bedell's career in Ireland, both as Provost of Trinity College, Dublin, and as Bishop of Kilmore, was derived. In the Archiepiscopal Library at Lambeth there is a letter from Bedell to Despotine, " De Prædicationibus Jesuitarum apud Sinenses, &c." Cod. 595.

Dr. Despotine succeeded well in his medical practice at Bury St.

* Reliquiæ Wottonianæ. † Op. Cit.
‡ Tanner MS. lxxiii. 129-140, Bodleian Library, Oxford.

Edmund's, and died wealthy. From his will,* proved at Bury St. Edmund's, July 22, 1650, it appears that his wife Susan and his daughters Katherine and Anne were living at the date of his will, December 13, 1648, but that Isabell, the second daughter, was dead.

CHAPTER V.

MARRIAGE—INCUMBENCY OF HORNINGSHEARTH—LITERARY LABOURS—DE DOMINIS—THE DIODATI FAMILY.

On his return from Venice, Mr. Bedell resumed his duties as preacher at St. Mary's in Bury St. Edmund's, and about a year thereafter married. The following is the entry of his marriage in the register of St. Mary's parish :

" 1611. January 29, Married, Mr. William Bedle, Clk. and Leah Mawe, Vid."

Mrs. Leah Mawe's first husband, Robert Mawe, Esq. Recorder of Bury St. Edmund's, was buried at St. Mary's, in that town, on the 1st of June, 1609 (P. R.).

At the time of his marriage Bedell was forty years of age, and his wife Leah thirty. According to the text, Mrs. Bedell was a daughter of John Bowles, Esq. of Earsham, co. Norfolk,† but Mr. Alexander Clogie, who married her daughter by her first husband, says in his Memoir of Bishop Bedell that she was a daughter of the family of L'Estrange. Bishop Burnet and all other biographers of Bedell repeat the statement. The assertion of Mr. Clogie, on this point, however, is not to be relied on as any authority.

* Wills and Inventories from the Register at Bury St. Edmund's. Edited by Samuel Tymms, F.S.A. A volume of the Camden Society for 1850-51.

† The Rev. W. P. Goode, Rector of Earsham, kindly searched the P. R. for me, but did not find an entry of the baptism of Leah Bowles, nor one of her marriage to Robert Mawe.

Mrs. Bedell's family by her first husband, Mr. Robert Mawe, consisted of, 1°, Nicholas, baptized at St. Mary's, Bury St. Edmund's, February 25, 1601-2. He entered the medical profession, and in the Roll of the College of Physicians of London by Dr. Munk we find the following account of him : " Nicholas Mawe, M.D., a native of Suffolk, was educated at Peterhouse, Cambridge, of which he was matriculated Pensioner in July, 1619. He proceeded A.B. in 1622 3, A.M. in 1626, M.D. in 1634, and was admitted a candidate of the College of Physicians, 15th of September, 1634 ;" 2°, John, baptized at St. Mary's, Bury St. Edmund's, June 19, 1603, died young ; 3°, Leah, baptized at St. Mary's, Bury St. Edmund's, November 16, 1604 ; 4°, Robert, baptized at St. Mary's, Bury St. Edmund's, December 10, 1606, died young ; 5°, Edward, baptized at St. Mary's, Bury St. Edmund's, March 22, 1607.

The daughter Leah and this son Edward accompanied their mother and step-father to Ireland, where they will come to be noticed again.

The family of the Rev. William Bedell and his wife Leah consisted of three sons and one daughter: 1°, William, baptized at St. Mary's, Bury St. Edmund's, February 14, 1612-13 (P. R.). Dr. Samuel Warde, Master of Sidney College, Cambridge, was his godfather. Of this the eldest son, and his family, a full account will be found in Chapter XIX. 2°, Grace, baptized at St. Mary's, Bury St. Edmund's, May 29, 1614 (P. R.), buried at Horningshearth, April 25, 1624 (P.R). 3°, John, baptized at St. Mary's, Bury St. Edmund's, August 9, 1616 (P. R.), died at Kilmore in the beginning of the year 1635 ; 4°, Ambrose, baptized at Horningshearth 21st of March, 1618 (P. R.)* Of this son Ambrose a biographical notice is given in Chapter XVIII.

In a letter to Dr. Samuel Warde, dated Bury, this last day of

---

* For the verification of the above entries in the P. R. of St. Mary's, Bury St. Edmund's, I am indebted to the Rev. John Richardson; and for that of the entries in the P. R. of Horningshearth I am indebted to the Rev. S. D. Brownjohn.

November, 1613,* Mr. Bedell mentions that some of his writings are at Geneva, in the hands of Sr Diodati, "as my cosin Alistone can tell," who had recently been at Geneva. Understanding from his cosin Alistone of Warde's being in London, he takes the opportunity to request, through Warde, leave from Sir Henry Wotton to publish "a Relation of Venice," and, by reason of his public services when Chaplain to the Embassy there, remarks that he considers himself entitled to preferment. Among the Venetian State Papers of the date of Bedell's residence in Venice, in the Public Record Office, there are three writings, one in Latin and two in Italian, on the History of Venice.† One of the latter is entitled "a Relation of Venice." In the Library of the Servi at Venice, Griselini informs us, there are five volumes of Father Paulo's MSS. in one of which there is, among other matters, a History of Venice. The writings here mentioned on the History of Venice among the Venetian State Papers, were probably copied or extracted from Paulo's manuscript, and may have been the groundwork of what Bedell proposed to publish.

The Rectory of Horningshearth falling vacant in February, 1615-16, by the death of the Rev. Thomas Rogers, who had been Rector of the parish since December 11, 1581, Mr. Bedell was presented to it by the patron, Sir Thomas Jermyn,‡ whose name is intimately associated with that of Bedell as his warm and constant friend. In the Diocesan Registry of Norwich there is a MS. (one of the Tanner Collection) from which the following is an extract,

* Tanner MS. lxxiv. 31, in Bodleian Library.
† No. 117, De origine Imperii Venetorum, Nos. 125 and 133-141.
‡ Sir William Hervey, an ancestor of the Marquis of Bristol, married Susan, daughter of Sir Robert Jermyn, of Rushbrook, co. Suffolk, and sister of this Sir Thomas Jermyn. By this marriage the Jermyn property came to the Herveys, including the right of presentation to the rectory of Horninger, or Horningshearth. The present Bishop of Bath and Wells, the Lord Arthur Hervey, was many years Rector of that family living.

but corrected as to the year, which is erroneously put down as 1625 instead of 1615.*
"*Horninger Magna & Parva* Lib. xxii. 56, 13 Mart. 1615, Guliel. Bedell ad præs. Thomæ Jermyn Mil."
The course of Mr. Bedell's life at Horningshearth is very fully detailed in the text. His leisure time he occupied in literary labours, which here claim some notice.

While resident at Horningshearth, Bedell's correspondence with his old college friend James Waddesworth, above referred to, took place. After Waddesworth's death, Bedell published the letters under the following title, and dedicated the book " To the Most High and Excellent Prince, Prince Charles." " The Copies of Certain Letters which have passed between Spaine and England in Matter of Religion. Concerning the General Motives to the Roman Obedience. Betweene Master James Wadesworth, a late Pensioner of the Holy Inquisition in Sevill, and W. Bedell, a Minister of the Gospel of Jesus Christ, in Suffolk." London, 1624.

In the text, at page 10, it is stated that these letters were to have been reprinted and published along with "this present history." But the author's intention of publishing the history, and reprinting the letters along with it, was never carried into effect. The Rev. Gilbert Burnet (afterwards Bishop of Salisbury), however, reprinted the correspondence at the end of his Life of Bishop Bedell, published in 1685. This was the year in which James II. succeeded to the throne, on the death of his brother Charles II., and in which their cousin of France, Louis the Fourteenth, revoked the Edict of Nantes, under which the Protestants of that country had enjoyed toleration during the preceding seventy-five years. The time was, therefore, not propitious for the republication of the passage in Bedell's last letter (p. 133, Original Edition), which argues for the lawful-

---

* I am indebted to the kindness of my former colleague at University College Hospital, Mr. Cadge, the distinguished surgeon, of Norwich, for procuring me this extract.

ness of resisting religious persecution by Princes, and repelling force with force. And all the less propitious for the republication of the said passage under the auspices of Gilbert Burnet, who had been recently deprived of his preachership at the Rolls, and his lectureship at St. Clement's Danes, by order of the King, on account of his having (in 1683) attended Lord William Russell on the scaffold, and who, on the accession of James II., found it prudent to leave England and retire to Holland. Accordingly, Sir Roger L'Estrange, the Censor of the press, would not allow the republication of the passage without interpolations calculated to give it an air as if Bedell had been only repeating the arguments of others, but not endorsing them.

The interpolations occur in the tenth chapter of the tenth and last letter (p. 133 of the original edition, and pp. 445-6 of Burnet), where the author is speaking "of the Reformers in France and Holland." This tenth letter comprises pp. 39 to 162 of the book and is an elaborate dissertation against Popery, divided into twelve chapters. The passage is here copied from the original edition as it stands in respect to spelling. The interpolations are placed within crotchets, as they were in Burnet, but in order that they may be the more readily distinguished by the reader, they are here, in addition to that, printed in small capitals :—" And tell mee," says Bedell, " in good sooth, Master Wadesworth, doe you approve such barbarous crueltie ? Doe you allow the *butchery at Paris* ? Doe you thinke subjects are bound to give their throats to bee cut by their fellow subjects ? or to [OFFER THEM WITHOUT EITHER HUMBLE REMONSTRANCE OR FLIGHT TO] their Princes, at their meere wills against their owne Lawes and Edicts ? You would know *quo jure* the Protestants warres in France and Holland are justified [I INTERPOSE NOT MINE OWN JUDGMENT, NOT BEING THROUGHLY ACQUAINTED WITH THE LAWS AND CUSTOMES OF THOSE COUNTRIES, BUT I TELL YOU WHAT BOTH THEY AND THE PAPISTS ALSO, BOTH IN FRANCE AND ITALY, HAVE IN SUCH CASES ALLEDGED]. First, the Law of *Nature*, which [THEY SAY] not onely alloweth, but inclineth and inforceth

every living thing to defend itself from violence. Secondly, that of *Nations*, which permitteth those that are in the protection of others, to whom they owe no more but an honourable acknowledgement in case they goe about to make themselves absolute Sovereignes, and usurpe their libertie, to resist and stand for the same. And if a lawfull Prince (which is not yet Lord of his Subjects' lives and goods) shall attempt to despoile them of the same, under colour of reducing them to his owne religion, after all humble remonstrances, they may [THEY SAY] stand upon their owne guard, and, being assailed, repell force with force, as did the Maccabees under *Antiochus*. In which case, notwithstanding, the person of the Prince himselfe ought allwaies to be sacred and inviolable as was *Saul's* to *David*. Lastly, if the inraged Minister of a lawfull Prince will abuse his authoritie, against the fundamentall Laws of the Country, [THEY SAY] it is no rebellion to defend themselves against force, reserving still their obedience to their Sovereigne inviolate. These are the Rules of which the Protestants that have borne Arms in France and Flanders, and the Papists also, both there and elsewhere, as in Naples, that have stood for the defense of their liberties, have served themselves. How truly, I esteem it hard for you and mee to determine, unlesse we were more throughly acquainted with the Lawes and Customes of those Countries than I, for my part, am."

[Note.—" THIS PASSAGE ABOVE IS TO BE CONSIDERED AS A RELATION, NOT AS THE AUTHOR'S OPINION: BUT YET, FOR FEAR OF TAKING IT BY THE WRONG HANDLE, THE READER IS DESIRED TO TAKE NOTICE, THAT A SUBJECT'S RESISTING HIS PRINCE IN ANY CAUSE WHATSOEVER IS UNLAWFUL AND IMPIOUS."]

When the Revolution in 1688 took place, the Rev. Gilbert Burnet returned to England as chaplain to King William, and was soon after (1689) raised to the Bishopric of Salisbury * in succession to Dr. Seth Ward. Being now on the right side of politics, Burnet

* Archbishop Sancroft regarded Gilbert Burnet as "a Presbyterian in a surplice," and, unwilling himself to assist at his consecration, issued a commission empowering any three of his Suffragans to act in the matter. Under the authority of this instrument Burnet was consecrated Bishop.—*Macaulay's History*.

took the opportunity to modify Sir Roger L'Estrange's note denouncing as unlawful and impious a subject's resisting his Prince in any cause whatsoever. Accordingly the copies of his Life of Bedell that remained on hand had the leaf (pp. 445-6) containing the note, cancelled and replaced by a new printed one with the note altered thus:—" This passage above is to be considered as a *relation*, not as the author's opinion, lest it should mislead the reader into a dangerous mistake."

The interpolations within crotchets in the body of the passage were allowed to remain, and the copies of the book thus altered were issued with a new title-page dated 1692.

Dr. George Hickes (Discourses, *ut supra*,) gave vent to virulent censures against Burnet in respect to the interpolations under notice; but, in doing so, the Dean appears to have been under the impression that the interpolations were made by Burnet of his own mere motion, and that, like a time-server, he denounced a subject's resisting his Prince in any cause whatsoever as unlawful and impious when the Government was severe against resistance, as it was before the Revolution of 1688, but changed his tone when, after the Revolution, more liberal ideas came into vogue. Burnet in his Vindication (Reflections on a Pamphlet by George Hickes, &c. London, 1696, 8vo.) says: " In reprinting Bedell's book against Wadsworth, I could not but take notice of the case of subjects resisting their Prince, fully stated and justified by Bedell and that in a book dedicated to Charles I., then Prince of Wales. I told Mr. Chiswell my publisher that I would not suffer the book to be printed without the passage on resistance. He (Mr. Chiswell) showed it to Sir Roger L'Estrange, who would not let it pass without several interpolations to give it an *air* as if Bedell had been only reflecting the arguments of other men. Besides which he (Sir R. L'E.) caused a marginal note to be added at the end of the paragraph p. 446 of Bedell's letters, which was framed by Sir Roger L'Estrange himself. I was very ill-pleased with all this, but (continues Burnet) I could not help it. All I could do was to get the interpolations put within crotchets." This it will be admitted is a sufficiently complete vindication of Burnet so far as regards the interpolations and the marginal note at pp. 445 and 446 of his Life of Bèdell as it appeared in 1685; but it is not easy to understand why Burnet did not, in the re-issue of his Life of Bedell, dated 1692, strike out the interpolations and the note altogether, and so restore the passage to the form in which Bedell originally published it, in the volume he dedicated to Charles, Prince of Wales, in 1624.

Another literary labour of Bedell while resident at Horningshearth was his translation from the Italian into Latin of the two last Books of Father Paulo's History of the Council of Trent. This (a continuation of a General History of Councils of the Church, which is lost) was first published in the original Italian in London in 1619, under the following title: " Historia dell Concilio Tridentino. Di Pietro Soave Polano." Paulo, it is said, completed the History in 1615, and communicated the manuscript to Mark Antony de Dominis, Archbishop of Spalatro or Spalato, who had it printed and published in London, as above,* and dedicated it to King James I. The work is printed in folio and extends to 806 pages. The feigned name " Pietro Soave Polano," under which the History was published, is an anagram of " Paolo Sarpio Veneto."

Mark Antony de Dominis, Archbishop of Spalato, had come to London about the year 1616, having received through Sir Dudley Carleton, the English Ambassador at Venice, some encouragement from King James. While in Venice, Mr. Bedell became acquainted with De Dominis, who was then residing in that city to be out of the way of Papal vengeance, for having taken part with the

* Without the knowledge or permission of the author, it has been alleged, but this is to be doubted. Griselini (Op. cit.) at the end of his Life of Father Paulo enumerates, among various other literary remains of that eminent man, the following: " La Storià del Concilio di Trento autografo di mano di F. Mario Fanzano (Father Paulo's amanuensis), con emmendazioni interlineari e marginali dell' autore. Fu trovato il codice fra i Manoscritti spettanti al Patrizio Veneto Zuanne Sagredo. Ora e possiduto della illuminatissima N. D. Veneziana Catterina Sagredo, Pesaro, Barbarigo."

Venetians in their dispute with Rome. It was said by Clogie and repeated by Burnet, and, though Dr. Hickes challenged the assertion, there does not appear to be any reason to doubt it, that Mr. Bedell suggested corrections of many ill applications of texts of Scripture, and of quotations from the Fathers, in the work "De Republica Ecclesiastica," which De Dominis was engaged in writing at the time in Venice, and which he afterwards published in London. Clogie and Burnet, however, were mistaken in saying that De Dominis as well as Despotine accompanied Bedell from Venice to England. As just said, De Dominis did not arrive in England until about 1616.

He came to England in the character of a Protestant and was well received by King James, who appointed him first to the Mastership of the Savoy Chapel, and, six months after, made him Dean of Windsor. De Dominis, however, restless and inconstant as he was, went back to Rome on the elevation of his old fellow-student Ludovici to the Papal throne as Gregory XV. Here he was at first favourably received, but after Pope Gregory's death in 1623 he was imprisoned in the Castle of St. Angelo, where he died in 1624. Being asked on his death-bed in what Faith and Religion he was abiding, he took a crucifix, and, kissing it, said, " I do die a member of the Roman Catholic Church." Notwithstanding this confession, his study was searched after his death, and certain papers, it is alleged, were found which did imply his opinion to be that there was "*Inequalitas personarum in Sanctâ Trinitate.*" This being added to the crime of his former revolt, it was thought fit by the Church to proceed against him. Advocates were retained on both sides, and after much discussion it was adjudged that De Dominis died in a state of heresy, and his body was condemned to be burned.*

Bedell, in his Latin Translation of Father Paulo's History of the Venetian Interdict, mentions De Dominis as " Infelix Archiepiscopus Spalatensis."

* Goodman's Court of King James, *ut supra*, vol. i. p. 354.

In 1620 an English translation of Father Paulo's " Historia dell Concilio Tridentino" was published in London, of which the following is the title : " The Historie of the Councel of Trent. Conteining eight Bookes. In which (besides the ordinarie Acts of the Councell) *are declared many notable occurrences which happened* in Christendome, during the space of fourtie yeares and more. And particularly, the practices of the Court of Rome to hinder the Reformation of their errors, and to maintaine their greatness. Written in Italian by Pietro Soave Polano, and faithfully translated into English by Nathanael Brent." Folio, pp. 825. This English translation was dedicated both to King James and to the Archbishop of Canterbury.

The translation of Father Paulo's History of the Council of Trent from the original Italian into Latin was made, the first six Books by Mr. Adam Newton, who had been preceptor of Henry, Prince of Wales (see p. 103), and the last two Books by Mr. W. Bedell, as above stated. The following is a copy of the Title-page of the Book (which is in folio, and contains 667 pages) :—

PETRI SVAVIS POLANI
Historiæ Concilii Tridentini
Libri Octo
Ex Italicis summa fide et accuratione Latini facti.

Veniet qui conditam, et seculi sui malignitate compressam VERITATEM, dies publicet. Etiam si omnibus tecum viventibus silentium livor indixerit; venient qui sine offensa, sine gratia judicent. Nihil simulatio proficit, paucis imponit leviter extrinsecus inducta facies; veritas in omnem partem sui semper eadem est. Quæ decipiunt, nihil habent solidi. Tenue est mendacium: perlucet, si diligenter inspexeris. SENECA, in fine Epist. LXXIX.

Augustæ Trinobantum.
M.DC.XX.

Considering the large size of the history, the translations above described could scarcely have been made in the short space of one year from the printed Italian edition, after its publication in 1619. Most probably, as both the original and the translations appear to have been brought out in concert, under the auspices of King James, the translations were made from the printed sheets of the Italian edition as they came from the press. Isaak Walton, in his Life of Sir Henry Wotton, says that Paulo's History of the Council of Trent was communicated by the author in portions as he wrote it off to Sir Henry Wotton, William Bedell, and others, and that the portions were forwarded, inclosed in letters, to King James. This had been during the period from the end of 1607 to the end of 1610.* It was probably in reference to this that Nathanael Brent, the English translator, says, in his dedication to the King, that the author wrote the History "in contemplation of your Majesty's service;" and, in his dedication to the Archbishop of Canterbury, that "for the sake of his Majesty the King (as some reasons induce me to believe) the work was principally composed." The incident mentioned by Isaak Walton, whatever were the real facts of the case, was probably the foundation of the story told by Mr. Clogie, and repeated by Bishop Burnet, that Father Paulo gave Bedell, on his leaving Venice, besides other gifts, the manuscript of his History of the Council of Trent. Dr Hickes (op. cit.) among his other strictures on Burnet's Life of Bedell, says that the History of the Council of Trent (by Paulo) was not extant when Bedell left Venice, as may be gathered from a letter of Sir Henry Wotton † in 1618 or 1619, in which the History is spoken of as a work then in hand, or but newly finished, whereas Bedell left Venice in 1610. The Dean, however, is here again at fault, for what Sir Henry Wotton refers to is the proximate publication of the History in London, not the writing of it by Father Paulo, who, we have seen, had finished

* Among the Venetian State Papers for this period at the Public Record Office I have not met with any such writings.
† Reliquiæ Wottonianæ.

the writing of it long before. Sir Henry Wotton's words to the King are, " Paulo's History of the Council of Trent is ready to come abroad * * *, wherein your Majesty had a hand, for the benefit of the Christian world." What Sir Henry here refers to is that King James promoted and encouraged the composition of the work, as far as it lay in his power, through himself, while the Ambassador at Venice, and William Bedell, the Chaplain to the Embassy—the same thing which is referred to by Sir Nathanael Brent the English translator in his dedications. How far the History may have been extant in 1610 has been above shown.

Though Dean Hickes was thus not correct in the matter, the blundering inaccuracy of Clogie and Burnet cannot be denied.

A French translation of Father Paulo's History of the Council of of Trent, by John Diodati, was published at Geneva in 1621, folio, and was entitled, " Histoire du Concile de Trente, Traduite de l'Italien de Pierre Soave Polan.* Par Jean Diodati." This translation, of which I have seen only the fourth edition (Paris, 1665), is esteemed for its fidelity.

The publication of the History of the Council of Trent made a great noise in the Christian world, and revived the animosity of the Court of Rome against Father Paulo, for, although the History was published under a feigned name, it was quite well known at Rome who the author was. *A propos* of this, the anecdote related in the Life of Father Paulo,† and repeated with amplification and embellishment by Sir Henry Wotton, in a letter to his friend Dr. Collins, King's Professor of Divinity in Cambridge,‡ may be here quoted : in 1622, the year before Father Paulo died, the Prince of Condé, being in Venice, had a desire to see so eminent a personage, but his visit could not be received without leave of the Senate. This being granted, it was arranged that Father Paulo should

---

* The name " Pietro Soave Polano," by being Latinized and Frenchified, has lost its anagrammatic point.
† English Translation, London, 1651, p. 152.
‡ Printed in Burnet's Life of Bishop Bedell.

receive His Royal Highness at the house of Signor Angelo Contarini, a Cavalier lately returned from an embassy to France, and who had been appointed by the Senate to attend on the Prince during his stay in Venice. In the course of the interview the Prince asked Father Paulo who was the real author of the History of the Council of Trent. Not choosing to answer such a home question directly, Paulo merely observed that at Rome, as he had been given to understand, it was well enough known who the author was, and, as the Prince was on his way to visit that city, he would learn all about it there.

Besides the last two Books of the History of the Council of Trent, Mr. Bedell translated into Latin Father Paulo's History of the Venetian Interdict. This translation, which he dedicated " Serenissimo Potentissimoque Principi Carolo, D. G. Magnæ Britanniæ, Franciæ, et Hiberniæ Regi, Fidei Defensori," * was published under the following title : " Interdicti Veneti Historia de motu Italiæ sub initio Pontificatus Pauli V. Commentarius, Authore R. P. Paulo Sarpio, Veneto. Recens ex Italico conversus.† Cantabrigiæ, 1626, 4to.," pp. 225.

In his dedicatory observations, Bedell says that when in Venice he received the commentary from the author to read, but on condition that he should not transcribe it. Father Paulo did not wish it then to be published for fear of the resentment of the Court of Rome. After Paulo's death the work in Italian was published in Venice in 1624.‡ Nothing, therefore, now preventing it, Mr. Bedell felt himself at liberty to publish a Latin translation.

* There is in the Library of Trinity College, Dublin, Dr. Dickson informs me, a copy of this work containing Bedell's autograph presentation to the College, when Provost.

† An English translation of Father Paulo's History of the Venetian Interdict was published in London, in 1626, under the following title: " The History of the Quarrels of Pope Paul V. with the State of Venice, in seven Books. Faithfully translated out of the Italian, and compared with the French Copie;" 4to. pp. 435. The translator gives only the initials of his name, C. P.

‡ Istoria dell Interdetto Veneto.

Mr. Bedell also translated into Latin a small tract by Father Paulo about Roman Catholics bearing arms. The translation is entitled, " Quæstio quodlibetica, an liceat stipendia sub Principe Religione discrepante mereri. Eodem Authore, pp. 30. Ibid. 1630. Among the Tanner MSS. there is a letter to Dr. Samuel Warde, dated May 7, 1628, which Mr. Bedell sent along with the MS. of the translation of this tract, desiring to have it published at Cambridge.

Mr. John Diodati, with whom, in conjunction with Fathers Paulo and Fulgentio the Servites, Mr. Bedell had the Conferences in Venice, mentioned at p. 111, being on a visit to London in 1627, made inquiry after Mr. Bedell; but none of the Clergy there happened to know anything of such a person. At this Mr. John Diodati wondered, for he expected that a Divine distinguished for so much learning and devotion as Bedell was would have been well known. Chance, however, brought the two friends together, for they one day unexpectedly met each other in Cheapside. Mr. Alexander Clogie, who tells the story on the authority of "a person of honour who was well acquainted with Diodati," informs us further that Mr. Diodati introduced Bedell to Dr. Moreton, then Bishop of Lichfield and Coventry, but afterwards Bishop of Durham. The person of honour referred to by Clogie as his informant, I am disposed to believe, was Sir Robert Harley of Brampton Bryan, Herefordshire, or some other member of the same family, for the following reasons: 1. Mr. Clogie, as Vicar of Wigmore, was well acquainted with the Harley family, as appears from both Lady Brilliana Harley's Letters and from unprinted documents, for obtaining a copy of which from the Lady Frances Vernon Harcourt I am indebted to the Rev. J. J. Trollope, the present Vicar of Wigmore. 2. The Harley family, in the time of Lady Brilliana, were acquainted with a Dr. Diodati, as appears from some of her Ladyship's letters of about the date of 1645-6. This Dr. Diodati was no doubt - Dr. Theodore Diodati, the brother of Mr. John

Diodati, the Theologian. He married an English lady and settled in London as a Physician. From the Roll of the College of Physicians of London, it appears that Theodore Diodati graduated M.D. at Leyden, October 6, 1615, and was admitted a Licentiate of the College on the 24th of January 1616-17. He was buried in the Church of St. Bartholomew-the-Less on the 12th of February 1650-1. He had a son Charles, also a Physician, who died before him in 1638, and who was a friend of John Milton the Poet. In the Roll of the College of Physicians of London, there is another Theodore Diodati, the son of the Theologian of Geneva, and nephew of the Dr. Theodore Diodati just mentioned. He was M.D. of Leyden, February 4, 1643, and Honorary Fellow of the College of Physicians of London in December 1664. He is mentioned in his uncle Theodore's will, which was dated June 26, 1649. When the Rev. John Diodati was in London, in 1627, he had been no doubt on a visit to his brother Dr. Theodore Diodati, who would therefore be cognisant of the incident above-mentioned.

It may here be observed that the Christian name " Theodore " was probably derived from Theodore Beza, the translator of the New Testament into Latin, who was a friend of the Diodati family and Instructor of John.

The Rev. John Diodati was born June 6, 1576, and died at Geneva, October 3, 1649.

CHAPTER VI.

Bedell's Removal to Ireland and Provostship of Trinity College, Dublin.

Mr. Bedell had held the living of Horningshearth for twelve years when he received an invitation to be Provost of Trinity College, Dublin. On the death of Sir William Temple, January 15, 1626, who had been Provost for seventeen or eighteen years, dissensions arose as to the right of electing his successor between the Senior and Junior Fellows of the College. The result was that the former chose one person, and the latter another, to be Provost. But the King intervened, and by his mandate, May 29, 1627, nominated Mr. William Bedell, a Bachelor of Theology, of Emmanuel College in Cambridge, to the place, with the approval of the Chancellor, the Most Reverend Dr. George Abbot, Archbishop of Canterbury, and the Vice-Chancellor, the Most Reverend Dr. James Ussher, Archbishop of Armagh. It was early in March 1626-7 that Bedell was invited to be Provost, as appears from a letter from him to his friend Dr. Samuel Warde, dated March 15, 1626-7 (Tanner MS. lxxii. 176, in the Bodleian Library, Oxford). He hesitated at first, but, the King's letters approving his nomination being communicated to him, Bedell agreed to accept the appointment; and, having received notice of his election, set out from Horningshearth for Dublin, about the end of July, by himself, and arrived at his destination on the 12th of August 1627. On the 16th of the same month he was sworn and admitted to the office of Provost * of the College of the Blessed Trinity, near Dublin, by the unanimous consent of the Fellows.

Thus was Mr. Bedell wafted to Ireland. The undercurrent which led to his invitation appears to have set in in some such manner as the following : Sir Thomas Jermyn had no doubt exerted his influence at Court in raising up a favourable impression in the King's mind towards the Parson of Horningshearth, who had recently dedicated to his Majesty his Latin translation of Father Paulo's "Istoria dell Interdetto Veneto." In the next place, Bishop Moreton, to whom Diodati had introduced Bedell, appears to have drawn the attention of Archbishops Abbot and Ussher, the Chancellor and Vice-Chancellor of Trinity College, Dublin, to the high character and qualifications of the man; so that they, on the occasion of the difficulty about the Provostship of that Institution, preferred a request to the King to interpose in favour of Bedell, respecting whose fitness for the office his Majesty was already well-informed.

* Dublin University Calendar.

How this request was backed by Sir Henry Wotton we have seen in his letter quoted in the text, p. 25.

Bedell returned to England in September of the same year, to settle his affairs, and to take over his family. But his previous hesitation to leave his native country returning, he had an inclination to give up the Provostship, and in a letter to Archbishop Ussher, dated April 1, 1628, expressed a desire not to return to Dublin, alleging as his reason broils in the College (p. 28), and, as he thought, his non-acceptableness. Encouraged, however, by the Primate he consented to retain the Provostship. Among the Tanner MSS. in the Bodleian Library (lxxii. 275), there is a letter from Bedell to Dr. Samuel Warde, dated April 28, relating to the differences at Dublin College, and his scruples about resigning his living at Horningshearth; and another (lxxii. 282), dated May 13, 1628, taking farewell on going to Ireland, and stating that he had named him (Warde), Dr. Despotine, and Mr. Sotheby, overseers of his will.

Bedell returned to Dublin with his family and resumed his duties as Provost on the 7th of June, and on the 18th of the same month, 1628, finally severed his connexion with England by resigning his Rectory of Horningshearth.

Dr. Samuel Warde, in a letter to Archbishop Ussher, dated May 16, 1628, remarks on Bedell's appointment to the Provostship of Trinity College, Dublin, with so much point that I cannot refrain quoting his words, though they have been more than once elsewhere printed: "I assure your Lordship I know not where you could have pitched upon a man every way so qualified for such a place. He is a sincere, honest man, not tainted with avarice or ambition; pious, discreet, wise, and stout enough, 'si res exigat.' He will be 'frugi,' and provident for the College; and, for converse, of a sweet and amiable disposition, and well experienced. In a word, he is ' homo perpaucorum hominum, si quid judico.'"

During his Provostship Bedell laboured with earnest diligence to reform the constitution of the College, and to improve the discipline. Among the MSS. in Trinity College Library there is a small folio volume (F. 4. 31), containing Bedell's Statutes, dated September 23, 1628, in his own handwriting, and signed thus, " Guilielmus Bedell Præp." (See page 27.) He also encouraged instruction in the Irish language, with the view of providing preachers of the Gospel whom the natives could understand, and thus more effectually spreading a knowledge of the truth among them. How industriously the Provost devoted himself to this part of his mission appears from certain letters of his to Archbishop Ussher. July 30, 1628. Here he refers to the progress in the Irish language in Dublin College, and the translation into Irish of the Psalter, for the Psalms had not been included in the Irish translation of the Book of Common Prayer already published in the Irish tongue. In a postscript to a letter dated Trinity College, Dublin, August 12, 1628, Bedell says, " I am become Mr. King's scholar in the Irish tongue. In respect whereof it may please your Grace to let me have the use of the manuscript Psalter in the Irish letter. I shall inure myself to the character, and observe the differences as I go from our translation, and consider if it might be fit constantly to follow that in the Irish translation or no." The Provost, moreover, inaugurated an Irish lecture to be read publicly in the Hall of the College, enjoined attendance at prayers in Irish in the Chapel, and directed a chapter of the New Testament in Irish to be read by one of the native scholars at dinner in the hall.

In 1628 Provost Bedell was elected one of the Burgesses to represent the University in Parliament; but he excused himself, and a Mr. FitzGerald was chosen instead.

By patent, dated the 20th of May, 1629, the King appointed Dr. Bedell to the Bishoprics of Kilmore and Ardagh, and, in reference to a successor in the Provostship, " His Majesty," says Laud, in a letter to Ussher, " would fain have a man go on where Mr. Bedell leaves;" * * * " the King likes wondrous well of the Irish lecture by Mr. Bedell." The King himself, in a letter to the Board of Fellows,* says: " In the College of the Blessed Trinity, near Dublin, we are informed that, by Mr. Bedell's care and good government, there hath bene wrought great reformation, to our singular contentment."

In the same letter, the Fellows of Trinity College received an inhibition against electing a successor to Dr. Bedell till they should understand his Majesty's further pleasure. Jealous lest their silence in this the second suspension of their privilege should in time make it worthless, the Fellows deputed two of their number to supplicate his Majesty to grant them freedom in election, and requested Bedell to give them a letter of recommendation to Bishop Laud of London. In the letter he gave, dated Trinity College, the 2nd of June 1629, (and which is preserved in the Public Record Office,) Bedell says, " I could not wth mine oth but give way to this their desire, and some furthermore also by these lines I beseech y^r Lord^p to vouchsafe their audience and y^r favourable assistance in their suite, wch their proposition upon the hearing shall seeme to y^r Lord^p to meritt." Annexed is a fac-simile of the signature to this letter:

The supplication of the Fellows was successful, for, in accordance with their prayer, the King gave authority, dated Westminster, the 29th June, 1629,† for the election of Dr. Robert Ussher to the Provostship.

* Dated April 16, 1629.
† Document in the Public Record Office, London, among the Irish State Papers for 1629.

CHAPTER VII.

ELEVATION TO THE EPISCOPATE AS BISHOP OF KILMORE AND ARDAGH—EXTORTIONS OF THE COURT ECCLESIASTICAL —RESIGNATION OF ARDAGH.

It was after about two years' tenure of the stormy office of Provost of Trinity College, Dublin, that Bedell was called to the higher, but, as it proved, more perilous one of Bishop of Kilmore and Ardagh; which two sees were again, for the occasion, united under one Bishop, by the King's patent.

The objection to making Bedell a Bishop referred to in the text, p. 30, seems to have arisen from his opposition to Arminianism and a reputation he had acquired for Calvinism. At p. 58, the imputation of Puritanism, indeed, is stated to have lost him the Deanery of Christchurch in Dublin. At p. 40, Dr. Bernard's "Character" of Bishop Bedell * is referred to, as giving a just account of his conformity to the Liturgy of the Church of England. The Bishop gave this direction, Dr. Nicholas Bernard informs us, viz.: "to observe whatsoever was injoyned in the *Rubrick* without addition or diminution; not to be led by *custome*, but by *rule*. And in speciall he ordered that the whole *Doxology* to the Blessed *Trinity*, Glory be to the Father, &c., should be always read by the *Minister* alone, without the *respond* of the people, and the like for the Psalms, Te Deum, and with the rest appointed to be read between and after the *Lessons*, though the custom had prevailed otherwise in most churches.

* Certain Discourses, &c.; including a Character of the late Bishop Bedell, of Kilmore. By Nicholas Bernard, D.D. and Preacher of the Honourable Society of Grayes Inne, London. (London, 1659.) Dr. Bernard was Dean of Kilmore, but incurring the Bishop's displeasure on account of his holding a number of benefices without being resident on any (Letter of Bedell to Laud dated September 2, 1637, in the Public Record Office), he exchanged, in 1637, with Dr. Henry Jones (afterwards Bishop of Meath) his Deanery of Kilmore for that of Ardagh. Dr. Bernard suffered much in the rebellion, and fled to England.

"The *Communion Table* was placed by him, not at the east end, but within the body of the *Chancell*; and for other Innovations elsewhere introduced he observed them not. His judgement being, that those were as well *Non-Conformists* who added of their own as those who came short of what was enjoyed, as he that *adds* an inch to the measure dissownes it for a *rule* as well as he that cuts an inch *off*.

"He was a careful observer of the *Lord's Day* both in *publick* and *private*. At one of the clock in the afternoon, he had then the Book of *Common Prayer* read in the *Irish* tongue in the church for the benefit of the *Irish*; at which he was constantly present himself, who in that little space had obtained the knowledge of the language."*

Though, as Dr. Bernard says, the Communion-table (upon which lay neither basins nor candles, Mr. Clogie † informs us,) was not placed at the east end, but within the body of the chancel, it would appear that Bishop Bedell still held sacred the upper end of the chancel; for, in his letter to Archbishop Laud, dated September 2, 1637, (in the Public Record Office,) commenting on the evils of plurality and non-residence, he incidentally observes: " When I was a minister in Suffolk, I placed the Communion-table in the upper end of my chancel. In Kilmore Cathedral, finding the Bishop's chair in that part, I said that I would never sit there, it being the ancient place of the altar."‡ This, it is to be observed, was probably the origin of the slander raised by his enemies against him that he wished to pull down his predecessor's seat in the chancel and to set up an altar instead. To return from this digression: though Bedell's appointment was dated May the 20th, 1629, he was not consecrated Bishop until the 13th of September following. In regard to this, he says in a letter to his friend Dr. Samuel Warde,§

* Certain Discourses, &c., *ut supra*, page 350.
† Memoir, &c. p. 139.
‡ See also Decree 11 of the Diocesan Synod: " Ut Sacrarium in Consistorium non convertatur, &c." in Chapter IX.
§ Tanner MS. ccxc. Bodleian Library.

dated October 6, 1629 : " The delay of my Consecration so long was occasioned partly by the desire of our Fellows to have a *free* election ; * partly out of my Lord Primate's and mine to renew the College nester-leases before an unknown successor should come; which, I thank God, I have happily effected."† Dr. Bedell was consecrated at Drogheda by the Primate, Archbishop Ussher of Armagh, assisted by Bishop Echlin, of Down and Connor, Bishop Buckworth, of Dromore, and Bishop Spottiswood, of Clogher.‡

Bishop Bedell, in the letter to Dr. Samuel Warde of the 6th of October, 1629, just quoted, the first since his coming to Kilmore, thus describes his first impressions of the place : " I ame come into a country fertile enough and pleasant, but where popery hath possessed not only the ancient inhabitants, but also our English, which planted here at the first almost universally, and our plantations are yet raw, and our churches ruined. My Cathedral church is such another as Horningerth was, but without steeple, bell, or font. You may imagine the rest. The Popish Bishop of this Diocese is lately chosen Primate, and dwells within a mile or two of me. I am in deliberation to write to him and offer some intercourse, as I see the African Churches and Bishops did to the Donatists." Some months' further experience of his Dioceses did not lead Bedell to form a more favourable estimate of their state, as appears from a letter he wrote to Bishop Laud, dated April 1, 1630.§ This letter also shows that if Bedell made any neighbourly advances to the Roman Catholic Primate, as he said in his letter to Dr. Warde he was contemplating, they had come to nothing, for he now complains of the encroachments and intolerance of the Popish clergy, saying, that they are " more numerous by far than we, and in full exercise of all jurisdiction ecclesiastical, by their vicar-generals and

---

* See in preceding chapter Bedell's letter to Laud, then Bishop of London.
† Another cause of the delay is mentioned at page 30.
‡ Bishop Bedell's predecessor in the Sees of Kilmore and Ardagh was Dr. Thomas Moygne, Fellow of Peterhouse, Cambridge, who had been preferred from the Deanery of St. Patrick's, Dublin, in 1612.
§ Public Record Office.

officials, who are so confident as they excommunicate those who come to our courts, even in matrimonial causes, which affront hath been offered myself by the Popish Primate's Vicar-General, for which I have begun a process against him." This letter Bishop Bedell concludes with the warning that " His Majesty is now with the greatest part of this country, as to their hearts and consciences, King but at the Pope's discretion."

In the letter to the Lord-Deputy Wentworth, written three years and a half after this one (dated November 5, 1633),* vindicating himself from the imputations against him for his share in the matter of the petition of the Protestants of Cavan, deprecating the oppressive charges for soldiers, as explained in pages 49-51 of the text, Bishop Bedell expresses himself still more strongly to the same effect, saying, " I that know, that in this Kingdom of his Majesty the Pope hath another Kingdom, far greater in number, and (as I have heretofore signified to the Lords Justices and Council, which is also since justified by themselves in print,) constantly guided and directed by the orders of the New Congregation *De propaganda fide*, lately erected at *Rome*, &c. * * *. Shortly, I that know that this Clergy and these Regulars, have, at a general meeting, like to a Synod, as themselves style it, holden at Drogheda, decreed, that it is not lawful to take the Oath of Allegiance, and if they be constant to their own learning, do account his Majesty, in their own hearts, to be King but at the Pope's discretion."

The letter to Laud, dated April 1, 1630, and a copy of this one to Wentworth, which Bedell had sent to Laud, now Archbishop of Canterbury, having been found among the Archbishop's papers, were read, on the occasion of his trial, at the bar of the House of Lords, by his prosecutors, as accusatory Articles, to show how Laud had been warned by the Bishop of Kilmore against the encroachments of Popery in Ireland, though without effect.†

* Strafford's Letters and Despatches, vol. i. pp. 146-151; folio, London, 1739.
† See " A Breviate of the Life of William Laud, Archbishop of Canterbury," Necessary Introduction; and also " Canterburies Doome," &c. by William Prynne, Esqnier, London, 1644 and 1646, folio.

EXTORTIONS OF THE COURT ECCLESIASTICAL. 151

But to return: In his letter to Laud (April 1, 1630), Bedell alludes also to the oppressions suffered by the poor Catholics,* from the extortions of the Court Ecclesiastical of the Protestant Establishment, "which," says he, "in very truth, my Lord, I cannot excuse, and do seek to reform." Bishop Bedell's attempt to carry out this reform led to his litigation with the Chancellor, Mr. Alane Cooke, which is related at length in the text. The following brief summary of the transaction, in Bishop Bedell's own words, is extracted from a letter (in the Public Record Office) to Archbishop Laud (at the time Bishop of London), dated Kilmore, August 7, 1630:—

* * * * * *

"By ye dayly complaint of my neighbours, and some of my tenants, and of the clergy," says Bedell, " I was inforced to demand the sight of his (the Chancellor's) Patent, which had been granted him by the previous Bishop."

* * * * * *

" On examination of the document," continues Bedell, " I found a vast heape of authority conferred upon him, without due forme,

---

* Protestant Non-conformists also (settlers from England and Scotland in Ulster) would appear to have suffered from the extortions of the Courts Ecclesiastical in Ireland, and that even in as great a degree as the Catholics. In a petition to the Commons' House of Parliament in 1641, the Protestant [Non-conformist] inhabitants of the counties of Antrim, Downe, Tyrone, &c. complain that " oure soules are starved, our estates undone, our families impoverished, and many lives among us cut off and destroyed," all through the "over-ruling Lordly power " of the Bishops (of the Establishment) and their subordinates. They also complain of the persecution and exile of their ministers. (See a Pamphlet in 4º in the Library of the British Museum, to be found in the Catalogue under the name " Antrim.") Among the Irish State Papers for 1638, in the Public Record Office, there is " A Catalogue of the Inhabitants dwelling in Antrim the last Easter, with those that did partake of the Communion marked with a starr." There is another paper, endorsed, " Rec^d. Jan. 22, 1638-9. The names of the Inhabitants and Communicants within the parish of Antrim at Christmas, 1638, showing that more Scotts conforme to receive the Communion, as is ordered in the Church of Ireland, than formerly." Letters to Archbishop Laud, about the Non-conformists in the counties above mentioned, also occur.

Latine or common sense." * * * " Nothing left to the Bp. but a meere shaddow of authority." * * * * " Accounting the patent void or surreptitious, or revoking it, in case it had any validity, I did inhibit Mr. Cooke to do any thing by vertue of it, as my Vicar, and the Clergy to assist him therein. Upō this, he appealed to my Lo. Primate's Court,* from whence I was inhibited and cited to appear to answer him; he being in the Citation styled Vicar of the Courts of Kilmore and Ardagh lawfully established; For this so apparent a forejudging the cause ere it was heard, I entered a recusation before a publick notary, wch I sent to my Lord Primate, yet submitting ye cause to his owne censure *omni appellatione remotâ*, if my adversary were so pleased. This he refused. Thus did it hang till Hilary Terme. In the mean season I went about my Dioces my selfe, and sate in mine own Courts, redressing the disorders and mittigating the fees (whereof yet I tooke no peny, but sequestered them only), and in a short space have, as I hope, disposed the people to some better opinion of o^r religion and jurisdiction then before they had conceived.

"The case at Dublin was divided in pleading by my counsayle; 1. That no Bishop may grant commission longer then during his owne tyme; 2. That my predecessor holding 2 Bishopricks, united only for terme of life, could make no greater estate then his owne. That by his death the Bishopricks were againe divided and anew united by his Ma^{ty}, so as in them I am not his successor. The other part would make a Vicar Generall a standing office, and sayd the Dean and Chapter anciently might choose a Bishop, much more then cōfirme a Bps. Vicar for life. Especially they urged precedents in England, and some here. The Lo. Chancellor seemed unwilling to have this case determined here, wch he said was never yet adjudged in England. Those of the counsayle y^t are of the profession of the

---

* In a letter to the Lord Primate, dated Febr. 15, 1629-30, Bishop Bedell expressed himself against the abuse of ecclesiastical jurisdiction, in terms identical with those which occur here and there in the letter to Laud under notice.

law, required it might be argued againe at the beginning of Michaelmas Terme, wch was granted.

"Since that Mr. Cooke hath procured me to be cited again to the Lo. Primate's Court, where I appeared July 29, alledging that ye cause is depending before ye LL. Justices and Counsell, and refusing againe the Chancellor, Mr. George Synge,* to be either Judge or Assistant therein; as having been Mr. Cooke's Master and Patron, and now his familiar friend, and having discovered some spleen against me in certain letters wch since this cause came into the Court he had sent me. Y^r L^p hath here the historicall part of this business. Whereto if I shall be bold to add the prognostical, it is this, that although I have his Maties Patents as large for me as I can desire, the canon law as clear as the sunne (whose maxims are these: Vicarius perdit jurisdictionem morte Ep̄i.: Vicarius removeri potest ad libitum Ep̄i, etiamsi sit constitutus cum juramento de non revocando: Vicarius mortuo Ep̄o non potest perficere causas inchoatas vivo Ep̄o. And *de facto* Mr. Cooke, after the death of my predecessor, tooke a new commisson frō ye Lo. Primate to execute the jurisdiction *sede vacante*. Lastly, though I have the common law æquall, if this be but a commission, and as ye Lo. Chiefe Baron sayd openly by ye law one Judge cannot appoint another in his steede, yet because in lands and possessions the grant of the Bp. wth consent of Dean and Chapter is good, it will be carried so here also.

* * * * * *

"The Lo. Chancellor persuades me to compound wth Mr. Cooke, wch for the incredible scandall that would follow I can never doe.

* * * * * *

"My Lord, if this were mine owne particular case alone, I should not be so bold as to request y^r favour and assistance hereunto. But it is the common interests of BBps. who through their owne suffrance do now but serve for cyphers to make up the wronges and extortions of their officers.

* * * * * *

* See text, page 34.

"For my part, God is my Witness, y^t if I thought I could be excused in cōscience for the misgovernm^t of the people whom God and his Ma^{ty} have committed unto me, I could easily suffer Mr. Cooke to exercise the jurisdiction, though there be left me nothing but the name of it; but when the blame also, and the shame of religion lies upon it, I hope good men will not account me pragmaticall, if I be sensible, and desire to fulfill my profession made at my consecration, that I would be *gentle and mercifull for Christ's sake to poore and needy people, and such as be destitute of helpe.* These poore people (to whom to be put into the *Bishop's booke*, as they call it, hath beene more then their imaginary Purgatory) do beseech y^r Lp., and by you his Ma^{ty} to pitty them. Religion intreates you to remove this scandall; the Church to reforme this disorder. I have sayd and done what I can. I leave the successe to God."

*　　　*　　　*　　　*　　　*　　　*

Bishop Laud's reply* to Bishop Bedell is dated from "Fullham House, September 11, 1630," and is sufficiently friendly, frank, and well considered, though, as stated in the text, p. 35, affording only some small verbal encouragement. Laud, thinking that not much can be done to remedy the difficulty, advises Bedell to adopt the suggestion

the Lord Chancellor to compound the matter, "and in that composicōn bynde up Mr. Cooke y^t ye people may have justice and ease. I doe not yet see what ill is in that, or what scandall can follow upon it, for I shall not advyse the making of any other composition then that which shall be free from corruption on your part, and for the just and orderly setling of your jurisdiction on his.

"None can be asked for counsayle but a Bishop or a Civillian. And if a Bishop be asked, he is likely to say for you, but if you ask a civillian I am sure he will be for Mr. Cooke."

In another letter (Public Record Office) to Bishop Laud, dated from Dublin, December 6, 1630, Bishop Bedell says: "If my Lo.

* Copy in the Public Record Office.

Primate be so pleased, he may decide the case by the Canon Lawe. If he put it over to the Comon Law, I am advised to send the case into England and require the opinion of lawiers of that profession, wch I have done by Sr Thomas Jermyn. * * * * * Y^r Lo^p hath beene a true prophett concerning ye bringing all the civilians and canonists upō my topp, for Mr Cooke libelleth against me y^t I seeke to roote out all ye professors of y^t learning."

* * * * * *

This suit between Bishop Bedell and Dr. Alane Cooke was prolonged for several years. There is in the Public Record Office a letter, dated Dublin, May 24, 1639, to Archbishop Laud on the subject, in which Bishop Bedell states that he had appealed from the Lord Primate's Court to the Chancery. And along with this there is a copy of the petition of the Bishop of Kilmore, " to the King's Most Excellent Ma^{ty} in his High Court of Chancery."

The final decision is stated in the text, p. 56.*

Besides the suit with his Chancellor, Bishop Bedell felt it his duty to institute proceedings for the recovery to the Bishoprics of lands which had been, some forcibly seized and kept possession of by Sir Edward Bagshaw and Sir Francis Hamilton,† and some illegally leased out for large fines or for favour at inconsiderable rents by his predecessor, Dr. Moygne, as mentioned in the text, pp. 48-49.

In his anxious endeavours to discharge his duties honestly, Bishop Bedell appears to have been, on the one hand, but faintly seconded, even in quarters where he might reasonably have expected support; and, on the other hand, assailed with bitter revilings. By some he was denounced as a Calvinist, by some as an Arminian, by

---

* Mr. Clogie (Memoir, &c. p. 86,) mentions that in 1646 he met Dr. Alane Cooke by chance in London, who spake as reverently of Bishop Bedell as any could do, and said that he thought there had not been such a man upon the face of the earth till he tried him; and that he was too hard for all the civilians in Ireland; and had he not been borne down by mere force, he had undoubtedly overthrown all the Consistory Courts by lay Chancellors, and restored to all the Bishops their several jurisdictions. He seemed to me to bemoan the Bishop's death.

† Clogie's Memoir, &c. pp. 39, 40.

some as a Puritan, by some as a Papist. He was, indeed, a Calvinist, inasmuch as he accepted the Calvinistic Articles of the Church of England; and a Puritan, inasmuch as he conformed to the Rubric, but would neither go beyond nor fall short of it. If thus a Calvinist, he could not be an Arminian; if a Puritan, not a Papist. Bedell was benevolent and beneficent to all men, whether Jew or Gentile, Protestant or Papist, Conformist or Non-conformist. In thus endeavouring to imitate Jesus, he was, indeed, a "Latitudinarian," though not in the sense in which Dr. Hickes (out of animosity to Bishop Burnet) afterwards sought to represent him.

Under feelings raised by such a thankless reception of his beneficent labours, Bedell's mind sometimes reverted to the quiet of his incumbency at Horningshearth. But he was not of a temper to be cast down; and influenced solely by the desire to discharge efficiently every duty, delegating nothing to others that he could do himself, he had not been Bishop long before he resolved to resign the Bishoprick of Ardagh in order to free himself from the distractions involved in the attempt to recover it from the plundered state in which he found it, and thereby to be in a condition the better to devote himself to the work of governing and correcting the abuses in the Diocese of Kilmore alone. In a letter to Laud (Public Record Office) on the subject, dated Dublin, May 10, 1631, Bishop Bedell accordingly intimates his desire to give up Ardagh, and expresses his opinion that that See could be better managed by a separate Bishop. At the same time he mentions Dr. Richardson * as the fittest man for it he knows of.

On the 28th Feb. 1632, accordingly, Bp. Bedell resigned the see of Ardagh. The following is a copy of the instrument of his resig-

---

* John Richardson, D.D. of the University of Dublin, Archdeacon of Derry, Rector of Ardstra, and Vicar of Granard. In 1639 he received the Archdeaconry of Down and Connor, instead of that of Derry, which he had held since 1622. See Sir James Ware's Antiquities of Ireland, vol. i., The Bishops; and Archdeacon Henry Cotton's Fasti Ecclesiæ Hibernicæ, vol. iii. pp. 49-52, 183-4, 231, 257, 337; and vol. v. pp. 208-9.

nation, from the original, preserved among the See Records of Armagh * : —

" CORAM VOBIS Reverendissimo in Christo Patre ac Domino Jacobo providentia divina Armachano Archiepiscopo totius Hiberniæ Primate,

Ego Gulielmus Episcopus Kilmorensis et Ardaghensis vestræ Armachanæ Provinciæ in Regno Hiberniæ humiliter et veraciter expono. Quod cum Serenissimus et potentissimus Princeps ac Dominus Carolus Dei Gratia Magnæ Britanniæ Franciæ et Hiberniæ Rex dictos Episcopatus mihi ex motu suo proprio et Regio beneplacito contulisset eosdemque in meam gratiam et propter eorum tenuitatem pro ea vice tantum univisset annexuisset et consolidasset ita ut eorundem duorum Episcopatuum æque principaliter Episcopus a vobis consecrarer et eosdem pro uno tantum ad vitam duntaxat meam naturalem cum omnibus eorum respective juribus membris preeminentiis privilegiis jurisdictionibus commoditatibus et hereditamentis quibuscunque tam spiritualibus quam temporalibus retinerem eorum tamen Episcopatuum respective obsequiis semper salvis Tametsi me uni Episcopatui administrando parem non existimarem ne dum ut duos capesserem tamen quoniam mihi conscius eram hoc munus nec ambienti neque cogitanti mihi impositum, nihil aliud quam fidem et diligentiam in utriusque Ecclesiæ administratione præstandum putavi Et pro virili parte operam dedi ex eo tempore ne quid alterutra detrimenti caperet Pro Ardaghensi quidem cujus reditus tenuiores erant aliquam mihi navasse videor : tum restitutis quibusdem possessionibus in feodum firmum et perpetuum alienatis tum vero antiquo illius Ecclesiæ Registrario recuperato. Sed quum multa alia utriusque Ecclesiæ jura persequenda restent et ista duarum Ecclesiarum unio utriusque commodis officit,

---

* For this again I am obliged to the courtesy of the Rev. Dr. Reeves, of Tynan, whose numerous other contributions are of such a character that without them this work would have been very incomplete.

quod improbe et cupide videatur amplius petere cui jam bini sint Episcopatus, cujus rei magnum argumentum capio, quod multis meis laboribus et impensis nullum hactenus ne in ruderibus quidem Ardaghensis Ecclesiæ aut ædium Episcopalium locum nancisci potuerim ubi vestigium ponam Cumque ista jurisdictionis ac possessionum Episcopalium in una persona conjunctio magnam in præsentia confusionem pariat ac majorem imposterum paritura sit; Presertim vero quoniam rerum experimentis comperi, quod ad temporalium utriusque diocesis curam et administrationem congruam, solus impar sim nisi in Litibus perpetuis ætatem conterens populi mihi commissi curam et officium Pastorale velim negligere. HASCE igitur ob causas, et alias nonnullas graves et justas animum et conscientiam meam moventes; Ego Gulielmus Episcopus antedictus non vi aut metu coactus, aut cujusquam precibus adductus, nec ullo terreno aut carnali affectu permotus, sed pure simpliciter sponte libere et utilitatem Ecclesiarum predictarum et officium meum præ oculis habens, Episcopatum Ardaghensem cum omnibus juribus tam spiritualibus quam temporalibus ad eundem pertinentibus, in manus vestras (Reverendissime Pater) ac per vos in manus Serenissimi Domini nostri Regis Caroli resigno: tituloque ac nomini et dignitati ejusdem cedo, et a cura ejusdem me per præsentes exonero: salvo tamen semperque mihi reservato omni jure titulo siue interesse quod in Episcopatu Kilmorensi cui prædictus Episcopatus Ardaghensis in mea persona hactenus unitus fuit, mihi ex Majestatis suæ gratia, et vestra Reverende Pater consecratione competit. Et peto a vobis humiliter ut hanc meam spontaneam cessionem siue resignationem pure simpliciter libereque factam admittere; et Regiæ Majestati suæ significare velitis, quo unionem Ecclesiarum siue Diocessium prædictarum in persona mea factam dissolvi; et jurisdictiones et possessiones earundem secerni, et Ecclesiæ Ardaghensi de alio quovis Pastore idoneo pro suo bene-placito provideri gratiose dignetur præcipere. In quorum omnium fidem et testimonium nomen meum subscripsi et sigillum meum Episcopale quo hactenus usus sum præsentibus apposui. Datum vicesimo octavo die Februarii Anno Domini Millesimo sexcentesimo tricesimo secundo.

GUILIEL. KILMOREN.

In a letter to Dr. Warde on the subject of the resignation of Ardagh, dated Kilmore, February 2, 1633-4,* Bishop Bedell says: "And because I found my suits for the rights of the B^{rick} of Ardagh had so cold success, as in three years I could not get so much as a place where to set my foot in the Diocese, although the leases were made contrary to an Act of State, and were upholden by forgery and perjury, I accounted it my best course to quit the B^{rick} to Dr Richardson, who hath the best living † in it and good friends.

"And to tell you the whole truth, I was loth that myne own example sh^d. serve for a pretext to the established practice of many of our Nation, who have gotten 4, 5, 6, 8 benefices apiece, and commonly vicarages, and w^h. is yet worse maintain no curates unless it be sometimes one for two or three livings."

Dr. John Richardson was raised to the Bishopric of Ardagh by Patent dated May 14, 1633, and consecrated in the *autumn* of the same year at Armagh by Primate Ussher, continuing to hold his preferments in Commendam.‡

Four years after this, Bishop Bedell, in a letter, to Archbishop Laud, dated September 2, 1637,§ says, that, by the care of Bishop Richardson, Ardagh is now as good as Kilmore or better; thus showing how well the affairs of the See of Ardagh had been managed under a separate Bishop. Laud in his reply, dated October 12, 1637,|| to this letter, expresses his satisfaction that the revenue of the Bishopric of Ardagh had been so much improved, and hopes that in time other benefices in Ireland will become rich

* Tanner MS. lxxi. 189, in Bodleian Library.
† The Vicarage of Granard.
‡ See Sir James Ware's "Ireland," and Archdeacon Henry Cotton's "Fasti," *ut supra*, vol. v. p. 231.
§ Public Record Office.
|| Draft in the Public Record Office. Also Laud's Works, vol. vii. p. 374.

enough to do away with any excuse for pluralities and non-residence. The poorness of some livings Laud recognises as an excuse for the existing abuses, remarking that poverty breeds contempt.

As a tail-piece to this chapter, Bedell's autographs, as Bishop of Kilmore and Ardagh, and as Bishop of Kilmore alone, are subjoined.

CHAPTER VIII.

FAMILY BEREAVEMENTS.

In the midst of Bishop Bedell's struggles to secure the due fulfilment of the duties pertaining to his sacred office, Death began to knock at his door.

First his second son John died. In a letter (Tanner MS. lxx. 74, in Bodleian Library) to Dr. Samuel Warde, dated Kilmore, October 11, 1635, the Bishop writes: " Since my last to you, I have sent before my second and best beloved sonne from the Colledge at Dublin to a higher Universitie, as I hope. God bring me well to him. It was a little after Christmas last."

The next death in the Bishop's family was that of his stepdaughter Leah in little more than a month after her marriage to the Rev. Alexander Clogie,* Vicar of Denn, in the county of

* See Chapter XVII.

Cavan. The marriage was solemnized in Dublin by the Bishop himself, who, in order to be authorised to do so by the Archbishop of Dublin, obtained a licence from the Consistory, November 23, 1637.*

Mrs. Leah Bedell, the Bishop's wife, did not long survive her daughter. She died on the 26th of March 1638, and was buried at Kilmore in the remotest part of the Cathedral churchyard beside her son John. In the text we have notices of Mrs. Bedell in her earlier days. In the following quotation from one of her husband's letters to Dr. Samuel Warde, we have a glimpse of her motherly gladness on the occasion of her eldest son by her first marriage, Nicholas Mawe, having distinguished himself at Cambridge. The letter † is dated "Hornin[th]" 28th April, 1628, and Bedell says: "I thank y[u] for y[r] newes of M[r] Mawe's dysputacion, w[h] made his mother a glad woman." Mr. Clogie, her son-in-law, supplies a further account of her. He praises her for her humility, virtue, and godliness, and dwells much on the reverence she always manifested towards her husband. The Bishop himself preached her funeral sermon, taking for his text Eccl. vii. 1: "A good name is better than good ointment."

It is above mentioned (p. 15) that Dr. Nicholas Mawe, Bishop Bedell's eldest step-son, married and entered on medical practice in London, but died not long after. I have not been able to ascertain the date of his death. He is not stated in the Roll of the College of Physicians to have attained the Fellowship. The last notice of him I have found is in the letter, dated Kilmore, October 11, 1635, to Dr. Samuel Warde, in which Bishop Bedell announces the death of his son John, and refers to his step-son Dr. Nicholas Mawe, in London, to get him some books. He probably died before his mother, so that Mrs. Bedell may have had to mourn the death of both her eldest son and only daughter by her first marriage, ere she herself was called away.

* Clogie's Memoir, &c. p. 159.   † Tanner MS. lxxii. 275, Bodleian Library.

CHAPTER IX.

DIOCESAN SYNOD.

In the text, Bishop Bedell's labours in his Diocese are described in detail, and the suit with the Chancellor, Dr. Alane Cooke, reported at length. Another principal occurrence during his Episcopate, which is only glanced at in the text (p. 41), may here be more fully noticed. In his anxiety for the well-ordering of his Diocese, the Bishop inaugurated a plan of holding Diocesan Synods yearly. The first, and, as it would appear, the only one, was held at the Cathedral Church of Kilmore on the 19th of September, 1638, and, after deliberation on Diocesan matters, decrees relating to discipline were passed. In the Public Record Office there is in the Bishop's own handwriting a document, which was sent to Archbishop Laud, containing minutes of the proceedings of this Diocesan Synod, with the decrees passed by it, and the names of the clergymen who subscribed them. There are also references to the ecclesiastical authorities on which each decree is founded.

The following is a copy of this document:[*]

Acta Ecclesiastica in Ecclīa Cathedrali Kilmoreñ.
Septembris 19°, 1638.

Quo die post peractas publicas pr̄ces, & synaxin ab Episcopo celebratam, jussit Epūs in medium proferri S. Biblia, & in mensâ sacrâ proponi: cumq. se ad conventus hujus causam exponendam accingeret, accessit Margeria King, uxor Murtachi King Vicarii parochiæ de Templeport, & supplicem libellum ei porrexit, in præsentia totius cōventus, in quo de vi & injurijs viro suo & sibi illatis, a Guilielmo

---

[*] It is indorsed thus: "Rec^d: Decemb: 20: 1638. Synodus Diœcesana Kilmoren: Septemb: 19: 1638. Actus ejusdē Synodi." In Clogie's Life of Bishop Bedell, and also in that by Burnet, there is a copy of the Decrees alone, but it does not contain the names of the clergymen who subscribed them.

Bayly Vicario de Anagheliff conquerebat'. Exclusis laicis & quotquot non erant de capitulo, Epūs cum Presbyteris tractavit super Articulis quibusdam in hoc conventu sanciendis. Intervenit ibi dictus Guilielmus Bayly & inter Presbyteros consedit: Et postquam absolvissent tractare, lectus est libellus dictæ Margeriæ, & interrogatus est G. Bayly an hæc ita se haberent? Qui respondit, multa in dicto libello contineri, partim vera, partim falsa. Interrogatus de singulis, vim factam negavit. Agnovit se procurante l'ras a Supremis Commissariis R. Ma^{tis} pro causis Ecclesiasticis decretas, ut dictus Murtachus comprehensus in custodiam traderetur. Se præsentem orasse Lictores, ut ipsū leniter tractarent, habitâ ratione valetudinis ejus. Agnovit se cum tribus aliis Equitibus abegisse boves et equas Margeriæ prædictæ. In quos dicebat ipsam cum servulis impetum fecisse, & auditam ejus vocem jubentis unum é suis, ut quēdam quocum manus conserebat occideret: Cum Epūs eum admoneret excōicationis quam olim incurrerat, adeoq. non esse ei jus in hoc conventu suffragandi; respondit se absolutum ēc, idq. postea manifestum fore. Cum alia quædam peragenda restarent, propter temporis angustias ulterius processū non est in hoc negotio. Proposita est locatio quædā duarum pullarū fundi Epalis, facta ab Epo Dionysio Sheriden, Vicario de Killasser, a capitulo confirmanda. Lectæ sunt tabulæ locationis. Res dilata ē in tempus pōmeridianum.

Cum iterum post prandium convenissent, lecta sunt Latinè capitula antea synodo proposita, & suffragia viritim rogata. De quarto pro majori parte ampliabant, reliquis subscripserunt, nisi q^d Fidelis Teate S. Theologiæ D^r de mulieribus in sacrario non sedendis non ē assensus.

De causâ G. Bayly, ipso non comparente, denuo tractatū est. Epūs commemoravit ante annū in Visitatione Dromlahani propter vim et intrusionem in dictam Vicariam de T. declaratum fuisse ipsū G. Bayly non modo illâ quam occupaverat, sed insuper Vicariâ de Anagheliff quam prius obtinuerat ipso jure privatū. Verum hujusmodi declarationē executioni non fuisse demandatam. Consensu omnium decretum est, ut ad causam dicendam proximâ Curiâ Cavanam citaretur, et prout causa postularet procederetur.

De Negotio locationis, visum est capitulo tractandum prius cum Prorege & Consilio, quorum si consensus accederet, se quoq. eam locationem sigillo capituli (quod in presentiâ non aderat) confirmaturos.

Proposuit Epūs de querelâ Cleri et populi ob iniquas exactiones in ultima Visitatione Metropolitica : et representati sunt breviculi aliquot ad eam rem facientes. Epūs consuluit ut lr̃as ad Reverendiss^m Prim. Armachanū Archiepūm super hoc negotio conscriberent. Electus est Decanus Kilmoreñ, qui cum Archidiacono & D^{re} Teate epistolam conciperent communi nōie mittendam.

Negotium de Decimâ ex pastione animalium, quod demandatum fuerat Geor. Creichtano, Vicario de Lurgan, prosequendum apud Proregem et Consilium nōie Clēri ; Item et aliud q^d gerebat Decanus Kilmoreñ de portione decimarū quam vendicat Comes Westmediæ a compluribus ecclesijs, nomine Prioratus sive Monasterii de Fower, dilata sunt in secundū Octobris, propter temporis angustias.

Cum jam advesperasceret, gratijs ab Epō Deo redditis, ob pacificum hujus Conventus exitum, ab omnibus discessum est.

DECRETA SYNODI.

In nōie Dñi Dej & Salvatoris nostri Jesu Chr̃i.

Regnante in perpetuum ac gubernante Ecclesiam suam, eodem Dōio nostro Jesu Chr̃o, annoque imperij Serenissimi Principis ac Dñi Caroli D. G. Magnæ Britāniæ et Hibniæ Regis decimo quarto. Cum ad Ecclesiam Cathedralem Kilmoreñ monitu Guilielmi Ep̃i convenisset Capitulum totius Diœceseos ad Synodum Diœcesanam celebrandum, post fusas ad Deum preces pro publicâ pace, Regisque et familiæ Regiæ incolumitate, et peractâ S. Synaxi, Verba fecit Ep̃us de ejusmodi Synodorum antiquitate, necessitate et authoritate.

Et cum venisset in consultationem quibus rationibus et fidei sinceritas, & morum sanctitas, & decor domus Dej, & Ministrorum libertas conservari posset, nihil conducibilius visum est, quam ut ea quæ à Patribus benè ac prudenter antiquitus instituta sunt, quasi postliminij jure revocarent^r. Atque tractatu inter nos habito, ad extremum in hæc capitula unanimiter consensum est.

Synodum Diœcesanam sive capitulum quotannis feria quarta secundæ hebdomadæ Mensis Septembris in Eccliâ Kilmoreñ tenendam. Eum diem huic Conventui statum et solennem fore, sine ullo Mandato. Si res poscat in cæteris quoq. ordinationum temporibus Presbyterium contrahi, Episcopi mandatum expectandum.

Concil. Lateran. sub Innocen. c. 6, Sicut olim.
Concil. Basil. c. 8, Synodales.

In Epi absentia aut morbo Vicarius ejus si Presbyter fuerit, præsidebit, alioquī Archidiaconus, qui de jure vicarius est Episcopi.

De offic° Archidiaconi, l. i. tit. 23, c. 1° and 7°.

Vicarius Epi in posterum nullus constituat^r aut cōfirmet^r qui Laicus sit, nec quisquam prorsus nisi durante duntaxat beneplacito.

Concil. Chalced. c. 26.
Concil. Hispalen. 2 c. 9, Nona actione, &c.
Ve Bertachinu'. pars 7, c. 9.

Ut Archidiaconus * de triennio in triennium personaliter visitet: Singularum Ecclesiarum ædiumque mansionalium sarta tecta tueat^r. Libros et ornamenta in Indiculo descriptos habeat; defectus omnes supplendos curet, Episcopalis procurationis dimidium habeat, eâ conditione ut Episcopus eo anno non visitet.

De Offic. Archidiaconi, c. 1°.
Concil. Oxonie', c. 22.

Ut secundum pristinam et antiquam hujus Diœceseos Kilmoreñ constitutionem, in tribus ejus regionibus tres Decani sint, ab ipsis Ministris cujusq. Decanatus eligendi; qui vitam et mores Cleri jugi circumspectione custodiant et ad Epūm referant, ejus mandata

* De hoc capite ampliat Capitulum.

accipiant, et quoties opus erit, per Apparitorē Decanatus ad compresbyteros suos transmittant.

> Regist. Kilmor.
> De Offic. Archidiac. c. Ad hæc.
> Vᵉ Concil. Oxon. c. 16.
> De Offic. Archipres. c. Ut singul.

In quoq. Decanatu in oppido ejus principali conventus sive capitulum sit Ministrorū, quolibet saltem Mense: ubi lectis plenè publicis precibus, concionentʳ per vices, absque longis precibus et proemijs.

> Vᵉ Lindwood De Constitut. c. Quia.
> Concil. Oxon. 16, 29 et 24.

Advocationes ecclesiaȓ nondum vacantium quæ ad collationē Epī spectant, nemini conferantʳ aut confirmentur.

> Concil. Lateran. sub Alex. Tit. de Jure Patr. 11, &c.
> Tit. ult. 103.

Possessiones Eccłiæ non alienentur aut locentur contra regni jura, nempe terrarū mensalium nulla sit Locatio, nisi quoad Epūs in vitâ aut sede sua supersit, cæterarum, in plures annos quam leges sinunt aut prioribus locationibus triefiio minus nondum expletis.

> Vᵉ Decretal. l. 3º, Tit 13, c. Nulli, &c.
> c. Ut super.

Ut corpora defunctorū deinceps in Ecclesijs non humentur, sed nec intra quintum pedem a pariete Ecclesiæ extrorsum.

> Concil. Bracar, 1. c. 36.
> Concil. Mold. c. 24º vˡ 9º, Antiquus in his, &c.
> Concil. Mogunt. 1. c. 32.
> Concil. Matised. 2. c. 17, Comperimus.
> Concil. Tribur. 1, c. 17, Secundum, &c.

Ut mulieres in sacrario non sedeant, sed infra căcellos; et quidem a viris secretæ.

> Concil. Laodicen. 44.
> Concil. Aquisgran. 82.
> Capitular. Car. l. 1, c. 17.
> Vᵉ Concil. Turonen. 2, c. 4, Ut laici, &c.

Ut sacrarium in Consistorium non convertat^r, aut sacra mensa Notarijs aut Scribis sit pro pluteo.

    Capitular. l. 1, c. 71. Ex Concil. Lugd.
    C. Decret. de immunitate Eccl. in Vl.
    Concil. Colon'. sub Herma'no, Tit. 3°, De Metrop.
        cap. 24, Cum in, &c.

Ne in funeribus mulieres planctum aut ululatum faciant.

    Concil. Toletan. 3, c. 22.
    Capitular. Car. l. 6, c. 194.

Ut ossa defunctorū in cæmeterijs non coacervent^r sed tradant^r sepulturæ.

    Capitular. l, 6. 195.

Ut * matricula sit, in quam referant^r nōia eorum qui ad S. Ordines admissi sunt, aut instituti ad beneficia, sive ad curā animarum coaptati ; clericorum item parochaliū, et Ludimagistrorū : neque deinceps ad l'ras testimoniales in Visitationibus exhibendas adigant^r.

    Concil. Agathen.* c. 2.
    Capitular. Addit. 4, c. 100.
    Dist. 50ᵃ. c. Contumaces.
    Lindwood, De Censibus, c. Item licet, &c.
        c. Sæva, &c.

Ne quis Minister oblationes ad funera, baptismū, Eucharistiā, nuptias, post puerperium, aut portionē Canonicam cuiquam locet.

    Decretal, l. 3. Tit. 30°, c. Quamvis.
    Concil. Oxon. c. 37.

Ne quis ejusmodi oblata acerbe exigat, p^{r}sertim a pauperibus.

    Concil. Latera'. sub Innocent. c. 66.
    Concil. Oxon'. 26.
    Concil. Vasen. 2, Præcipiendu' est, c. 13ᵃ, 9, 2ᵈᵃ.
    Concil. Tribur. 16 Abhorrendus, &c.
    Grat. cᵉ, 13, 9, 2, c. 12.

Ut fas sit Ministro a S. Cænâ repellere eos, qui se ingerunt ad Synaxin, neque nōia sua pridie Parocho significarunt.

    Concil. Cabilon. 2ᵘ, c. 46.

Ut pueri a septimo saltem ætatis anno donec confirment^r per manuum impositionem, stent inter Catechumenos, factoque Catalogo, singulis Dominicis certus eorum numerus sistatur in Ecclesiâ examinandus.

Si quis Minister quenquam ex fratribus suis alibi accusaverit priusquam Epō denunciet, ab ejus consortio cæteri ōes abstinebunt.

Concil. Chalced. c. 9.
Ve Grat. c^a, n. q. 1, c. 38, De persona Presbyt.
et c. Pervenit.

Clerici comam ne nutriant & habitu clericali prout Synodo Dubliniensi constitutum est incedant.

Concil. Oxon. c. 30.
Lindwood, Tit. De Offic. Indi. c. Ordinarij.

Oeconomi Parochiarum provideant, ne in Ecclesiâ tempore cultus divini, pueruli discursent: atque canes arceant^r, constitutis * ostiarijs, vel mulctâ imposita, si quis semel atque iterum admonitus canem secum in Ecclesiam introduxerit.

* V* Concil. Laodicen. c. 22. & 43.
Capitular. l. i. c. 71.

Ut nulla excōicationis sententia feratur ab uno solo Ministro, sed ab Epō, assistentibus quotquot ex Capitulo fuerint p^{r}sentes.

Matth. 18, 17.
1 Cor. 5, 4.
Capit. Car. l. 1º, c. 142.

Haec Decreta Synodalia, quoniam ex usu hujus Diœceseos futura credimus, et ipsi observabimus, & quantū in nobis est ab alijs observanda curabimus adeoque manus suæ quisque subscriptione corroboramus. Septemb. 19º, 1638.

Guiliel. Kilmorēn Epūs.

Tho. Price, Archidiacon. Kilm. Hen. Jones.

DIOCESAN SYNOD. 169

Omnibus his subscribo præter-
quam nono * decreto:— Faithfull Teate.
Martin Baxter.
Georg. Creichton.
Alexander Clogie.
Daniel Crean.
Al. Comine.
Tho. Brady.
Denis Shiriden.

It is here seen that the Ministers present delayed judgment on the fourth decree, but subscribed to all the others, except Dr. Faithfull Teate,† who objected to that by which it is ordered that women should sit not in the chancel, but below the rails and apart from the men. Dr. Teate's reason for this was, Mr. Clogie alleges, that he had erected a new seat for his wife in the chancel but a little before, and was loath to remove it.

The convening of this Diocesan Synod gave occasion to a great outcry against Bishop Bedell on the part of his adversaries. Notwithstanding the moderation and legality of the whole proceedings the Bishop and every minister that assisted at the Synod, it was declared, ought to be cited before the High Commission Court or the Star Chamber. This frightened the ministers, but the Bishop was ready with a reply.‡ His explanation to Archbishop Laud, dated Dublin, December 20, 1638, accompanies the Minutes of the Proceedings and the Decrees of the Synod above copied from the document in the Public Record Office, and is here quoted:—

* The decree to which Dr. Teate did not assent was that against women sitting in the chancel. This decree in the above series it will be seen stands tenth and not ninth; the fourth, being reserved, was not counted.

† The son of this Dr. Faithfull Teate or Tate was Nahum Tate, one of the authors of the metrical version of the Psalms.

‡ "You had better let him alone," Archbishop Ussher warned Bedell's assailants in Dublin, "for fear, if he should be provoked, he should say much more for himself than any of his accusers can say against him." (Harris's Ware's Works, i. 236.)

CAMD. SOC. Z

"Concerning my bringing into the Castle-Chamber and *Præmunire* for our Diocesan Synode, the bruite is much ceased since men have a little looked on their books. A Prelate of great note said to one of my clergy here, If we might hold a Diocesan Synode, why not a Provinciall? and if that, why not a Nationall? The argum̃t indeed is *a minore ad majus*, but affirmative. Yet touching Provinciall Synodes, enjoined by the canons of ye universal church, allowed by the laws Imperiall, and those of other Christian countries, practised by y^r Gr^s predecessors in England, and by the Archbp̃s of this Kingdome, yea (as I am informed) by ye Popish titular clergy here this day, I cannot conceive what jealousy of State there should be against them, being sufficiently limited by the Act of submission of the clergy and subordinated to the Crowne. And if there be any scruple in the law touching the assembling of Suffraganes by their Metropolitane, for causes merely Ecclesiasticall, his Majesty by his Roiall authority declaring his pleasure therein, might (if in his high wisdome he should thinke fitt) take away all doubt and restore the ancient order of the Christian Church, and bring much ease to his subjects, wthout neede of other extravagant courses. These conceptions I humbly submit to y^r Grace's mature judgment. To retorne to Episcopall Synodes: Among other things, since I came to this place, I have mett wth a just Treatise De Synodo Epi, in that great work of the Tractates of the D^{rs}, printed at Venice, in 16 Tomes; It is Tome 2º. The author's name is Henricus Botteus; he wrote, as may appear, part 3ª, No. 74, ye year after Rome was sackt, anno 1527. Amongst others, these are his positions: that such a Synode *est de jure divino*. And, *Papa non po't Ep'is auferre potest'em faciendi suas Synodos*. Item, *Ep'us non debet petere licentiam ab Archiep'o pro congreganda sua Synodo. Synodus est præparatorium ad Visitationem, &c. Quædam Visitatio generalis &c. Episcopus omittens convocare Synodum debet puniri suspensione*, &c. And it is very likely that those y^t penned o^r late canons, or those from whom they were taken, had this in their mindes when they appointed y^t ye constitutions lawfully enjoined by ye Bp. of the Dioces in his Visitation, should be observed, &c. But I forget myself and y^r Grace's many employments."

CHAPTER X.

EFFORTS TO SPREAD THE GOSPEL THROUGH THE MEDIUM OF THE NATIVE LANGUAGE—IRISH TRANSLATION OF THE OLD TESTAMENT.

From the time of Edward the Sixth down to that of James the First, the necessity of imparting religious instruction to the Irish in their own language had been repeatedly recognised. Queen Elizabeth, in the 13th year of her reign, sent over a font of types, in the Irish character, in the hope, as she expresses herself, "that God in his mercy would raise up some one to translate the New Testament into their mother tongue." And Sir H. Sidney, "the good Lord Deputy," suggested that Irish-speaking ministers should be appointed in remote parishes. But, notwithstanding all this, we find King James, in the 17th year of his reign, complaining that Irish-speaking ministers had not been trained in Trinity College, Dublin, as had been intended by Queen Elizabeth.

We have above seen that Bedell had not been Provost long before he applied himself to the study of the Irish language. In this he succeeded so well as to become a proficient, as regards the reading and writing of it, but did not, as was to be expected at his time of life, acquire much facility in speaking it. On being made Bishop he undertook the task of having a translation of the Old Testament made into Irish, as appears from a letter to Archbishop Ussher, dated February 15, 1629-30, in which he mentions that Mr. James Nangle was occupied with the translation of the Psalms, and Mr. Murtach King with that of the Historical Books of the Old Testament.

In 1631 the Bishop printed, not exactly a catechism, but a short summary of Christian doctrine, in English and Irish. Of this tract there is a copy in the British Museum. A description of it and its contents is here given, drawn up with the work before me.

It is comprised in a single sheet, small octavo: —

(First Leaf.)

The
A, B, C,
or
The Institution
of a Christian.
(Irish title in Irish letters.)

Dublin:
Printed by the Company of Stationers. 1631.

On the back of this title-page is a wood-engraving, coarsish but clever and well-drawn, representing a tree laden with apples, and children gathering the fruit from it: two are up the tree plucking off the apples, three are catching them as they fall or picking them up from among the fallen leaves, one is sitting looking up at the tree, and one, also sitting, is eating of the fruit. The artist's initials are R. B. This picture was, no doubt, intended by the Bishop to illustrate the saying of St. Augustine, which he had often in his mouth: "Fruit, not Leaves, I seek."

(Second leaf.)

The A, B, C.

| A a, B b, &c. in Roman Characters. | The corresponding letters in Irish Characters. |

A SUMMARY OF CHRISTIAN DOCTRINE. 173

Abbreviations :—

&	ā	y^e	y^t	y^u	The same in Irish.
and,	an,	the,	that,	thou,	
w^t	w^c	. i .			The same in Irish.
with,	which,	vizt, that is.			

Numerals:—
Roman ———————
Arabic ———————
Roman ———————
Arabic ———————

MDCXXXI.
1631.

On the reverse side of this second leaf the paging commences.

Page 1 on the left, in English, and page 2 on the right, in Irish, face each other, and contain :—

The profession of a Christian :
In the name of the Father, &c.
The Catholike and Apostolike Faith :
The Creed.
The Lord's Prayer begins.

Page 3 on the left in English, and page 4 on the right in Irish, face each other, and contain the rest of the Lord's Prayer, and the 1st and 2nd Commandments, with the commencement of the 3rd.

Page 5 on the left in English, and page 6 on the right in Irish, facing each other, contain the rest of the Commandments.

Page 7 on the left in English, and page 8 on the right in Irish, facing each other, contain " The Summe of the Gospell," Galat. 3, 10, John 3, 16.

Page 9 on the left in English, and page 10 on the right in Irish, facing each other, contain 2 Corinth. 5, 19.

Page 11 on the left in English, and page 12 on the right (by a typographical error numbered 11) in Irish, facing each other, contain Acts 13, 38, The recommending the soule into the hands of God; Luke 18, 13; Mat. 9, 24; Luke 17, 5; Psal. 31, v. 7; Acts 7, 59; Grace before meat, Psal. 145, 15.

Page 13 is the last, and is divided into two columns, the first of which is in English, and the second in Irish. It contains Grace after Meat and the Benediction, The Grace of our Lord Jesus Christ, and the love of God, and the Communion of the Holy Ghost, be with us all. Amen.

At the end of this page is a flowered tail-piece.

In a reprint of this tract, we are informed in Burnet's Life of Bedell, there were added some of Leo's and Chrysostom's homilies, in English and Irish. This augmented edition of the work I have not seen.

Bishop Bedell did what he could to induce such of his clergy as were resident on their livings to set up Irish Schools in their parishes. In a letter to his friend Dr. Samuel Warde (Tanner MS. lxxi. 189, Bodleian Library), dated February 2, 1633, the Bishop says that he trains his children up as he may to understand the Irish tongue, in the hope that they may endeavour to open the eyes of some part of the Irish Nation.

In a convocation held at Dublin in 1634, there were no small debates on the subject of the version of the Bible and Liturgy into Irish, for the benefit and instruction of the natives. The Bishop of Kilmore advocated the measure, founding his arguments on the principles of theology and the good of souls. Dr. John Bramhall,* then Bishop of Derry, and afterwards Archbishop of Armagh, on the contrary, opposed the measure, from politics and maxims of state, as inexpedient, and because there was a statute of Henry the Eighth obliging the native Irish to learn English.†

* Dr. Bramhall appears always to have acted in a cold and unsympathising—even secretly inimical—way towards Bedell's beneficent labours, as appears from his letters to Laud in the Public Record Office, and occasional expressions in Bedell's own letters.

† Dr. Antony Dopping, Bishop of Meath, in a letter dated December 14, 1685, to the Rev. * * *, in the Works of the Hon. Robert Boyle.

IRISH TRANSLATION OF THE OLD TESTAMENT. 175

Convocation, countenanced by Primate Ussher, siding with Bishop Bedell, ordered, that when the people of a parish are all, or mostly all, Irish, the Liturgy shall be read in Irish, and that when the minister does not know Irish, and many Irish are in the parish, such a clerk may be chosen as shall be able to read in Irish those parts of the service as shall be appointed to be read in that language.

The New Testament in Irish had already been published in 1602; and in 1603 King James ordered it to read in the parishes of the Irishrie. This Irish New Testament was that the translation of which had been, in pursuance of the recommendation of Queen Elizabeth, commenced by Nicholas Walsh, Bishop of Ossory, continued by Nehemiah O'Donnellan, Archbishop of Tuam, assisted by John Kearney, sometime Treasurer of St. Patrick's, Dublin, and completed by William O'Donel or Daniel, the successor of O'Donnellan in the Archbishopric of Tuam, the expense being borne by the Province of Connaught and Sir William Ussher, Clerk of the Council.* Archbishop Daniel also translated the Book of Common Prayer into Irish, and had it published at his own charges in 1608-9.

Encouraged by the decision of Convocation that where all or most part of the people are Irish, the Bible and Common Prayer Book in the Irish tongue, so soon as they may be had, shall be provided by the parish, Bishop Bedell went on diligently with the work of translating the Old Testament into Irish. The translation was made from the authorised English version, and was completed about the year 1638. (See text, p. 61.) While preparation was being made to print the translation, which the Bishop intended to do at his own expense, Lord Wentworth, afterwards Earl of Strafford, the then Lord-Deputy, influenced by misrepresentations, interfered to delay the good work. An ill-feeling towards the Bishop himself, on the part of certain persons, no doubt had some-

* Hon. Robert Boyle's Life and Works, Appendix No. III.; and Preface to the Second Edition of the Irish New Testament.

thing to do with this opposition. For already in 1630, as appears from a letter to Archbishop Ussher, dated Kilmore, March 29, Bedell refers to the slanders of some persons discontented against him, which had found vent in the accusation of his being too zealous in the endeavour to dissipate the gross errors that obscured the minds of Roman Catholics; but the ostensible grounds on which the Irish translation of the Old Testament was objected to were the meanness, unworthiness, and incapacity of the person whom Bishop Bedell employed to make it.

Mr. Murtach King, the principal translator, was an old man of about seventy, who, it is said, had formerly been a Roman Catholic priest. By the account in the text (p. 61) he was converted to the Reformed religion by Bishop Bedell, though, by Mr. Clogie's account, his conversion dated back to King James's time. However that may have been, King was recommended as above-said to Bedell as the best Irish scholar then living. Bedell himself had taken lessons in Irish from him, and was thus well able to judge of his qualifications. Being satisfied with Mr. King's attainments and conversation in life, the Bishop not only employed him, but also admitted him to Holy Orders, and gave him the living of Templeport, after having publicly examined him in all points of the Christian faith, in the Cathedral Church of Kilmore, as Mr. Clogie informs us.*

The following is the entry in the Regal Visitation of 1633-4 of Mr. Murtach King's ordination and preferment : †

Dioc̃ Kilmore.
Epūs confert. Valet 60ˡⁱ } Vicaria de Tem- { Mr. Murtachus Kinge
   per annum.   pleport.   Vicarius.

Murtachus Kinge admissus fuit ad sacrum Diaconatus ordinem per Gulielmum Kilmorensem et Ardaghensem Epūm, 23º die Septemⁱˢ 1632. Et ad sacrum Presbyteratus ordinem per eundem Epūm,

* Memoir, p. 104.
† This extract has been supplied by the Rev. Dr. Reeves, of Tynan, to whom I am indebted for so much original information relating to the subject of this work.

22 Sept. 1633. Idem Murtachus collatus fuit per eundem Epūm ad Vicariam de Templeport, 29 Septem^{is}, 1633. Inductus fuit in eandem vicariam eisdem die et anno.

Mr. Murtach King was not only decried but positively persecuted, notwithstanding all the protection which the Bishop could afford him. The benefice of Templeport, like the Vineyard of Naboth, appears to have been a moving cause of the persecution of Mr. Murtach King. A Mr. Bayly, a Scotchman, whom Bishop Bedell had collated to the living of Anagheliff, on condition that he would reside in the parish, and not hold any other benefice, not content, did, nevertheless, within a month after entering into this solemn engagement, purchase a dispensation at the Prerogative Court in Dublin to hold an additional benefice, and, casting covetous eyes on Templeport, went about with the assistance and counsel of others to disseize Mr. Murtach King of his living. Pretending now a lapse of the benefice of Templeport to His Majesty the King, Mr. Bayly, by his interest, obtained a grant of it from the Lord Deputy for himself under the broad seal. See p. 47.

In his letter to the Archbishop of Canterbury, dated September 2, 1637 (in the Public Record Office), above quoted, Bishop Bedell refers to this proceeding of Mr. William Bayly against Mr. Murtach King, and in another letter (also in the Public Record Office), dated Dublin, November 12, 1638, says, that by artifice of Lady Lambart and Mr. W. Bayly, Mr. Murtach King was inveigled to send in a resignation; and that " Bayly accused Mr. Murtach King as a man unlearned in Holy Scripture and Divinity, not able to read prayers, neglecting his cure, not conforming his wife and children to the religion established, and in his heart affecting superstition more than the truth, and with many more like Articles * such as malice can suggest." Again, in a brave letter to the Lord Deputy

---

* There is in the Public Record Office a copy of these Articles, which had been sent by Bishop Bramhall, of Derry, to Archbishop Laud. The paper is indorsed "Receeved February 28, 1638-9, from the Bp. of Derry, Articles of the High Commission Court in Ireland against King."

CAMD. SOC. 2 A

Wentworth, dated December 1, 1638, the Bishop laid bare the whole nefariousness of the transaction. This letter has been printed but not accurately. From the copy of it in his own handwriting (preserved in the Public Record Office), which Bishop Bedell sent inclosed to Archbishop Laud, the following extracts are taken:—

* * * * * *

"The occasion is not my long suite (wch I have comitted to God) or any other matter of profitt, but God's honour, and (as He is Witnes) yours. I have lately received letters from my L^d of Canterbury, whereby I perceive his Grace is informed, y^t Mr King whom I employed to translate ye Bible into Irish is a man so ignorant y^t ye translation cannot be worthy publick use in ye Church; and besides obnoxious, so as ye Church can receive no creditt from any thing y^t is his. And his Grace adds, that he is so well acquainted wth y^r Lop^s disposition y^t he assures himselfe you would not have given away his living had you not seene just cause for it.

"I account myselfe bownd to endeavour to satisfy his Gr. herein, and desire, if I may be so happy to do it, by satisfieing you. * * * *

"Touching Mr King's seclines (wch it concerns me the more to cleare him of, y^t I be not accounted a seely man myselfe), I beseech y^r Lop. to take information, not by men w^o never saw him till yesterday, but by the ancient eith^r Church or Statesmen of this kingdome, in whose eies he hath lived these many years, as are the L. Primate, ye Bp. of Meath, ye L. Dillon, Sr James Ware, and the like: I doubt not but y^r Lo^p shall understand y^t there is no such danger, y^t ye translation should be unworthy because he did it. Being a man of y^t knowne sufficiency for the Irish especially, either in prose or verse, as few are his matches in the Kingdome. And shortly, not to argue by conjecture and divination, let the worke itselfe speake, yea, let it be examined *rigoroso examine*, if it be fownd approveable, let it not suffer disgrace from ye small boast of the workeman; but let him rather (as old Sophocles, accused of dotage) be absolved for the sufficiency of the worke.

"Touching his being obnoxious: it is true y^t there is a scandalous information put in against him in the High Commission Court by his despoyler, Mr. Bayly (so my Lo. of Derry, in my hearing, told him he was), and by an excom̃unicate despoyler, as myselfe, before th' execution of any sentence, declared him in ye Court to be; And Mr. King being cited to answer, and not appearing, as by lawe he was not bownd, was taken *pro confesso*, deprived of his Ministry and living, fined 100^{li}, decreed to be attached and imprisoned. His adversary Mr. Bayly, before he was sentenced, purchased a new Dispensation to hold his Benefice, and was ye very next day after (as appears by ye date of the instrum^t) both presented in the King's title, although ye Benefice be of my collation, and instituted by my L. Primate's Vicar, shortly after inducted by an Archdeacon of another Dioces. Within a few dayes he brought downe an attachm^t, and delivered Mr. King to a Pursivant.* He was haled by ye head and feete to horse-back, and brought up to Dublin, where he hath remained under arrest these 4 or 5 Moneths. He hath often offered to purge his supposed contumacy by oth and witnesses, that by reason of his sicknes of ye flixe (whereby he was brought to death's dore) he could not appeare and prosecute his defence, and y^t by the cunning of his adversary he was circumvented and secured. Entreating y^t he might be restored to his liberty, and his cause into ye former estate. But it hath not availed him. My Reverend Colleagues of ye High Commission doe some of them pitty his case. Others say, the sentence past cannot be reversed, least ye credit of the Court be intacked. They bid him simply submit himselfe and acknowledge his censure is just. Whereas the B^{ps} of Rome themselves, after most formall proceeding, doe grant *restitutionem in integrum*, and acknowledge y^t *sententia Ro'æ Sedis potest in melius com'utari*. My Lord, if I understand what is right divine or humane, these be wrongs upon wrongs, which if they reached only to Mr. King's person were of less consideracōn. But when through his side y^t great worke, ye Translation of God's booke, so necessary

* See the Minutes of the Diocesan Synod in the preceding chapter, p. 163.

for both his Maties kingdomes, is mortally wownded, pardon me (I beseech y^r Lo^p) if I be sensible of it.

* * * * * *

" For conclusion (good my Lord) give me leave a litle to apply the parable of Nathan to K. David, to this purpose. If the wayfaring man y^t is come to us (for such he is, having never yet been setled in one place,) have so sharpe a stomack, that he must be provided for wth Plurality, sith there are heards and flocks plenty, suffer him not (I beseech you) under ye collour of the King's name, to take the cosset-ewe * of a poore man to satisfy his ravenous appetite.† "

* * * * * *

Notwithstanding the incredible injustice here exposed, it appears that Bayly, having appealed from Bishop Bedell's sentence of excommunication, was absolved and confirmed in his ill-acquired benefice. Nay, ere long, he was raised to the Episcopate, being in 1644 consecrated at Oxford Bishop of Clonfert. He had even been designed, it is said, for the See of Kilmore, upon Bishop Bedell's death, but the patent was revoked.‡

* A pet lamb brought up by hand.

† According to what are alleged to have been the true facts, the case of the Bishop of Killala, above related in the text at pp. 52-4, was, in some respects, a counterpart of this of Mr. Murtach King. The Bishopric of Elphin in Ireland having fallen vacant, the Earl of Strafford claimed it for Dr. Henry Tilson, his chaplain, whereas King Charles designed the preferment for another. At this juncture, the scandal against the Bishop of Killala occurred, (see pp. 52-4), and was seized upon as a pretext to deprive him of his Bishopric in order to create a vacancy for the King's nominee, John Maxwell, the refugee Bishop of Ross in Scotland; and by this notable expedient the wishes of both King and Viceroy, which had come to be to a certain extent at issue, were reconciled.

‡ Mr. William Bayly must have had great interest with King Charles. I do not know whether he was of the same family as Dr. Lewis Bayly (the paternal ancestor of the Marquis of Anglesey's family), who came from Scotland with King James the First as tutor to Prince Henry, and was made Bishop of Bangor. Bayly's career of preferment stands thus :—Jan. 7, 1634, Coll. Vicar of Annageliff; and again, by presentation of the Crown, instituted and inducted, Aug. 7, 1637; and

Before the impediments thus thrown in the way could be overcome, so that the printing of the translation might be proceeded with, the Rebellion broke out, and the publication of the Old Testament in Irish was altogether prevented for the time by the venerable Prelate's death, which soon followed thereon.

CHAPTER XI.

The Irish Rebellion of 1641.

The rebellion broke out on Saturday the 23rd of October, 1641, all over Ireland, and none were more forward than the Rebels in the county of Cavan. All the forts and other places of strength were quickly in their hands except Keilagh and Croghan, the castles of Sir Francis Hamilton and Sir James Craig, who were able to hold out. The house of Bishop Bedell was at first respected, and thither, as well as to Keilagh and Croghan Castles, the neighbouring Protestants, English and Scotch, flocked for protection.

The plan of the rebels to surprise the Castle of Dublin, and to seize the arms therein stored, having been by timely information frustrated, and two of their principal leaders taken into custody, those in the county of Cavan thought fit to temporise. Accordingly, having drawn up a "Remonstrance" to the Lords Justices and Council, calculated to put a gloss upon their proceedings, in the hope of suspending the opposition of the Government, they made

again June 15, 1638. Presented by the Crown to the Vicarage of Templeport Aug. 7, 1637; and again June 15, 1638. Bishop Bedell in his letter to Archbishop Laud, dated Novr. 12, 1638, refers to the instrument of this latter presentation as having been produced by Mr. W. Bayly. The renewed presentations by the Crown here mentioned, were made to counteract the sentences of excommunication and privation pronounced against Mr. Bayly by Bishop Bedell. See "Acta Ecclesiastica," in the preceding chapter.

application to Bishop Bedell to undertake the presentation of it, but he fairly excused himself * on account of his age, whereby he was not fit to travel to Dublin with that expedition which they expected; and also because that many of the poor English of Belturbet, who had retired to him and depended on what security and subsistence he could afford them, would by his absence be exposed to want and other injuries. This, says Dr. Henry Jones, the Dean of Kilmore, whose narrative I am quoting, " the rebels interpreted as a put off, yet did the gravity and respect which his presence commanded restrain them from what some in their councell had before propounded in case he should give out and decline that service for them." Dean Jones himself was next in their eye, being a prisoner with his family in their hands. He was accordingly designed and commanded upon this employment. " I must confess, says the Dean,† it was such as was in every respect improper for me to undergo, but considering that I might gain the opportunity of laying open to the Lords what I had observed of the proceedings of the rebels in the county of Cavan, and which could not otherwise be so safely communicated, I did accept the employment." Dr. Jones accordingly went to Dublin accompanied by Mr. John Waldron of Farnham, delivered " the Remonstrance," and after ten days' stay in that city returned with an answer from the Lords Justices and Council. " Return I must," says the Dean,—" my wife and children remaining as hostages " in the hands of the rebels. The Remonstrance was as follows:—

* The Beginnings and Proceedings of the Rebellion in the county of Cavan rom the 23rd of October 1641 until the 15th of June 1642. By Henry Jones, D.D. London, August 11, 1642. See also Dr. Edmund Borlace's History of the Irish Rebellion, London, 1680, folio, p. 32; and Sir James Ware's History of Ireland.

† Op. cit. This narrative of " the Beginnings and Proceedings of the Rebellion in the county of Cavan " is a different work from Dr. Henry Jones's deposition concerning the Rebellion, dated March 3rd, 1641-2, forming Appendix IX. in Sir Richard Cox's Hibernia Anglicana, or History of Ireland, vol. ii. p.p. 38-44. In this deposition Dr. Jones states what he had heard of the long hatching of the rebellion, and of the plans and intentions of the Rebels.

"The humble Remonstrance made by the Gentry and Comonaltie of the countie of Cavan, of their grievances comon with other pts of this Kingdome of Ireland.*

" To the Right Honble the Lords Justices and Councell.

" Whereas wee his Maties loyall subjects of his Highness Kingdome of Ireland have of long time groaned under many grievous pressures occasioned by the rigorous gov^{t}ment of such placed over us, as respected more the advancement of theire owne private fortunes than the honour of his Matie or the welfare of us his subjects, whereof wee have in part in humble mañer declared ourselves to his Highness, by the agents sent from the Parliament, the representative body of this Kingdom: Notwithstanding which wee find ourselves of late threatened with far greater and more grievous vexations, either to captivating of oure Consciences, our loosing of our lawfule Liberties, or utter expulsion from our native seates, without any just grounds given on our parts to alter his Maties goodness soo long continued to us; of all which wee find greate cause of feare in the proceedings of our neighbour nations, and doe see it already attempted upon us by certaine petitioners for the like Course to bee taken in this Kingdom; for the effecting whereof in a compulsory way, rumours have caused feare of invasion from other parts, to the dissolvinge the bond of mutual agreem^t which hitherto hath bin held inviolable betweene the severall subjects of this Kingdome, and whereby all other his Maties Dominions have been linked in one.

" For preventing therefore of such evills growinge upon us in this Kingdome, wee have, for the preservation of his Maties honor, and our own liberties, thought fitt to take into oure hands for his Highness Use and Service, such forts and other places of strength, as, comeing into the possession of others, might proove disadvantageous and tend to the utter undoing of the Kingdome. And wee doe hereby declare, that herein we harboure not the least thought of

* Paper in the Public Record Office, endorsed :
" 6 No. 1641.
Coppie of the Remonstrance of the Rebells in the county of Cavan."

disloyalty towards his Matie, or purpose any hurt to any his High-ness subjects in theire profession, goods, or libertie, only wee humbly desire that your Lo'pps will bee pleased to make Remonstrance to his Matie for us, of all our grievances and just feares, that they may bee removed, and such a course setled by the advise of the Parliament of Ireland, whereby the liberties of oure consciences may bee secured unto us, and wee eased of our other burthens in civill government.

"As for the mischiefes and inconveniences that have already happened through the disorder of the comon sort of people against the English inhabitants or any other person, wee, with the Noblemen and Gentlemen of this and each other several countie of this kingdome, are most willing and reddy to use our and theire best endeavours in causing restitution and satisfaction to bee made, as in pt. wee have already don.

"An answere hereunto is most humbly desired w'th such present expedition as may by youre Lopps. bee thought most convenient for avoidinge the continuance of the barbaritie and uncivilitie of the comonalty who have comitted many outrages and insolences without any order, consenting or privitie of ours. All which wee most humbly leave to your Lopp's most grave Wisdomes.

"And wee shall pray, &c.

(*Signed*)—" Phillip Rely,—Mullmor O'Reilly,—Edmond Relly,—Hugh Relly,—Owen Relly,—Hugh Reilly, — Phi. Relly,—Ed. Reilly,—Torlagh Relly."

This Remonstrance was presented to the Lords Justices and Council on the 6th of November, 1641; and the following is the Preamble and substance of their reply to it, dated the 10th of November 1641 :—

"By the Lords Justices and Councell.*

"Wm. Parsons, Jo. Borlase.

* Paper in the Public Record Office, endorsed:—
"Novr. 10, 1641.
Coppie of the answer to the Remonstrance of the Rebells in the county of Cavan."

"Henry Jones, Deane of Killmore, and John Waldrom, of Farnan, in the countie of Cavan, Gent. attended us the Lords Justices and Councell at this Board, and presented unto us a writinge stiled: 'The humble Remonstrance made by the Gentry and Comonaltie of the County of Cavan of their grievances comon with other pts. of this Kingdome of Ireland,' and signed by (here follow the names above given).

"Upon consideration whereof and of other intelligence we had from those parts before the said Jones and Waldrom came hither, we observe:"

Here follow the observations which were, in substance, that the subscribers to the Remonstrance had without authority presumed to make use of His Majesty's name, and that they had no right to speak in the name of all the gentry and commonalty of the county of Cavan or other county, and that there were no grounds for their alleged fears. They were also reminded of the illegality of taking into their own hands forts and other strong places without the King's authority.

The Lords Justices and Council, however, added that, as the Remonstrants had not participated in the cruel outrages perpetrated against the English, their Remonstrance would be forwarded with a favourable representation of their case to the King, provided they (the Remonstrants) would lay down their arms, make restitution to those who had been despoiled, and return home.

This reply is signed:—
"Lancelot Dublin,*—Ormond,—Ossory,—R. Dillon,—Cha. Lambert,—Ad. Loftus,—Jo. Temple,—Cha. Coote, —Rob. Merydith."

The names of the Lords Justices, "W^m. Parsons, and Jo. Borlase," are at the top.

Dean Jones in his Narrative † expresses his belief that the rebels did not expect or even wish any other answer; their Remonstrance

* Dr. Bulkeley, Archbishop of Dublin.
† Ut supra. See also Sir James Ware's History of Ireland; and Dr. Edmund Borlace's History of the Irish Rebellion. London, 1680, fol. p. 32, ut supra.

being tendered rather to win upon the people (whose cause they pleaded) than to give any reasonable account or satisfaction to the Lords concerning their proceedings. In fact during the presentation of this Remonstrance the rebels were mustering their forces—all men from sixteen to sixty years of age—to meet at Virginia the Monday following, notwithstanding they had empowered the Dean of Kilmore to assure the Lords Justices that there would be a cessation of all proceedings until the return of their Lordships' answer. Afterwards, says Dr. Jones, as many cruelties and outrages were committed in the county of Cavan as elsewhere.

Mr. Clogie's account of this transaction,* in which he is followed, of course, by Bishop Burnet, and other biographers of Bishop Bedell, is of the most unfounded character, inasmuch as the Bishop is represented as having written the Remonstrance for the Rebels, and sent it by a special messenger of their own, a chief rebel, to the Lords Justices.† Whereas we have seen from the narrative of Dr. Jones, the Dean of Kilmore, that Bishop Bedell refused to have any share whatever in the transaction, and certainly, in its style, the Remonstrance is very unlike the writing of Bedell. Mr. Clogie, after his blundering and inaccurate fashion, appears to apply to this Remonstrance of the Rebels the part which Bishop Bedell took in revising and remodelling the Petition of the Protestants of Cavan, which was presented to the Lords Justices some eight or nine years before. (See text, pp. 49-51.)

There is, in the British Museum, a book, 8vo. pp. 162, printed in London in 1747, but without a publisher's name, entitled " A brief Account from the most Authentic Protestant Writers of the Causes, Motives, and Mischiefs, of the Irish Rebellion, on the 23rd Day of October, 1641, Delivered in a Dialogue between a Dissenter and a Member of the Church of Ireland, as by Law Established. Together with an Appendix." Appendix No. 1 is " A Remonstrance of the Gentry and Commonalty of the County of Cavan,

* Memoir, &c. p. 184.
† Possibly a chief rebel may have accompanied Dr. Jones and Mr. Waldron as an escort, but no such person appears on record, or is even hinted at by Dean Jones.

Written by Bishop Bedell in 1641,"* and a quotation from Bishop Burnet's Life of Bishop Bedell is given as the authority for attributing the authorship of the document to Bishop Bedell. Under the guise of candour, "the Churchman" labours to make it appear that in the Rebellion of 1641 the Irish were the lambs and the English the wolves ; whilst Bishop Bedell, thanks to Mr. Clogie and Bishop Burnet, is set before us as a witness in support of " the Churchman's " argument! On this I will make no comment, but beg here only to observe that one cherished object of the labour I have bestowed in editing this life of Bishop Bedell has been to rescue his memory from such indiscreet and uninformed friends as Mr. Alexander Clogie and Bishop Burnet.

About this time Dr. Swiney, the Roman Catholic Bishop of Kilmore, wrote to Bishop Bedell, offering to take up his residence with him in the Episcopal house, and so be a means of protection to him. This offer Bedell received in good part, but declined accepting it.†

In the midst of the violence which prevailed, Bishop Bedell, like the true shepherd, fled not when the wolf came down on the fold, but stood at his post, doing what he could to protect his flock. But at last the Rebels peremptorily commanded him to send the Protestant refugees away from his house, and to betake himself and family to Dublin, and, on his refusal, they, on the 18th of December, seized him and his sons and step-son-in-law, and sent them prisoners to Loughoughter ‡ Castle, which they had taken possession of.

The Roman Catholic Bishop now took up his residence in the

---

* In the Catalogue of the British Museum Reading Room this work is entered under different heads: 1°, Bedell (William), Bishop of Kilmore and Ardagh. A Remonstrance of the Gentry and Commonalty of the County Cavan. 2°, Dissenter, &c. 3°, " Irish Nation, &c." 4°, James Howell, on the Irish Rebellion of 1641.

† See Clogie's Memoir, p. 188, for Bishop Bedell's letter in reply to Dr. Swiney, dated Novr. 11, 1641.

‡ In English, *Upper Lake*.

Episcopal house, and, in the course of the rifling that ensued, Bishop Bedell's library was destroyed, dispersed, or lost, as described in the text, p. 77, with the exception of his MS. Hebrew Bible, now in the Library of Emmanuel College, Cambridge, and also the MS. of the Irish Translation of the Old Testament, both of which were saved by the care of Mr. Denis Sheridan.

How the other Bishops of the Establishment in Ireland fared in the Rebellion may, in conclusion of this chapter, be briefly glanced at.* Some did not escape personal ill-treatment, and almost all suffered loss of property.

Province of Munster.—Archbishop Hamilton of Cashel, Bishop Adair of Waterford and Lismore, Bishop Chapell of Cork and Ross, and Bishop Synge of Cloyne, quitted Ireland. Bishop Webb of Limerick died of dysentery, a prisoner in the hands of the rebels. Bishop Fulwer of Ardfert survived to be made Archbishop of Cashel at the Restoration. Bishop Jones of Killaloe remained safe in Dublin, where he departed this life at the advanced age of 104.

Province of Connaught.—Archbishop Boyle of Tuam, and Bishop John Maxwell of Killala, afterwards Archbishop of Tuam, found refuge in Galway, the latter after being nearly killed. Bishop Tilson of Elphin, and Bishop Dawson of Clonfert and Kilmacduagh, quitted Ireland.

Province of Leinster.—Archbishop Bulkeley of Dublin remained safe in Dublin city, and died in 1650 at the age of 82. Bishop Ussher of Kildare, Bishop Williams of Ossory, and Bishop Andrews of Ferns and Leighlin quitted Ireland; but Bishop Williams returned to his See after the Restoration. Bishop Sibthorp of Kilfenora survived the rebellion to be translated to Limerick.

Province of Ulster.—Archbishop Ussher of Armagh was in England when the rebellion broke out, and remained there. Bishop Bramhall of Derry quitted Ireland, but returned at the Restoration

* Cotton's Fasti and Sir James Ware's History of Ireland, *ut supra.*

and was made Primate. Bishop Lesley of Raphoe also survived to be translated to Clogher. Bishop Richardson of Ardagh was in England when the rebellion broke out, and did not return to Ireland. Bishop Leslie of Down and Connor passed unhurt through the rebellion, and was afterwards translated to Meath in 1660. Bishop Buckworth of Dromore, and Bishop Spottiswoode of Clogher, quitted Ireland. Bishop Martin of Meath, after the rebellion, was Provost of Trinity College, Dublin.

CHAPTER XII.

Last Illness and Death.

Bishop Bedell with his two sons and his step-son-in-law, Mr. Clogie, was detained in Loughoughter Castle from the 18th of December until the 7th of January, when they were liberated under the circumstances and conditions mentioned in the text. The Bishop's own residence being now usurped by the Roman Catholic Bishop, he took up his abode in the house of Mr. Denis Sheridan at Drum Corr, in the parish of Kilmore, and within a mile of the Church. Here the Bishop's sons' wives had remained during the imprisonment of their husbands. How kindly and affectionately Bishop Bedell was received and waited on in Denis Sheridan's house is related in the text.

On Sundays the 9th, 16th, 23rd and 30th of January, the Bishop preached to his family. On Monday the 31st of January, he was taken ill; on Tuesday the 1st of February, fever declared itself, and on the 7th he died.*

From the description, as given in the text, of the illness which carried off Bishop Bedell, it is to be inferred that it was malignant typhus fever. This with other forms of pestilence prevailed in Ire-

* Clogie's Memoir, pp. 217-225.

land as an attendant on the political disasters in that country of 1641 and subsequent years.* "The malignant epidemic fever began with cold and shivering," then followed a weakness and "spots on the skin, pain in the head, delirium. Depletion was hurtful." The forced crowding together in the Rev. Denis Sheridan's house of so many persons, refugees from the country round, and the privations they suffered from deficiency of food and severity of the weather—for the winter of 1641 in Ireland was "most bitter cold and frosty,"† were incidents which no doubt operated as the cause of the outbreak of the typhus fever which attacked young Edward Mawe, and was from him communicated to his step-father, the Bishop, while affectionately nursing him in his sickness. What became of Edward Mawe himself, whether he recovered or died of the fever, I have not been able to ascertain.

Dr. Stokes, the distinguished Professor of Physic in Trinity College, Dublin, to whom I sent a copy of the description of the fever, as given in the text, with a request for his opinion, kindly wrote in reply, saying: "It may safely be assumed that the fever of which Bishop Bedell died was typhus, or what is called petechial fever; doubtless intensified by the crowding together of many persons under one roof;" and like other continued fevers more dangerous in the old than the young.

In the text the fever is designated by the name of "Irish ague;" but here "ague" seems to be used as a name for fever in general, and not for intermittent fever in particular. The name "Irish Ague," Dr. Stokes observes, "is clearly improper. Ague is not contagious, and it is a curious fact that, except in a few localities in low sea shores, ague cannot be enumerated among the diseases of Ireland. I never heard of or met with a case of it as occurring in the great bog districts of Ireland."

Mr. Ambrose Bedell, in his deposition, we shall see, expresses his belief that his father's illness and death were occasioned by the

* Census of Ireland. Blue Book, vol. xxix. 1856, p. 107.
† Temple, History of the Irish Rebellion. See Blue Book, *ut supra*.

...iserable accommodation he had in Loughoughter Castle, where there was neither door, nor window of glass, nor shutter of wood, to keep out the wintry winds, the snow, or the rain; and where they must have perished from cold, had it not been that Mr. Castledyne, a fellow-prisoner and who had formerly been a carpenter, procured, as Mr. Clogie informs us, some tools and boards and made extemporaneous shuts for the large windows.

The harsh usage which the venerable Bishop—the friend of all his neighbours, Papist as well as Protestant—was thus subjected to, does not, however, really appear to have seriously affected his health and strength, if we may judge from the anecdote related by Mr. Clogie,* viz. that a week before the Bishop sickened, he was out taking a walk with his sons and Mr. Clogie, and in returning leaped so nimbly and vigorously over a broad ditch that, says Mr. Clogie, it amazed us all and put us to a stand still to follow him. Possibly the privations the Bishop endured in Loughoughter Castle may have predisposed him to be more susceptible of the infection to which he was exposed than he might otherwise have been. Still it is so far consolatory to think that Bishop Bedell did not actually die worn out from the hardships he suffered at the hands of the rebels, as has hitherto been supposed. We have seen, with sympathetic emotion, how his martyr-spirit rose above the terrors of the situation.

According to Mr. Clogie's† description, Bishop Bedell was tall in stature and appeared to be, nearly to the last, strong and hale for his age. His hair was gray, but he had suffered no loss of it. He wore his beard long and broad. He had not lost one tooth; and his sight continued good. From the fact that he never required spectacles it is to be inferred that he was naturally somewhat nearsighted, an inference which his small and beautiful handwriting confirms. The history of his deafness is given in the text, p. 3.

* Memoir, *ut supra*, p. 226. † Memoir, &c. p. 226.

CHAPTER XIII.

Bishop Bedell's Last Will and Testament.

In the name of God Allmighty the Father the Sonne and the Holy Ghoste Amen in the yeare of our Lord's Incarnation one thousand six hundred and fourtie the fifteenth day of February I William Bedell Bp. of Kilmore being in health of body but mindful of the frailty of this mortall life desirous to set an order in that outward estate which God of his greate mercie hath given me doe make this my last will and testament in manner and form following But first I bequeath my Soule to Allmighty God my mercifull and faithfull Creator Redeemer and Sanctifier by whose meere mercie through the meritts of my Lord and Saviour Jesus Christ I have assured hope that it shall be saved from the wrath to come whensoever it shall please him to call for it And for this corruptible flesh I appoint that it be comitted to the ground without any feudall pompe in the church yard of Kilmore at the south corner thereof in the same grave or hard by the corpe of my deare wife Leah and my sonne John about whose coffins and mine I doe appoint that there shall be a wall of stone raised up from the bottome and the ground raised up to the levell of the rest of the walke by the wall on the west side of the church yard and one or more large gravestones layd over W^{th} this inscripčon Guilielmi quondam Kilmoren Ēpi Depositum I knowe whome I have beleeved in and that hee is able to keepe that which I have comitted to him against the day of his glorious appeareing And as for my judgement in matters of Religion I doe referr myselfe to my former profession from a child my preaching and wrytinge being the Catholiq. faith grounded on Holy Scriptures and consonant to the confessions of the Churches of England and Ireland whereof I have often (without any equivocačon as God is wittness) made publique acknowledgement And for my worldly goods ffirst I give to the Church of Kilmore five pounds $ster^l$ to be imployed for the paveing of the chauncell with hewne stone and if any

ployed for the paveing of the chauncell with hewne stone and if any remayne thereof for the furnishing the com̃union-table with linnen as farr as it will extend the sayd money to be payd within three monthes after my decease Item I give to the Church of Black Notly in England where I was baptized a Bell to supply one that is wanting of three which it aunciently had the money to be payd within one yeare after my decease Item I give to the Library of Emanuell Colledge in Cambridge where I was brought up and first Scholar after Fellow of that Societie my manuscript Hebrew Bible * and the foure Evangelists and Euclides Elements in the Arabique tongue Item I give, to the Library of Trinity Colledge neere Dublin my manuscript Priscian with foure more of my manuscripts such as my Executor shall think fitt Item I give to the Right Reverend Father in God the Lord Primat of Archmagh my manuscript Psalter † written in the Irish Character in testimony of my true and heartie affection to him Item I give and bequeath to my sonne Ambrose Bedell the annuitie which I purchased of Sr James Craig of fourtie pound per annum issuing out of the lands of Carne which were lately purchased to his use and out of the lands holden by Ralph Lowharret to have and hold to the sayd Ambrose and his heyres for ever Item I give to my son-in-law Edward Mawe fiftie pounds ster^l to supply his porc̃on spent in the time hee was with my cosen Gooday and my brother John Bedell which sume of fiftie pounds I will to remayne in the hands of William his brother for his maintenance unless some convenient wife may be

* This MS., which Bedell brought from Venice, is now in the Library of Emmanuel College, but the other books here bequeathed are not, it would appear, known to exist there. They had been lost or destroyed in the Rebellion.

† This appears to be identical with the Psalter in the library of T. C. D. containing Ricemarch's verses at the end. I am favoured with the following notice on the subject by the Rev. Dr. Reeves of Tynan : the beautiful manuscript Psalter preserved in the library of T. C. D., under sig. A. 4, 20 (among Ussher's MS. treasures), has the autograph " G. Bedellj." This, the penmanship of which is in the Irish style, is Ricemarch's Psalter. Ussher, in his "Religion possessed by the ancient Irish " (Works, vol. iv. p. 249), quotes from the Colophon verses; and in a note makes this reference: " MS. in bibliotheca eruditissimi antistitis D. Guilielmi Bedelli Kilmorensis et Ardaghensis apud nos Episcopi." This treatise of Ussher, it is to be observed, was

found for him whoe can manage his estate In which case I will that it be payd to him and his wife to beginne the world withall Item I give to Edwin Walford and each of his sisters Phœbe and Elizabeth to everie of them ten pounds the sayd summes for Phœbe and Elizabeth to be raised yearly out of the profitts of Whiteheads and payd into the hands of Mr. Richard Symons of Blacknotly to their use And I doe comitt to the care of my Executor the educacõn of the sayd Edwin Walford till he shall accomplish the age of one- and twentie years at which time I will it shall be payd to him unlesse it may be layd out for his preferrm^t in the meane time Item I give to Mary Jervice ten pounds to William Jervice and John Walford and to the two sonnes of my sister Willys to everie of them five pounds to my two godsonnes Samuel Sothby and William Sheriden to each of them fourtie shillings to my brother John Bedell my dear friends Dr Ward Dr Despotine Dr Aylett and Mr Samuel Sothby to each of them a ring of fourtie shillings price Item I give to each of my servants which shall be in my service at the time of my death a quarters wages above that which they have begun The residue of all my goods and chattles of what nature soever I give to my sonne William Bedell whom I make sole executor of this my Testam^t which I have written with mine owne hand and sealed with my seale the daye and year above written. W. KILMOREN.

Whereas I have bequeathed the surplusage of my goods to my Executor my meaning is notwithstanding that whatsoever I doe recover in the suite wth Mrs. Moigne shall not be accompted any part of my goods but if I recover anything and depart this life ere I doe imploy it according to my vow to the Edition of the Irish Bible that summe I charge him to apply to that end and noe other.*

W. KILMOREN.

first printed in 1631 when Bedell was Bishop of Kilmore and Ardagh. Again, in his "British Ecclesiastical Antiquities" (Works, vol. v. p. 17), first printed in 1639, when Bedell was Bishop of Kilmore alone, Ussher writes: "In Britannico vero quod describendum curavit Ricemarchus Sulgeni Menevensis Episcopi filius, &c." and in a note to this adds: "Habetur MS. in Bibliotheca D. Guil. Bedelli Kilmorensis apud nos Episcopi."

* In a letter to the Lord Deputy Wentworth (Strafford's Letters and Despatches,

Administration with this will annexed granted to William Bedell the Executor by the Court of Probate in London on the 13th day of April 1654.
Proved in Dublin on the 17th day of January, 1656.

CHAPTER XIV.
FUNERAL AND TOMB.

Bishop Bedell, it has been just seen, left directions in his will that he should be buried beside his wife and son, and that his funeral should be conducted without pomp. According to his wishes he was buried beside his wife and son, though it appears to have been with some difficulty that the permission of the intruding and now paramount Popish Bishop was obtained, he objecting that the churchyard was not to be defiled any more with the bodies of heretics. As regards the absence of pomp, it cannot be said that the deceased Bishop's directions were observed. The cortège of Irish rebels, and the volley of musketry over his grave, with the ejaculation " Requiescat in pace Ultimus Anglorum," constituted a kind of funeral pomp, barbaric no doubt, which, however, his executor was powerless to prevent. To this scene in the churchyard of Kilmore, on the 9th of February, 1641-2, a certain pathos was imparted, when, in the enthusiasm of the moment, Edmund Ferrely, a Roman Catholic priest, remembering the kindness he had experienced from Bishop Bedell, and the instructive conversations on religion he had so often had with him, was heard fervently breathing out the prayer: "O sit anima mea cum Bedello."*

vol. ii. p. 151, folio, London, 1739), dated February 22, 1637, Bishop Bedell refers to his suit with Mrs. Moigne, concerning two unjust leases given to her by her late husband, his predecessor (see above, p. 155), and says, "I had devoted and dedicated all that I should recover herein to God, to be employed in the edition of the Irish Bible."

* See note in the edition of Burnet's Life of Bishop Bedell, published in Dublin, 1758, communicated to the publisher by Mr. Bedell Stanford, grandson of Isabella the youngest daughter of the Bishop's eldest son, the Rev. William Bedell, Rector of Rattlesden.

Bishop Bedell entertained a strong feeling against the practice of burying in churches, believing it to be injurious to the living, not honouring to the dead, and a profanation of the house of God. One of the decrees passed in his Diocesan Synod, it has been above seen, was, that the bodies of deceased persons should not be buried in churches, nor outside churches within five feet of the wall of the building. We have seen that he buried his wife and son in a remote corner of the churchyard of Kilmore, and directed that he himself should be laid beside them, thus setting an example in his own case in rebuke of the pride and superstition suggesting the custom. Bedell's college friend Joseph Hall, Bishop of Norwich, participated in the same opinions on the subject, saying in his will, " My body I leave to be interred without any funeral pomp, at the discretion of my executors, with this only monition, that I do not hold God's house a meet repository for the greatest saints." Notwithstanding this " monition," Bishop Hall appears to have been buried in the chancel of Heigham church.* Dr. Edward Wettenhall, who was Bishop of Kilmore and Ardagh from 1699 to his death in 1713, and previously (1678) Bishop of Cork and Ross, in his will, dated May 10, 1709, directed that, should he die at Kilmore, his body should be interred near " good Bishop Bedell's." Dying in London, however, he was buried in Westminster Abbey. Another Bishop of Kilmore, Dr. Denison Cumberland, who died in 1774, was interred beside Bishop Bedell. Mr. Richard Cumberland, the Bishop's son, in his Memoirs,† says, " In a small patch of ground, inclosed within stone walls, my father's corpse was interred beside the grave of the venerable and exemplary Bishop Bedell. This little spot, as containing the remains of that good and great man, my father had fenced and guarded with particular devotion, and he had more than once pointed it out to me as his destined grave, saying to me, as I well remember, in the words of the Old Prophet of Bethel, ' When I am dead, then bury me in this sepul-

* Jones's Life and Times of Bishop Hall, *ut supra*, p. 98.
† Vol. i. p. 275, 1807.

chre, wherein the man of God is buried ; lay my bones beside his bones.'"

In his will, it is seen, Bishop Bedell directed one or more large grave-stones to be laid over his grave, with this inscription: "Guilielmi quondam Kilmoren. Ep̄i Depositum. I know Whom I have believed in, and that He is able to keep that which I have committed to Him against the day of his glorious appearing."* By the word "*Depositum*" he meant, no doubt, the mortal coil shuffled off, on the ascension of the soul to God. Here these lines by Rogers may be appropriately quoted:—

"When by a good man's grave I muse alone,
Methinks an angel sits upon the stone,
Like those of old, on that thrice-hallowed night,
Who sate and watched in raiment heavenly bright:
And, with a voice inspiring joy, not fear,
Says, pointing upward, that he is not here,
That he is risen."

The tombstone over his grave shows that the Bishop's injunction was carried out, with the exception that the quotation from 2nd Timothy is omitted. The time when the tombstone was laid down there is no record to tell. Probably it was not until some years after his death, in consequence of the troubles created by the rebellion. The Bishop's property had, to a large amount, been destroyed (as shown by his son Ambrose's deposition, to be quoted below), and it was not until 1654 that his will was proved in London, and two years after that in Dublin.

The earliest description of the tombstone, so far as I have been able to ascertain, occurs among the manuscript notes in the copy of Bishop Burnet's Life of Bedell, in the possession of a gentleman in the county of Monaghan, above referred to, p. 88, written by a Mr. Thomas Bedell, about the year 1721. A rough drawing represents the sculpture and inscription on the grave-stone, as follows:

* Second Epistle of Paul to Timothy, 1st chapter, 12th verse.

A shield bearing, Per fess azure and argent a pale and three mullets counterchanged. Surmountiug the shield there is something which might be taken for a cap of maintenance, or an esquire's helmet, and over that a Bishop's mitre. Below the shield are crossbones, and below them a skull. On either side of which is a sandglass. Underneath is the incription:

Gulielmi Bed^ell
quondem . Kilmorens
is . Episco
pi Depositum.

The description next in date is by the minister of Killasser, in 1740. He says, "At the south angle of the churchyard (Kilmore), within a small walled enclosure, are deposited, in a vault, the remains of the good and great Bishop Bedell, over which is raised a tombstone, with his arms, and this modest inscription :

' Gulielmi Bedell, quondam Episcopi Kilmorensis, Depositum.'

" The present Bishop is now repairing the injuries which this venerable tomb has suffered by time. Between the Episcopal house of Kilmore and the garden there is a venerable old grove of sycamore trees, planted one hundred years ago by Bishop Bedell,* the largest of which stands in the middle of the terrace, and from thence, spreading its boughs into the churchyard, shades its planter's tomb."†

Of nearly one hundred years' later date is the description in Bishop Mant's History of the Church of Ireland. The woodengraving given in this work represents the shield as above described, and, surmounting the shield, something more like an

---

* In the text at page 17, it is stated that, by way of recreation, he used to occupy himself in planting, transplanting, &c. See also Mr. Clogie's Memoir, p. 145.

† See " A Description of Lough Erne," in Additional MS. 4436, British Museum, page 314. The Bishop of Kilmore referred to as repairing Bishop Bedell's tomb had been, if the date of the writing here quoted was 1740, Dr. Josiah Hort, who was translated to the Archbishopric of Tuam in 1742, and was succeeded by Dr. Joseph Story.

INSCRIPTION ON THE TOMB. 199

esquire's helmet. Above this, but not resting on it, is a Bishop's mitre. Below the shield is a clam-shell-like ornamental flourish, below which is a skull, and below this again cross-bones. On the left-hand side, just above the level of the skull, is an open book, and in the corresponding place on the right-hand side is a sand-glass. Underneath all is the inscription, which stands thus:

Guilielmi Bedll
quondem Kilmorens
is Episcopi
Depositum.

On each side of the slab is a sculptured representation of pillars in low relief, supporting as if the representation of an ornamental arch over the shield and mitre.

The two pictorial representations just described tally with each other, except in such slight deviations as might readily have been made in the act of sketching. The inscription in the letter-press accompanying the engraving in Bishop Mant's History, it is to be observed, does not so exactly tally with the inscription as given in the engraving. The following is the account given by a friend of Bishop Mant:—" I had much difficulty in reading the inscription; indeed it puzzled me twice, and I was perplexed, but determined to make it clear. The letters are all raised on a brownish slab broken in pieces, and the edges of the letters are so rounded by time that there is little shade from them, so as to recognise them from the plane surface. The bursting out of the sun, as the shadows from the index of a dial, relieved the letters a little for me, and made my success more complete. The inscription, then, is truly and really this:—

Gulielmi Bideli
quondem Kilmorens
is Episcopi
Depositum.

" As a few years will remove all, I wish you to keep this as the fruit of accurate inquiry, and the more especially as I could not obtain any aid in making the matter more easy. I have seen some notices of the inscription, but they are all incorrect. The grave is in a retired part of the churchyard, and a sycamore tree of at least twelve feet in circumference, the growth of ages, is flourishing near it, and flinging its time-honoured arms over the spot."*

This sycamore tree, said to be one of those which were planted by the Bishop himself, and known by the name of " Bedell's tree," stands in the Palace grounds. I have a photograph of it before me in which it is seen at the end of the walk by the side of the wall which intervenes between the palace grounds and the churchyard. The branches of the tree at the left side, as we face it looking down the walk, project over the adjacent wall into the churchyard, and so shade the tomb of Bedell.

A correspondent in Saunders's News-letter for April 4, 1871, thus describes the state in which he found Bishop Bedell's tomb at a recent visit. " The grave-yard is in quite a ruinous state, covered with weeds . . . Bedell's resting-place being elevated a little above the level has escaped in some degree the surrounding ruin. The inscription is almost covered over with grass and weeds, and the stone (which lies flat) is broken in two or three parts."

More recently, as I am informed, the slab has been brushed clean with soap and water.

Whether the grave-stone with the sculpture described in the copy of Burnet's Life of Bedell above referred to, and that described in Mant's History be identical, or whether the latter be a new edition of the former, cannot so far as I know be determined. Nor can it be determined whether the grave-stone described as above in 1721 was that originally laid down. Grave-stones by the exposure to the weather so rapidly undergo decay that we can scarcely suppose that that at least described in Mant's History was the original one. Probably the restoration by the Bishop of Kilmore about the year 1740, referred to in the " Description of Lough Erne," may have

* Bishop Mant, History of the Church of Ireland, vol. ii. p. 655. For the drawing of the *grave-stone*, see vol. i.

been complete enough to secure its preservation down to Dr. Mant's time.

Now, there is a nobler and more enduring monument to Bishop Bedell. On the west front of the new Cathedral Church of Kilmore is this inscription:—

Guilielmi Bedelli quondam Kilmorensis Episcopi in memoriam.

This new Cathedral Church, consecrated on the 17th of July 1860, was erected by the pious care of Dr. Marcus Gervais Beresford, formerly Bishop of Kilmore and now Archbishop of Armagh, aided by generous contributions from the many who sympathised in the design of Dr. Beresford's undertaking.

CHAPTER XV.

DEPARTURE OF BISHOP BEDELL'S SONS FROM THE COUNTY OF CAVAN.

After the Bishop's death his eldest son William with his wife continued to reside at Drum Corr, in the house of Mr. Denis Sheridan. Mr. Alexander Clogie also found a home there.

Sir James Craig, of Castle Croghan, who had long held out against the rebels, having died of fever, Ambrose Bedell, whose wife was a niece of Lady Craig, was entrusted with the command of Croghan Castle, along with Archdeacon Price.* The neighbouring Castle of Keilagh was held by Sir Francis Hamilton. In these two castles great numbers of British Protestants had found an asylum, but, in consequence of deficient food and want of room, fever broke out among them. Thus straitened with famine and sickness, the garrisons of Keilagh and Croghan were necessitated,

* Dean Jones's Beginnings and Proceedings of the Rebellion, &c. *ut supra.*

after a resistance for eight months, to propose terms of surrender to the rebels. On the 4th of May 1642 negotiations for this purpose were opened by Sir Francis Hamilton, requesting the rebel chiefs to permit Master Thomas Price, Archdeacon of Kilmore, and Master Ambrose Bedell, Chief in the Castle of Croghan, to pass with safety from thence to his Castle of Keilagh, to confer with him on the subject of the proposed capitulation. This having been agreed to, the representatives of the two castles of Keilagh and Croghan met and decided on treating with the rebels. Accordingly a conference took place. Sir Francis Hamilton, Sir Arthur Forbes, and two others from the Castle of Keilagh, and Master Price and Master Ambrose Bedell from the Castle of Croghan on the part of the British, met Philip McHugh O'Reilly, Mullmor O'Reilly, and four others on the part of the rebels. The terms of surrender agreed on were these:—The garrisons of the Castles of Keilagh and Croghan, with the refugees who had therein sought and found protection, and what other English and Scotch Protestants were still remaining about the neighbourhood, were to be allowed to march away to Drogheda with some arms, and all the moveable goods which they could conveniently carry away with them by horse or cart. Master William Bedell, Minister of Kinawley, and his wife, Master Alexander Clogie, Minister of Cavan, Mr. Bagshaw and his family Mr. Arthur Cullum,* and Mr. Castledyne,† were specially included by name in the agreement. Besides these, the company, which, according to the terms of capitulation agreed on, started for Drogheda on Wednesday the 15th of June 1642, consisted of Sir Francis Hamilton, Sir Arthur Forbes, and about eight hundred men, women, and children from Keilagh Castle; Lady Craig, Master Ambrose Bedell and his wife, ten ministers, including Archdeacon

* The Governor of Loughoughter Castle at the breaking out of the Rebellion, and who with his charge was seized by Mullmor O'Reilly, when he came on pretence of making a visit of courtesy.

† Who turned his former occupation of a carpenter to account for the benefit of Bishop Bedell, and his other fellow prisoners in Loughoughter Castle, by making shutters for the windows to keep out the cold and the rain.

Price, with about four hundred men, women, and children from Croghan Castle; and about one hundred and forty persons from other parts in the neighbourhood, making in all one thousand three hundred and forty souls. They were accompanied by a large escort of rebels.

On their arrival at Slane on the 22nd of June, wearied by their seven days' march and seven nights' bivouac in the open fields, they were met by Sir Henry Tichborne, the Governor of Drogheda, and a party of horse and foot, and by them conducted into the town.

Most of the people, including Mr. Clogie and the other ministers, proceeded on to Dublin. From Drogheda the Bedell family took shipping and went for England.

It now remains for us to follow separately the fortunes of William Bedell, Ambrose Bedell, and Alexander Clogie. But I cannot leave Kilmore without paying a tribute of respect to the minister of Killasser, Mr. Denis Sheridan, the kind host of Bishop Bedell and the preserver of the manuscript of the Hebrew Bible, and of the Irish translation of the Old Testament, and glancing at the career of his remarkable family.

CHAPTER XVI.

THE SHERIDAN FAMILY.

Of an ancient Irish stock, Denis Sheridan, though a Protestant and a minister of the Established Church of Ireland, still commanded in a great measure the affections of his clan or sept. When, therefore, the rebellion broke out, he was able through his influence with his countrymen to aid in protecting many of the British Protestants who flocked to his house for safety. And when Bishop Bedell was liberated from his imprisonment in Loughoughter Castle, his own house being now appropriated by the

Roman Catholic Bishop, Denis Sheridan's house, which had been all along the asylum of his sons' wives, was open to receive him and his sons also.

Mr. Denis Sheridan, it has been commonly said, was a Popish priest or friar, but that, becoming acquainted with Bishop Bedell, he was led by the Bishop's conversation and arguments to embrace the Reformed Faith. From the account in the text, however, it would appear that Denis Sheridan was brought up a Protestant, in the house of John Hill, Dean of Kilmore. Whether originally a Roman Catholic, or not, Denis Sheridan was ordained by Bishop Bedell, June 10, 1634, as a Minister of the Established Church, and two days after was collated to the Vicarage of Killasser, in the Diocese of Kilmore.

The following entry is extracted from the Regal Visitation of 1633-4:

Ēpus confert valet 40ˡⁱ ⎫   Vicaria de   ⎧ Mr. Dionitius Siriden
   per annum.   ⎭   Killasser.   ⎩   Vicarius.

Dionisius Shirridan admissus fuit ad sacrum Diaconatus ordinem per Wittum Kilmorensem Episcopum 10° Junij 1634. Collatus fuit ad Vicariam de Killassar per eundem Episcopum 13° Junij 1634. Inductus fuit 13° Junij 1634.

In addition to Killasser, " Denis Sheridan, Clerk, was, Sept. 20, 1645, presented by Patent (19°-24° Car. I. f. 8,) to the vicarages of Drunge and Larra, in the diocese of Kilmore, in the gift of the Crown by lapse, Dr. Faithfull Teate the last Incumbent being dead."

Mr. Denis Sheridan married about the year 1634. His wife was an English lady. Their son Thomas, in his speech before the House of Commons, on Wednesday the 15th of December, 1680, to be quoted below, defending himself against the charge of being a paid adherent of the Duke of York, and of being a participator in the Popish plot, incidentally stated that she was of a family named Foster. In the pedigree of the Sheridans of Cavan, in the College of Arms, Dublin, a copy of which is subjoined (p. 205), there is,

PEDIGREE OF SHERIDAN.

Oscar O'Sheridan of Castle Togher, ⚭ ...... daughter of O'Rourke, Prince of the Co.
Co. Cavan, only son and heir. | Leitrim.

    Anthony O'Sheridan, son ⚭ ...... daughter of O'Neil, Prince of
    and heir. | the Co. Tyrone.

    Conor O'Sheridan, son ⚭ ...... daughter of O'Donnell,
    and heir. | Prince of the Co. Donegall.

Anthony O'Sheridan, son and heir. ⚭ ...... daughter of O'Farrell of Moat Farrell,
| and Prince of North Annatly, Co. Longford.

Conor O'Sheridan, son and heir. ⚭ ...... daughter of The O'Connor Don of
| Cloonniallas, Co. Roscommon, Prince of
| Connaught.

    Anthony O'Sheridan, son ⚭ ...... daughter of O'Reilly, Prince of
    and heir. | the Co. Cavan.

    Conor O'Sheridan, son ⚭ ...... daughter of O'Rourke, Prince
    and heir. | of the Co. Leitrim.

    Anthony O'Sheridan, son ⚭ ...... daughter of O'Connor of Sligo,
    and heir. | Prince of Co. Sligo.

    Thadeus O'Sheridan, son ⚭ ...... daughter of Edmond O'Reilly
    and heir. | of Cavan in the Co. Cavan, Esq.

    Audven * O'Sheridan, son and ⚭ ...... daughter of Thomas O'Brady of
    heir. | Ballyhase in Co. Cavan, Esq.

    Denis O'Sheridan, son ⚭ Jane, daughter of Anthony
    and heir.   Atkinson.

---

* According to another account the Christian name of the father of Denis Sheridan, the friend of Bishop Bedell, was "Donald." See Dublin University Magazine for November 1852, article " Quilca and the Sheridan family."

we see, a Denis who corresponds, as regards date, to the Denis Sheridan under notice, but his wife's name, though English, is put down as Atkinson.

The children of Denis Sheridan of whom I have found notices are the following: 1°, William, the godson of Bishop Bedell, born in 1635. Bedell in his will, it has been seen, left him forty shillings. In 1652, being then seventeen years of age, he was entered at Trinity College, Dublin, as appears from the following extract from the Register:—1652, May 15°. Sheridan, Gulielm., Schol. Commensalis —filius Dionysii Sheridan, ministri—17 annorum, natus in Togher Comitatu de Cavan, educatus sub M^ris Sheridan, Bedlow, et Wilson. Tutor, Josephus Travers.

William Sheridan became Dean of Down, and was in January 1681 made Bishop of Kilmore and Ardagh. He received the degree of Doctor of Divinity T. C. D. in 1682. In 1691 he was deprived of his Bishoprics for refusing to take the oaths to William and Mary.[*] He died in London, October 3, 1711.[†]

2°, Patrick, the second son, was born in 1638, and entered at Trinity College, Dublin, along with his brother William: 1652, May 15°. Sheridan, Patricius, Schol. commensalis—filius Dionysii Sheridan, Ministri—14 annorum, natus juxta Enniskillen in Com. Fermanagh, educatus sub M^ris Sheridan, Bedlow, et Wilson. Tutor, Joseph Travers.

He was one of the four Masters of Arts nominated Fellows of

[*] On the deprivation of William Sheridan, the Bishoprics of Kilmore and Ardagh were again separated. The former was given to Dr. Wm. Smith, who was translated from Raphoe, and the latter to Dr. Ulysses Burgh, Dean of Emly. Dr. Burgh, who was consecrated in September 1692, dying a few months after, Ardagh was reunited to Kilmore under Bishop Smith, who died February 24, 1698, and was succeeded by Dr. Wettenhall (see p. 196). My kinsman, the late Rev. Richard Burgh Byam, Vicar of Kew and Petersham, was a great-great-grandson of Bishop Burgh.

[†] It is said in Bishop Mant's History of the Irish Church that the deprived Bishop of Kilmore died in poverty in London, but this is contradicted in the article on Quilca and the Sheridan Family, in the Dublin University Magazine for November 1852.

Trinity College, Dublin, by the Crown on the occasion of the Restoration of Charles the Second in 1660. In 1665 he took the degree of B.D.; in 1666-8 he was Vice-Provost of Trinity College, Dublin; and in 1679 was made Bishop of Cloyne, retaining the other preferments which he previously held.* Bishop Patrick Sheridan married in 1677 Anne, daughter and co-heir of Francis Hill of Hill Hall (brother of Mary the wife of Captain Ambrose Bedell) and relict of her cousin Moyses Hill of Hill Hall. He died s.p. and was buried November 22, 1682, in the College Chapel, Dublin. His widow died in July 1683.

3°. The third son of the Rev. Denis Sheridan has been hitherto overlooked. That the son Thomas was the fourth and not the third is shown by his entry at the Middle Temple. The third son (probably named Denis) and the fifth or youngest son James, to be mentioned below, were, it is said, Generals in the Imperial service.†

4°. Thomas Sheridan was born in 1646, and entered at Trinity College, Dublin, as appears from the following extract: 1660-1, January 17, Sheridan, Thomas, Pensionar.—filius Dionysii Sheridan, ministri—14 annorum, natus villa S^{ti} Jōhis juxta Trimiam, in Comitatu Medensi, Dublinii privatim educatus. Tutor, Laurentius White.

He graduated B.A. in 1664, became a Fellow in 1667, and in 1670, June 29, was admitted of the Middle Temple, London:—
June 29, 1670: Mr. Thomas Sheridan, filius quartus Dennis Sheridan de Drum Corr in Com. Cavan in Regno Hibñiæ gen. admissus est in Societatem Medii Templi.

* Dublin University Calendar, 1870, pp. 354-5.
† The authority for this is the minister of Killasher or Killassar, co. Cavan, about 1740, in the article entitled, a "Description of Lough Erne," in Add. MS. 4,436, Br. Museum. His words are that Denis Sheridan was ordained by Bishop Bedell, and was promoted to the living of Killasher, in the diocese of Kilmore, where he died at a great age, " and saw two of his sons generals in the Imperial service, a third Secretary of State and Commissioner of the Revenue, a fourth, Patrick Sheridan, Bishop of Cloyne, and the eldest (youngest is erroneously put down,) William, Bishop of Kilmore and Ardagh."

In this entry Thomas Sheridan is put down as the fourth son. Between the date of his brother Patrick's birth in 1638 and that of his own in 1646 there is room for an intermediate brother, who was no doubt the one before indicated.*

Thomas Sheridan obtained the situation of Collector of the Customs in Cork, by which he realized some fortune. He subsequently became acquainted with the Duke of York, afterwards James II, and visited him at Brussels during H. R. H.'s retirement there in 1679, in consequence of the strong public feeling manifested against him. Being thus known as an adherent of the Duke of York, Thomas Sheridan was accused of a participation in the Popish plot, and committed to prison in 1680. On the 15th of December, 1680, he was examined by the House of Commons, and, after his examination, made a speech, from which the following extracts relating to his family are made: †—

" I was born a gentleman of one of the antientest families, and related to many considerable, in Ireland. In one county there is a castle and a large demesne; in another a greater tract of land for several miles together yet known by our name. I need not say who was the head or chief—'tis too much, that my grandfather was the last that enjoyed the estate; and that my father, left an orphan at the beginning of King James's reign, found himself dispossessed and exposed to the world—that whole county with five others in Ulster being entirely escheated to the Crown. My parents, Protestants— my mother, a gentlewoman of England, of good fortune, a Foster, who for my father's sake quitted her country and relations—both famed for honesty, for their loyalty and sufferings in the late rebellion, when my father escaped twice narrowly with his life and at

---

* In Brady's Clerical and Parochial Records of Cork, Cloyne, and Ross, Thomas is erroneously stated to have been born in 1641; but this year was no doubt the date of a birth in Denis Sheridan's family, that, namely, of the third son.

† A short account or state of Mr. Sheridan's case before the late House of Commons. In a letter to J. T. London, 1681, small 4to. King's Pamphlets, in the British Museum.

last was forced to fly for relieving and protecting both the fortunes and persons of very many English.

"To my birth, I had a suitable education; I have slender pretence to letters; am not altogether a stranger to the civil law nor the laws of England, the means intended for my livelihood.

* * * * * *

"Born of Protestant parents, bred all along a member of the Church of England, and (by the grace of God) will live and die in this profession, for it is not so much owing to the chance of education, as to my choice being satisfied by reason, by Scripture, and the laws of my country,—no inconsiderable argument, that of all it is the most purely Christian.

* * * * * *

"It has been objected against me 'that by my interest in H. R. H. I got my brother made a Bishop in opposition to the Lord Levetenant of Ireland and contrary to merit.'

* * * * * *

"My brother has been as much and as injuriously defamed as I, though not so publicly. But he came off with honour."

* * * * * *

Parliament being abruptly dissolved, Thomas Sheridan was set at liberty.

On his accession to the throne, James the Second created Colonel Richard Talbot Earl of Tirconnell, and appointed him to be Lieut.-General in Ireland. Henry Hyde, the second Earl of Clarendon, was then Lord Lieutenant, but was superseded two years after (Feb. 1687) by Lord Tirconnell. About this time Mr. Thomas Sheridan was sent Secretary into Ireland, and Commissioner of H. M.'s. Revenue, but he had not been long there before Lord Tirconnell, wishing to have another person as Secretary, preferred charges against Sheridan, and eventually removed him from the offices to which he had been appointed. In vindication of himself Thomas

Sheridan appealed to the King. The result does not appear; but that the King was satisfied with Sheridan is evident from the circumstance that his Majesty in exile retained him as private Secretary.*

Thomas Sheridan is said to have married a natural daughter of King James, and to have had a son and a daughter. The son followed the fortunes of the Pretender, and the daughter married Colonel Guilliaume, Aid-de-Camp to King William the Third.

5°. James, the youngest son, was born in 1649, and entered at Trinity College, Dublin, in 1665:—"1665. Undecimo Maii, Jacobus Sheridan, filius Dionysii Sheridan clerici, natus annos sedecim, natus juxta Trimiam; Educatus sub M^{ro} Cary; Tutor, Michael Ward."

As above said, this James, the youngest son of Denis Sheridan, was no doubt one of the two sons said to have been Generals in the Imperial service. He is the only son of Denis Sheridan mentioned in the pedigree in the College of Arms, Dublin.

It has been said that Dr. Thomas Sheridan, the grandfather of Richard Brinsley Sheridan, was the son of James Sheridan just noticed, but the pedigree in the College of Arms does not substantiate the relationship. Dr. Thomas Sheridan, the friend of Swift the Dean of St. Patrick's, father of Thomas Sheridan "the Manager" as he has been styled, who was the father of Richard-Brinsley, appears to have been the son of a collateral branch of the Sheridan family. He was born in 1684, and was educated at Trinity College, Dublin, through the kindness, it is said, of his kinsman Dr. William Sheridan, the deprived Bishop of Kilmore. He died in 1738.

* In the Bodleian Library, Rawlinson Collection of Manuscripts, 139, B. 4, there are "Two memorials to the King from Thomas Sheridan, Secretary and Commissioner of the Revenue in Ireland, respecting the charges brought against him by the Lord Deputy, together with a letter from him to the President of the Council, a copy of the articles exhibited against him, the original report of the Irish judges thereon," &c. 1688, ff. 118, 121, 146, 175.

The following anecdote * here merits a place, as the verses by Dr. Sheridan afford a brilliant example of his ready genius: Soon after Swift and Sheridan became acquainted, they passed some days together at the episcopal palace of Kilmore on a visit to the then bishop. After Swift's departure, it was discovered that he had written the following lines on one of the windows looking into the churchyard towards Bishop Bedell's grave:—

> Resolve me this, ye happy dead,
> Who've lain some hundred years in bed,
> From every persecution free
> That in this wretched life we see,
> Would ye resume a second birth
> And choose once more to live on earth?

Whereupon, in reply, Dr. Sheridan wrote underneath:—

> Thus spoke great Bedell from his tomb:
> "Mortal, I would not change my doom
> To live in such a restless state,
> To be unfortunately great;
> To flatter fools, and spurn at knaves,
> To shine amidst a race of slaves;
> To learn from wise men to complain,
> And only rise to fall again:
> No, let my dusty relics rest,
> Until I rise among the blest."

CHAPTER XVII.

THE REV. ALEXANDER CLOGIE.

Mr. Clogie was a Scotchman, born in 1614, but in what part of Scotland I have not ascertained. In 1636 we first become acquainted with him, when he was admitted to Holy Orders by Bishop Bedell.

* Swift's Works, by Sir W. Scott, vol. xii. pp. 485-6. 2nd Ed. 1824.

On the 12th of November 1637 he was collated to the Vicarage of Dyne or Denn, co. Cavan, in the Diocese of Kilmore, and, in about a fortnight after, was married to Miss Leah Mawe, the Bishop's step-daughter. She, however, as stated in Chapter VIII., died in little more than a month after her marriage.

Mr. Clogie held the Vicarage of Denn until May 1640, on the 7th of which month he was instituted Vicar of Urney, or Cavan, instead. He seems to have lived in habits of intimacy at the Episcopal house, but was not Chaplain, for the Bishop discharged the duties of that office himself (see page 77). The period under notice was that during which Bishop Bedell was engaged carrying on the supervision of the translation of the Old Testament into the Irish language, by Mr. Murtach King. In this labour of supervision Mr. Clogie, as he himself informs us,* assisted. He thus appears to have known Irish, and, though he does not say that he previously knew Gaelic, it is probable he came from some district in Scotland where that language was spoken, and that, knowing Gaelic, he was enabled the more readily to acquire a knowledge of the Irish.†

Mr. Clogie, we have seen, was with Bishop Bedell and his family when the Rebellion broke out, and shared in their sufferings and imprisonment ‡ After the Bishop's death he continued at Mr. Denis Sheridan's house until the 15th of June, 1642, when, as above mentioned, he made one of the company of English and Scotch who departed for Dublin. At Drogheda we lost sight of Mr. Clogie; now we meet him again in Mr. Bladen's shop in Dublin, as related by himself in the following passage:—" Amongst other converts there was a learned friar called Daniel O'Creane,§ on whom

* Memoir of Bishop Bedell, printed from the MS. (No. 6400, Har. Coll.) in the British Museum, and edited by Mr. W. Walker Wilkins, p. 106, London, 1862.
† See p. 156 *et seq*. The Minister here referred to under the initials A. B. appears to have been Mr. Clogie himself.
‡ Memoir of Bishop Bedell just cited, p. 205.
§ Mr. Creane's name occurs among the signatures to the decrees passed at the Diocesan Synod of Kilmore, on the 19th of September, 1638. (See Chapter IX.) He was collated to the vicarage of Mullagh, *alias* Killinkere, by Bishop Bedell in

the Bishop had bestowed a good living. * * * He did not fall away upon the Rebellion, as many hypocrites and false converts did, but stood out manfully against all violence, and spoil, and terror, and escaped to Dublin, at length, naked and bare, and the first money that God sent him he laid out for an English Bible (*as I—Clogie—did see*) in Mr. Bladen's shop." *

On the 11th of Sept. 1643, Mr. Clogie appears to have been present when Lord Moore was killed in an attack against the rebels at Portlester. " I saw," says Clogie, " the cannon bullet taken out of his body."†

The next time we meet with Mr. Clogie is when he came from Ireland to England at the end of 1643, as Chaplain with the Horse,‡ after the Marquis of Ormonde had made the treaty for a cessation of arms with the rebels, on the 15th of September of the same year.

In 1645 he appears to have been with the troops before Hereford, when Col. Lawrence Crawford was slain there.§

In 1646 we find Mr. Clogie in London,|| for he relates that then and there he met Dr. Alane Cooke, the Chancellor of the Diocese of Kilmore, with whom Bishop Bedell had the protracted litigation (see pp. 55-6, 151). Dr. Cooke, Mr. Clogie says, spoke kindly of the Bishop, and lamented his death (see p. 155).

At last, in 1647, Mr. Clogie, after all his troubles, is settled in the Vicarage of Wigmore, county Hereford, where he enters on a new phase of life. Now thirty-three years of age, his incumbency extended throughout a period of fifty-one years more. The following

---

1631. (Reg. Visitation 1633-4.) The Rev. Daniel Creane married a daughter of Captain Perkins, and had a son named Ambrose, after Captain Ambrose Bedell, the Bishop's son. To this Ambrose Creane Captain Ambrose Bedell bequeathed £5.

* Op. Cit. p. 97. † Op. Cit. p. 176.

‡ Clogie, Op. Cit. p. 68. Master Thomas Price, who had been Bishop Bedells Archdeacon, and who was joined with Ambrose Bedell in command of the Castle of Croghan after Sir James Craig's death, came over to England at the same time as Chaplain of Infantry. Archdeacon Price was afterwards Bishop of Kildare. We shall meet with him again as Archbishop of Cashel.

§ Op. Cit. p. 177. || Op. Cit. p. 86.

inscription is on a stone slab inside the Communion-rails and immediately under the Communion-table in the church of Wigmore:—

" Here lieth in hopes of a glorious Resurrection unto Life eternall the body of that Holy, Reverend, and Learned Divine, Mr. Alexander Clogie, who departed this life October 24, 1698, aged 84. Minister at Wigmore 51 years."*

To whom Mr. Clogie was indebted for his introduction to the Vicarage of Wigmore I have not ascertained; but it is suggested by the Rev. T. T. Lewis, the editor of the Letters of Lady Brilliana Harley during the Civil War,† that it may have been through the Rev. Stanley Gower, the Rector of Brampton Bryan, and one of the Members of the Assembly of Divines at Westminster. Mr. Stanley Gower had been Chaplain to Archbishop Ussher, and to him Mr. Clogie might thereby have become known in connection with Bishop Bedell.

It is above stated that Mr. Clogie was a Scotchman. This had been surmised by the Rev. Dr. Reeves of Tynan, near Armagh, from certain passages in Clogie's Life of Bedell; but it is now shown to be a fact by a document communicated through the Rev. J. J. Trollope,‡ the present Vicar of Wigmore, by the Lady Frances Vernon Harcourt. It is to be premised that on the 6th of August 1650, " An Act was passed prohibiting all trade between *England* and *Scotland*, and the injoyning the departure of *Scotsmen* out of this Commonwealth." (Whitelock's Memorials, p. 452.) The document, which is a petition from the parishioners of Wigmore to the Parliament, that their Vicar, Mr. Clogie, though a Scottishman, may have licence to remain in England, is as follows:—

---

* In the burial of Mr. Clogie within the church, the example of Bishop Bedell was not followed.

† A volume of the Camden Society for the year 1853-4.

‡ For all the information here given about Mr. Alexander Clogie, I am indebted to the very obliging courtesy and kindness of the Rev. Mr. Trollope. Thomas Bedell's MS. notes (*supra* p. 89) first gave the reference to Wigmore.

Whereas wee are given to understand that there is an Act of Parliam[t] latelie made by yo[r] honours, that all Scottishmen shall speedilie depart out of this Comon Wealth of England unlesse they have a especial lycence from yo[r] honours: Wee the inhabitants of this parish of Wigmore in the countie of Hereff. are bould to become humble peticoers to yo[r] honours in the behalf of Mr. Alexander Clogie o[r] now Minister, a Scottishman borne but hath not lived in Scotland, as wee are informed, for sixteen years past, who is a man learned and of a godlie conversacon; That as he hath been sent wth the approbacon and good liking of the Parliam[t] amongst us where he hath exercized his ministrie both painfullie and powerfullie to the great comfort of o[r] poore soules for the space of allmost three years, so yo[u] will be pleased out of the goodnes and zeale for God's glorie to give him lycence to continue amongst us in this parish for time to come. By which worke of yo[rs] God shall be glorified, and wee of this poor parish shall be bound to pray for yo[r] honours' happines in this and the world to come.

Signed by 97 persons.

Endorsed Wigmore, peti[n] for Mr. Cloggie.

(in the hand-writing of Sir R. Harley or that of Sir E. Harley.)

Some eight years after his settlement at Wigmore, Mr. Clogie entered into a second marriage, of which the following is the record in the Parish Register of Wigmore:—

1655. The eleventh day of December, 1655, Mr. Alexander Clogie, Minister of the Gospel of Jesus Christ at Wigmore, was married to Mrs. Susanna Nelme, daughter to Mr. John Nelme, some tyme of Gloucester, citizen, according to the Act of Parliament, at Ludlow, in the county of Salop.

The children of this marriage were the following, as appears from the Parish Register of Wigmore:—1656, John; 1658, Brilliana; 1660, Shusanna; 1661-2, Leah; 1665-6, Thomas; 1671, Mary.

Mr. and Mrs. Clogie lived to see grand-children.

Mrs. Clogie survived her husband and died in 1711. Her burial at Wigmore is entered as follows:—25 July Anno D^{ni} 1711, buried Mrs. Cloggie, Vid.

The time when Mr. Clogie wrote his life of Bishop Bedell appears, from what he says,* to have been whilst Dr. Francis Marsh was Bishop of Kilmore and Ardagh, viz. between 1672 and 1681. That the Memoir was already written before 1679 is shown by Mr. Clogie's letter to Archbishop Sancroft of Canterbury, given below, and that it was written subsequently to 1672 may be inferred from his remark that, at the time he was writing it, above fifty years had run out since the publication of Bedell's correspondence with Wadesworth in 1624. This makes the time to be about 1675. Isaak Walton's Life of Sir Henry Wotton had been already published when Mr. Clogie was writing his Life of Bishop Bedell.

The following letter to Archbishop Sancroft of Canterbury is contained in the Tanner MS. xxxviii. 41, Bodleian Library, Oxford:—

Most Reverend Father in God my Honble good Lord,

I bless God with all my hart, that after almost 40 years oblivion it hath pleased him to raise and stirr up y^r Grace to revive the blessed memory of that worthy man of God, who was a faythfull servant in his house as another Moses, Dr Wm Bedell, L. B. of Kilmore, my Lord and Father, whose name to me is next y^t Sacred name y^t is above every name; it hath beene undoubtedly a great loss to the Church to have beene depryved so long of the knowledge of so worthy a person, so famous for all Christian excellencys in his generation as any since the Apłes days. Had I been so happy as to have known sooner y^r Grace's interest in him and sincere affection to him as his , all my interest and papers (the sacred reliques of him) had readily attended y^r Grace's hon^{ble} designe, in raysing up the name of ye dead. The short narrative of his life and death y^t by the motion of some noble p'sons I drew up, not for publick view, but private satisfaction (having lived wth him in the hour of tempta-

* Printed Memoir, *ut supra*, p. 49.

tion y^t came upon Ireland in '41, and being wth him in prison and at his death and buriall) I humbly submit to y^r Wisdom's correction and arbitram^t. I have sent y^r Grace (according to my promise) some of his papers y^t I rescued out of the fyre with the hazard of my lyfe. I have yet by me many loose papers of his owne writting, out of wh^{ch} many precous things things (sic) may be picked for the benefit of the Church, and since I have found favour in y^r Grace's eyes for Jonathan's sake, if in this, in giving the dead his due, or in anything else, I may be serviceable to y^r Lp., I doe most willingly resign my selfe to y^r Grace's disposal, and craving pardon for this presumption,

Most worthy Patriarch, I subscribe myselfe y^r Grace's (above all mortalls) most humble and obedient soñe and servant,

Alex: Clogie

Wigmore, June 9th, '79.

The noble persons to whom Mr. Clogie alludes in this letter, by whose motion he was led to draw up his narrative of the Life and Death of Bishop Bedell, were probably the Harley family of Brampton Bryan, with whom he appears to have lived, as Vicar of Wigmore, in habits of intimacy. The manuscript copy of his narrative in the Harleian Collection in the British Museum, which I have no doubt is in his own hand, had probably been presented by him to one of the Harleys, and thus came to form one of their celebrated collection. The copy sent to Archbishop Sancroft is probably that which is now in the Tanner Collection in the Bodleian Library bound up in the same volume with the MS. of our text.

To Mr. Clogie the Rev. Gilbert Burnet, afterwards Bishop of Salisbury, was indebted for the materials on which was founded his well-known Life of William Bedell, Lord Bishop of Kilmore, first published in 1685. Burnet settled as a resident in London in 1674, and it was probably some time after that when he and Mr. Clogie became personally acquainted, for there had evidently been, judging by Burnet's expressions, personal communications between the two. Burnet says, in his preface: " I had a great collection of materials put in my hands by a worthy and learned Divine, Mr. Clogie, that was much more the author of this book than I am. I confess my part in this was so small that I can scarce assume anything to myself but the copying out what was put in my hands." In the course of his work, again, p. 232, Burnet says: " And both he that collected these Memorials of Bishop Bedell, and he that copies them out and publishes them, will think their labours very happily employed if the reading them produces any of those good effects that are intended by them."

The Life of Bishop Bedell, as published by Gilbert Burnet, has supplied the materials for all the biographies of Bedell which have appeared. The latter therefore reproduce all the defects and errors of the former. We have seen that Archbishop Sancroft designed at one time to publish a treatise comprising the biography and works of Bishop Bedell, and that the manuscripts on the subject in the Tanner Collection in the Bodleian Library were of his Grace's collecting. This being known at the time, Dr. Edward Wettenhall, Bishop of Cork and Ross, in a letter to Archbishop Sancroft of Canterbury, dated April 24, 1686, hints his disapprobation of Burnet's Life of Bedell, in the following terms:—

" I have read Bp. Bedell's life, but I cannot think it is published by any whom your Grace employed. The present Bp. of Kilmore, in whose father's house Bp. B. died, told me lately he had several papers of Bp. B. which I have desired him to look up at his return home, which will give a fuller account." *

* Tanner MSS. in the Bodleian Library, Oxford, vol. xxx. folio 25.
The Bishop of Kilmore here referred to was Dr. William Sheridan; and Dr. Edward Wettenhall, the Bishop of Cork and Ross in 1686, who himself became Bishop of Kilmore and Ardagh in 1699, in succession to Dr. Smith, was he who directed in his will that should he die at Kilmore his body should be interred near " good Bishop Bedell's." *Supra*, p. 196.

I have above had occasion to examine into the validity of Dean Hickes' strictures on certain passages in Bishop Burnet's Life of Bishop Bedell, and to show that though they are in part justified they also in a much greater part betray the Dean's unacquaintance with the subject into which he ventured to rush as a critic, and manifest too glaringly the animus by which he was actuated against Burnet. In his vindication of the funeral sermon on Archbishop Tillotson, Burnet says:—" I published that life (of Bishop Bedell) just when I went out of England. . . . The whole materials were prepared for me many years before I meddled with them by an ancient and reverend clergyman, Mr. Clogie. . . . I declined to write on the subject for some years, but repeated importunities overcame me at last.

"I am not answerable for any mistakes which my author may have misremembered : so if any of these are wrong, they are another man's errors, they are not mine."

The blundering and inaccuracy of Mr. Clogie, however, are in some instances so glaring that any one acquainted with Ecclesiastical History—as a former Professor of Divinity, an actual Preacher at the Rolls, and a future Bishop of the Church of England ought to be—must at once have been led to examine more narrowly into the facts of his subject. Bishop Burnet therefore cannot be excused for contenting himself with copying merely and standing sponsor to the statements of Mr. Clogie.

In taking leave of Mr. Clogie we must not omit mention of a singular publication which appeared under his name a few years before his death, entitled: " Vox Corvi; or, the Voice of a Raven that thrice spoke these words distinctly; ' Look into Colossians the 3rd, and 15th.' A sermon preached at Wigmore, co. Hereford, by Alexander Clogie. London, 1694." Of this pamphlet there is a copy in the British Museum, and another in the Bodleian Library at Oxford. But these are not copies of the first edition. I have seen, through the kindness of the Rev. J. J. Trollope of Wigmore, the preface (without the sermon) of an edition dated 1691. This no doubt was the first, as the alleged incident on which the sermon was founded is stated to have occurred on the 3rd of February, 1691.

The sermon is directed against domestic brawls, and the alleged incident referred to was this:—A certain family in the parish of Wigmore had become notorious for the dissensions which existed among its members, when one day Thomas Kinnersley, a grandson of Mr. Clogie, ten years of age, who resided with him, went out into the wood-yard, where he sat down, and was amusing himself with "whittling" a stick, when his attention was drawn to a raven perched on the steeple of the Church, which, looking towards the house at variance with itself, screamed out distinctly to his hearing three times the words, "Look into Colossians the 3rd, 15th." Surprised and alarmed at this extraordinary occurrence, the child ran into the house, breathless, and told what he had heard. Whereupon reference was made to Colossians, chapter iii. and verse 15, and the text found to be this: "And let the peace of God rule in your hearts, to the which also ye are called in one body; and be ye thankful."

A wood-cut, different in the two editions above referred to, but in each case of artistic merit about equal to that which is usually displayed by the woodcuts on broadsides, represents: 1°, The parsonage, with Mr. Clogie, in canonicals and book in hand as if he were preaching, standing at the door; 2°, Thomas Kinnersley in the wood-yard "whittling" his stick and looking at the steeple where, 3°, the Raven is perched as above described, with a scroll held in its beak, on which the words already mentioned are written; 4°, the House at variance with itself, and its members at the door quarrelling with each other.

CHAPTER XVIII.

CAPTAIN AMBROSE BEDELL.

About the year 1640, Ambrose, the youngest son of Bishop Bedell, being then twenty two-years of age, married Mary, only daughter of Peter Hill, Sheriff of Down, and his wife the sister of Randall, first Earl of Antrim. Peter Hill was the oldest son of Sir Moyses Hill, the second son of Sir Moyses being Arthur of Hillsborough, the ancestor of the Marquis of Downshire, and of the late Viscount Dungannon. Mary, the only daughter of Sir Moyses, was the wife of Sir James Craig, of Croghan Castle, near Kilmore. On the occasion of Ambrose's marriage, his father bought the lands of Carne from the Rev. Martin Baxter, Vicar of Kildallon, " for the use of Ambrose and Mary his wife during their lives, and for the heirs of their bodies and right heirs of Ambrose Bedell for ever."

We have seen that Sir James Craig held his Castle out against the rebels, and gave shelter to many of the British Protestants. Fever breaking out among them, however, Sir James caught it, and died. After this Ambrose Bedell, in conjunction with Archdeacon Price, continued the defence until they were necessitated by famine and sickness to capitulate as above related. After the capitulation Ambrose went with the company from Croghan and Keilagh Castles and the neighbourhood as far as Drogheda. Thence he accompanied his brother to England, but did not remain long in that country, for we find him in Dublin on the 26th of October, 1642, making his deposition regarding the sufferings undergone and losses sustained by his family in consequence of the rebellion. The following are the principal points in this deposition: *—

"Ambrose Bedell, gent. sonne of the late Reverend Father in God William Lord Bp. of Kilmore, in ye county of Cavan (now,

---

* The original is preserved in the Library of Trinity College, Dublin, and has I believe never before been printed. For procuring me a copy of it I am indebted to Professor Stokes of T.C.D. who has been unwearied in forwarding my undertaking.

by the cruelties of ye rebells, deceased), sworne and examined, deposeth and sayth that in the beginning of the present rebellion and by means thereof his said father in his lyfetyme was deprived, robbed, or otherwise despoyled of his meanes, goodes, and chattels of the value and to his presente coste of foure thousand and three score poundes str. And this deponent was also deprived, robbed or otherwise dispossessed of the possession, rente, and profite of his lands and farme, and of his goodes and chattels, worth three hundred and thirty-one pound str. and is like to loose the future rentes and profitts of his said landes and farmes worth ninety-six poundes p. ann. untill a peace be established.

" And further sayth that Edmund McMulmore O'Rely of . . . Esqre came about the 19th or 20th of Novr.* last 1641 to the said Lord Bp's. house and commanded him to turne out of dores about 200 of aged p̃sons, women and children of Protestants, whom (with others before that tyme departed from him) he had since the beginning of the rebellion harboured and releived. The said Edmund alledging that the said Bp. must not kepe those English to devoure the meate (meaning the said Bp's. meate) which belonged to the souldiers meaning his the said Edmund's rebellious company. But the said Bp. professed that whyle he had a bytt for himself never a child there to his . . . . should want. And when all was gone he would trust in God for more. Whereupon the said Edmund told him that the next day he would show him the most woefulle spectacle that ever he beheld. To witt he would hang all those people before his own face. And accordingly the said Edmund came the next day, with about 200 foote and 20 or 30 horse, and entering the said house scised on the person of the said Bishop, and on all his goodes, turned the poore stripped people out of dores to shift for themselves, many of whiche perished by the highway with cold and hunger. Others were killed with the barbarous people, and some escaped to Dublin, as this deponent hath credibly heard. But this deponent with the said Lord Bishop his father, Mr. Wm. Bedell

* This appears to be a mistake for December.

this deponent's elder brother, and his brother-in-law Mr. Cloghy, Minister, were by the said Edmund carried prisoners to Clowater Castle. And this deponent and the said Mr. Cloghy cast in boults, where all of them abode for the space of three weeks. And immediately after the said prisoners were sett free out of that miserable castle, where they had noe glass windowes or shutters to keepe out the weather coming off the lough where it was seated, the said Lord Bishopp fell sick and died (as this deponent verily believeth) by occasion of such usages in the said castle. And this dep^t further saith that shortly after that his said father and the forenamed were cast into prison the pretended popish Bishopp of that Diocese came by the direction or consent of the said Edmund Rely into the said Bishop's house, seized on the rest of the goodes and bookes which were in the said house, and there liveth. . . . . And (this deponent) further saith that Sr James Craige, knight, that long had maintained Castle Croghan, being buried in the Church of Killesandra his corps were taken up out of the grave by the rebells and cutt in pieces, and after they had taken away his coffin and sheete, and had soe hackt and mangled him, they threw his mangled body into the grave again. And further saith that the rebells did often say that they woulde neither leave Englishe nor Scottishe, nor Protestants, nor any nation but themselves in Ireland. And this dep^t hath heard the rebells utter and use divers opprobrious words against the Lords Justices and Counsell of this Kingdome. And further saith that Mr. Luke Dillon of Trinity Island seemed long not to partake with the rebells, and tould this dep^{ts} father that he was loth to joine with them. But after when the said Luke Dillon's father was dead the said Luke Dillon sayde he had a letter from the Lord Dillon his brother, whereby he was advised to partake with the rebells to save the old Erle of Roscomon's goodes, and that thereupon the said Luke did joine and partake with the rebells of the Englishe pale * only: but not with

---

* The English pale was a territory comprehending the county of Louth in the Province of Ulster, and the counties of Dublin, Meath, and Kildare in Leinster.

the other rebells for that they were of different counsell and factions, and this dep' heard the meere Irishe rebells often say to the other rebells of the pale these words, viz: You churles with the great broeches, doe you think that if we were rid of the Englishe we would spare you? noe, we would cutt all your throats also, for you are all of one race with the other Englishe though we make use of you for the presente. And further saith that there were owing unto the said Lord Bishopp, this deponent's father, several sumes of monie by divers persons, some whereof are absolute rebells, and the rest owing by such as the presente rebellion hath disabled to make satisfaction, to the amounting in all to the sume of one thousand one hundred poundes or thereabout. And that the parties rebells that were soe indebted were and are these that followe, viz. Philip McMulmore O'Rely, of Lismore, in this county of Cavan, Esq., Hugh McTorlaghe Brady of Drumloght in the same county, Gent., Owen McWiltin O'Sheridan late of Lisbeg in the county of Longford, Gent., and Owen O'Sheridan of . . . . in the county of Cavan, a captain of rebells. And further saith that these persons hereafter named were and are notorious rebells, and acted in this presente rebellion, and doe partake, joine with, and carry arms with, for and amongst the rebells against the King's Matie and his loyale subjects, viz. (Here follows a number of names which it is unnecessary to quote.)   (Signed)   Ambrose Bedell.

The xxvi. October 1642.

John Watson.
Will. Aldrich.

After this Ambrose Bedell served in the Royal Army in Ireland as a Captain in the regiment of his wife's uncle Colonel Arthur Hill,* until 1649. He was thus one of the " Forty-nine Officers "

The rebels of the English pale were the descendants of the old English settlers in those counties who still adhered to Popery.

* This Colonel Arthur Hill, of Hillsborough, second son of Sir Moyses Hill, as above said, was ancestor of the Marquis of Downshire and of the late Viscount Dungannon. From him the name of Arthur descended in the Downshire and Dungannon families, from the latter of which the Duke of Wellington derived it, his

who claimed arrears of pay to a large amount. None of these arrears had been paid when Cromwell assigned lands to satisfy his own army. After the Restoration, however, the claims of the " Forty-nine Officers" were attended to, and Captain Ambrose Bedell had a grant of lands confirmed to him under the Acts of Settlement and Explanation, May 21, 19th Charles II. This grant comprised the townlands of Drumherine *alias* Drumhervise, Unagh *alias* Uragh, both in the Barony of Loughtee, county of Cavan; and Ballybollan, *alias* Uterclony, in the barony of Toome, county of Antrim, containing in all about 450 acres.*

Besides the lands thus acquired and the lands bought for him by his father, Captain Ambrose Bedell, on the 30th of April 1661, purchased from Thomas Richardson and his wife Anne (*née* Bagshaw) certain other lands in the parish of Drumlane, county of Cavan.†

After his retirement from the army, Ambrose Bedell appears to have resided on his estate at Carn Hill, a Justice of the Peace for the county of Cavan. Here he was residing when the letter (printed in the preface to the present volume) was addressed to him on the 5th of October, 1680, from Trinity College, Dublin, by Dr. Palliser,‡ relative to Archbishop Sancroft's design of publishing the Life and Writings of his father Bishop Bedell.

In 1682, having first made his will, Capt. Ambrose Bedell went to London to be touched by the King for the "Evil," as appears by a letter § from Archbishop Francis Marsh, of Dublin, previously Bishop of Kilmore, to Archbishop Sancroft of Canterbury, dated August 12, 1682, recommending Capt. Ambrose Bedell

mother being the eldest daughter of Arthur Hill 1st Viscount Dungannon, who was second son of the grandson of Colonel Arthur Hill. H. R. H. Prince Arthur, again, was named " Arthur," after the Duke of Wellington.

* Reports from the Commissioners respecting the Public Records of Ireland, 1821-1825, folio, p. 96. Ordered to be printed 17 June 1829.

† These lands were sold by Capt. Bedell Stanford, who died in 1857, to James H. Story, Esq.

‡ Tanner Collection, xxxvii. 147, Bodleian Library, Oxford.

§ Tanner Collection, xxxv. 68, Bodleian Library.

to his Grace's assistance to get him touched by the King; Capt. A. Bedell being, observes His Grace of Dublin, grievously afflicted with the evil.

In the letter from Capt. Ambrose Bedell to the Archbishop of Canterbury (Tanner Collection xxxv. 121) dated November 1, 1682, given in the preface, he speaks as if his health had been fully restored, and returns humble and hearty thanks to his Grace. However, the King's touch notwithstanding, Captain Ambrose Bedell died the following year at Cavan, aged sixty-five.

I have not ascertained when his wife died. Though Ambrose Bedell appears to have had a child or children before his father's death,* they were dead before him, as he left no issue.

In his will, dated June 20, 1682, and proved in Dublin October 20, 1683, Captain Ambrose Bedell directed that he should be buried in the churchyard of Kilmore beside his father. The testamentary disposal of his property will be noticed in the next chapter.

CHAPTER XIX.

The Rev. William Bedell and his Family.

William, the eldest son of Bishop Bedell, was godson of Dr. Samuel Warde, Master of Sidney Sussex College, Cambridge. In a letter to Dr. Warde, dated Kilmore, February 2, 1633, in reply to an offer made by him to entertain William at Cambridge, the Bishop says: " I do thank you very heartily for your kind and very friendly offer of entertaining my son, which I shall perhaps accept." William, however, who was then twenty-one years of age, does not appear to have been sent to Cambridge.

On the 1st of June, 1634, the Bishop ordained him Deacon, and on the sixth of the same month collated him to the Vicarage of

* Clogie's Memoir, *ut supra*, p. 4.

Kinawley, a parish situated at the head of Lough Erne, in the diocese of Kilmore, but chiefly lying in the county of Fermanagh.

The following extract from the Regal Visitation of 1633-4 has been supplied by the Rev. Dr. Reeves:—

Dioc Kilmore.
Decanat. de Dromlahen.

Epūs confert. Valet 100ˡⁱ per annum. } Vicaria de Kinally { Mr. Guliellmus Bedell, Vicarius.

Guliellūs Bedellus litteratus admissus fuit ad sacrum Diacanatus ordinem per Guliellmum Kilmorensem Episcopum 1º Junii, 1634. Collatus fuit, per eundem Episcopum ad vicariam de Kinally unacum omnibus decimis oblationibus et emolumentis ad rectorias de Knockninnay et Claindgorry et Ballegillaconing olim ad Episcopum Kilmorensem infra parochiam de Kinally pertineñ et nunc vigore literaȓ patencium Jacobi nuper Regis eidem vicarie assigñ et annex̃ 6º Jun. 1634.

Inductus fuit 7º Junii, 1634.

In reference to this admission of his eldest son William to Holy Orders, and his Collation to the Vicarage of Kinawley, Bishop Bedell in a letter to Dr. Samuel Warde, dated October 11, 1635, says: " Your Godson I have conferred a benefice upon; whereupon he is resident, and I hope he will prove a good minister and an honest man. I pray give some direction for the course of his studies, for I never yet knew how to study."

We have seen how anxious Bishop Bedell was that his Clergy should not be absentees from their parishes. But though the clergy, influenced by his own example of faithful discharge of duty, were many of them favourably disposed to conform to his wishes, this difficulty as to residence so presented itself that in many parishes there was no parsonage, nor even glebe land on which a parsonage might be built. Large parcels of ground indeed had been granted by King James, on the plantation of Ulster, to each church for glebe land, with a provision in the patent requiring the incumbent to build a mansion-house of a specified size for his personal residence. The distribution of the glebe lands however had been so inconveniently made by the surveyors and commissioners that in most cases there was not a foot of the glebe land situated in the parish to which it was assigned. To obviate the difficulty Bishop Bedell offered a portion of the Episcopal lands which lay in the neighbourhood of most of the parish churches, in exchange for the glebe lands which were situated so inconveniently out of the way, and to carry the plan out obtained a commission from the Lord Deputy and Council to see the exchange equitably made, so that the bishopric might have no damage, nor the present lessees of the glebe lands any just reason to complain. A general agreement on the subject having been come to between the bishop and the clergy, Mr. William Bedell was chosen to be sent into England with a petition to the King begging a confirmation of this exchange by a new patent.

Such was the occasion, so far as I can make out, of the visit of the Rev. William Bedell, Vicar of Kinawley, to England in 1637. He had a letter of recommendation,* from his father to Archbishop Laud, dated Septr. 2, and was entrusted by the latter to carry back a reply thereto, dated Oct. 12. But, being unable to return to Ireland so soon as he expected, Mr. William Bedell forwarded Archbishop Laud's letter to his father by a special messenger.

In a letter to the Archbishop, dated Dublin, December 20, 1638, Bishop Bedell incidentally mentions that he received this communication on the 30th of October 1637, and says, that his son had ague in England and was detained there in consequence, being advised by his physician not to return to Ireland until the following spring.

We have seen that William Bedell was already married when

* This letter and a draft of Laud's reply are in the Public Record Office, and are above quoted in Chapter VII. p. 159, in reference to the improvement of the revenue of the Bishopric of Ardagh under Dr. Richardson.

the rebellion broke out. But when, where, and whom he married I have not ascertained directly from any document. I am, however, inclined to think that he married when in England on the occasion just mentioned, and that his wife was a daughter of a Suffolk family named Barber. Mrs Bedell's Christian name was Mary, as appears from the entry of her burial, and also of that of her son James, in the parish register of Rattlesden, to be quoted below. That her maiden name was Barber may be inferred from the expression in her son James's will that his books were lying in the care of his " Uncle Barber." The first child of William Bedell and his wife Mary of whom I have found any record was his daughter Leah, who was baptized at Whepstead, co. Suffolk, on the 28th of December, 1643 (P. R.). According to Mr. Clogie's Narrative (p. 4), it would appear that William, as well as his brother Ambrose, had a child or children before his father's death. Any such child or children, however, must have died young.

The story of William Bedell, from his leaving Ireland after his father's death until his temporary settlement at Whepstead, is related with simple but touching pathos in the following letter to his godfather Dr. Samuel Warde, who at the time was himself overwhelmed by the troubles of the GREAT REBELLION which had commenced in England. See Chapter II. p. 95.

Reverend Sir,

I have received yours of the first of this instant month, in w^h y^u justly blame me of forgetfulnesse of those many obligations whereby I stand obliged to y^u, both in respect of my deceased father and myselfe and mine owne particular.* I desire to give y^u a breife

* The letter of Dr. Samuel Warde to which this is a reply would seem to have been written in a querulous tone. William Bedell however completely exonerates himself from the charge of neglect. I do not know whether he was ever able to make his promised visit to his godfather, but I fear that Dr. Warde remained dissatisfied with him, otherwise he would have left him a ring as he did to several other personal friends. I must confess that I felt disappointed on reading Dr. Samuel Warde's will (*supra*, p. 95) to find that he did not mention his godson William Bedell. The Bishop in his will did not forget Dr. Warde.

account of my present condition, wh. is not settled as y^u have heard. After I had some while rested me in Essex at my father's brother's house after my long and dangerous journey out of Ireland, I came into Suffolk, and being with an auncient friend of my father's (Dr. Despotine) I was desired to preach at Whepstead by some of the parish who had known my father. Now the minister of this towne, one Mr. Hinde, had a little before left his place in this manner: He furnished himselfe with an horse and pistolls and a sword, and borrowed some money, and takes his journey, with purpose after some weeks to returne. For what reasons I cannot certainly say, but for some cause or other, he is not yet returned. In his absence (which hath been since Christmas) I have at the entreaty of the parish supplyed his place, and upon their petition to ye Parliament I am appoynted to serve the cure, and to be payd for my paines out of ye benefits of ye living till Mr. Hinde appear. This is my settlem^t. And truly I confesse y^u may well marvell y^t y^u were not consulted with. But for y^r satisfaction: First, the thing was suddene and unexpected; Secondly, the people were wholly unprovided of a minister, so that I could never be at mine owne disposing since I first preached among them; And lastly, I was certainly informed y^t y^u were not at Cambridge, so y^t I knew not whither to goe unto y^u; and withall I neyther was furnished with horse nor money. Thus y^u may in fact understand my case. As for that poynt in y^r lett^r touching my father's death, I cannot at large satisfie y^u. Yet thus much in short: He died in ye rebells' hands, but had courteous useage in comparison of what other Englishmen found. I shall give y^u ye full relation shortly (if God please). For those wrightings y^r lett^r mentioneth, I think I heard my father speake of them. But what became of them or of the Bp. of Corke * himselfe I know not. S^r, the truth is, all my father's

---

* The Bishop here referred to was William Chappel, B.D., Fellow of Corpus Christi, Cambridge, Provost of Trinity College, Dublin, Feb. 1634-5, and Bishop of Cork and Ross, 1638. When the rebellion broke out he went from Cork to Dublin, whence he escaped to England in December. This was the Bishop of Corke

books and papers are wth ye rebells. And although I had some principall labours of his I durst not bring them (being to passe among ye rebells and being lyable to be searched at their pleasure) except I would extreamely have hazarded my life, w^h without y^t was danger enough. For conclusion, I am glad to heare of y^r health, and I shall shortly by God's helpe see y^u. But as for y^r imprisonment and ye cause thereof w^h y^r letter expresseth, they are matters above me. Therefore I can but desire God to direct y^u and to fit us all for times of suffering. Which I shall dayly doe in my poore prayers. Thus craving y^r blessing, I rest

Your dutyfull Godsonne
William Bedell

Whepstead, June ye 12, 1643.

Mr. Hinde, the rector of Whepstead here mentioned, not having returned, or, according to Walker's " Sufferings of the Clergy," (part ii. p. 274,) having been turned out, the Rev. Ambrose Salusbury was, about April 1644, preferred to the living, and the Rev. William Bedell was made Minister of Rattlesden, co. Suffolk, after doing clerical duty at Whepstead for about a year. The following is the record of his presentation extracted from Tanner's MS. in the Diocesan Registry, Norwich:—

" *Rattlesden.*

" Lib. Hall, 4 Mart. 1644, Gul: Bedellus, A.M. ad præs: Edw. Rivett, Arm."

Thus was Mr. William Bedell settled in the quiet Rectory of Rattlesden, after having suffered so much in that hurricane of human

who was so " very sharpe against ye offence " of the Bishop of Killal: see note, p. 54. Bishop Chappel was one of the persons supposed to have been the author of " The Whole Duty of Man." He died at Derby in 1649, aged 67.

passion, stirred up by national animosity and intensified by religious hate, which swept over Ireland, carrying death and devastation before it, and leaving famine, pestilence, and misery behind, where all had been previously blessed with peace and plenty. It is, indeed, a relief now to contemplate him and his family in the refuge he had gained in his own county and among his own people, where, being still young, he might look forward to many years of usefulness, "labouring," as Mr. Clogie said of him, in his Vicarage of Kinawley, "with that fidelity which became the son of such a father."

It was, I believe, during the earlier years of his quarter of a century's incumbency at Rattlesden that " The Relation of the Life and Death " of his father here published was composed by him. Dr. Despotine, from whom much information was derived, died in 1650, and was, therefore, still living during the first six years of the time. Dr. Despotine in his will, dated December 13, 1648, left five pounds to the Rev. William Bedell, of Rattlesden. See *supra*, p. 128.

The Rev. William Bedell's wife, Mrs. Mary Bedell, died in 1663. The following is the entry of her burial in the Parish Register of Rattlesden :— *

" 1663. Mary the wife of William Bedell was buried."

The Rev. William Bedell himself died in 1670-1. The following is the entry of his burial in the P. R. of Rattlesden :—

" 1670, March 16. Mr. William Bedell, after he had been Rector of this parish . . . . . . years, was buried."

A blank is here left in the Register. It will be seen that twenty-six years was about the time.

He left no will so far as I have been able to discover.†

---

* For this and the following extracts from the Parish Register of Rattlesden, relating to the Rev. William Bedell's family, I am indebted to the kindness and courtesy of the Rector, the Rev. John Barney.

† He succeeded his uncle John Bedell, his father's brother, in the family property in Essex. In an old rate-book of the parish of Black Notley in the possession of

The children of William and Mary Bedell were:—

I. Leah, baptized at Whepstead. The following is the entry of of her baptism in the Register of that parish:— *

"1643, Innocents' Day. Leah the daughter of William Bedell was baptized."

This daughter died unmarried at the age of twenty-eight. The following is the entry of her burial in the P. R. of Rattlesden:—

"1671, December 22. Mrs Leah, daught^r to Mr Wm Bedell, ye late Rector of this par^h, buried.

II. William. The following is the entry of his baptism in the P. R. of Rattlesden:—

"1645, February 22. William, the sonne of William Bedell and his wife, baptized."

When he grew up William was sent to Ireland to the care of his uncle Ambrose, whose heir presumptive he was, for his university education. The following is the record of his entrance as a Fellow Commoner at Trinity College, Dublin: " 26 Maii 1662, Gul^s

Mr. Watkinson of Staunton's, who obligingly permitted me to look through it, I found under the year 1670 a "Mr. Bedle" rated at sixteen shillings and eight pence. I have not found any later trace of Essex property being in possession of the family. The Bishop in his will refers to a property named "Whiteheads" belonging to himself, apparently in the parish of Black Notley. In the will of Mathew Elliston, or Alliston, of Castle Hedingham, the Bishop's uncle, dated Sept. 29, 1621, certain lands in the parish of Black Notley belonging to the Bishop's brother John, which the testator held in mortgage, are transferred to his second son John Alliston. This John Alliston, who was buried at Black Notley on the 15th October 1625, in his will proved at Braintree May 2, 1626, describes the said lands under the name of "Dewlands," and leaves them to one of his sons, unless they should be redeemed by John Bedel. John Alliston states that though the time for the redemption of the lands had already passed, his will, nevertheless, " is that if my said Cosen Bedel doe pay or cause to be payd unto mine executor the said sume of two hundreth pounds, the rent behind at the feast of the Annunciation of the Blessed Virgin Mary next coming, that then my said Cosen Bedel to have and injoy the said lands as in his former right."

* For the verification of this entry I am indebted to the kind courtesy of the Rector, the Rev. T. J. Steele.

Bedell Scholarium Commensalis filius Gulielmi Bedell Presbiteri natus annos sedccim. Natus Rattlesden in Comitatu Suffolciæ. Educatus in eodem Comitatu sub Magistro Coulson—(Tutor) Patricius Sheridan."

This Patrick, afterwards Bishop of Cloyne, was the second son of the Rev. Denis Sheridan, as above mentioned, p. 206.

Dr. Stokes, to whose kindness I am indebted for this extract, informs me that in the Record Book of entries there appear no names of Masters of Arts until 1672. As William Bedell was a Fellow Commoner he would be entitled to take the degree of M.A. in 1668, but of this there is no record, as at the time of the Revolution Trinity College was despoiled of many of its old documents. The William Bedell under notice is no doubt the William Bedell, M.A., who is mentioned in Archdeacon Cotton's Fasti Ecclesiæ Hibernicæ as Prebendary of Iniscattery or Kilrush, 1672, and who was the same year collated to the Prebend of Tullagh.*

William Bedell, M.A. was at the same time instituted in the vicarages of Kilballahone, Moyferta, Killmihill, and Killfieragh, all in the county of Clare.†

What became of Prebendary Bedell I have not ascertained. He probably died in 1674, the date of the avoidance of his benefices. There is no mention of him in his uncle Ambrose's will, nor in his brother James's will, which apparently refers to all the other members of the family living in 1682. There is no will of this William in the P. C. of Dublin.

III. John. The following is the entry of the baptism of this son in the P. R. of Rattlesden: 1648, July 9, John, the sonne of William Bedell and his wife, baptized.

In the list of Cambridge graduates there is a John Bedell, C. C., A.B. 1666, A.M. 1670. This was probably our John, who entered

---

* The Prebends of Iniscattery and of Tullagh are in the Diocese of Killaloe. The Bishop of Killaloe from 1669 to 1674 was Daniel Witter, previously Dean of Down. Dr. Witter was succeeded in his Deanery by Dr. William Sheridan.

† First Fruits Books, Record Office, Dublin.

the Church, and succeeded his father as Rector of Rattlesden. The following is the record of his presentation, extracted from Tanner's MS. in the Diocesan Registry of Norwich:—*

"Rattlesden.

"Lib. Reynolds. 24 Augt. 1671, Jōes Bedell, A.M. ad præs. Gul. Pooley, Arm."

The Parish Register of Rattlesden of 1671 is signed "Rector, Mr. John Bedell."

He died the following year, as appears from the entry of his burial:

"1672, Aug. 21. John Bedell, after he had been Rect^r of this parish a year or thereabouts, was buried."

I have not found that the Rev. John Bedell left a will.

IV. James. The following is the entry of the baptism of this son in the P. R. of Rattlesden:

"1651, March 30. James, the sonne of William Bedell and his wife, baptized."

I have not ascertained of what profession, if of any, James was. He died at the age of thirty-one. The following is the entry of his burial at Rattlesden in the P. R.:

"1682, Feb. 24. James, ye son of Mr. William Bedel, sometime Rector of this parish, and Mary his wife, was buryed."

The will of this James Bedell, dated December 28, 1682,† was proved in the Archidiaconal Court of Sudbury, at Bury St. Edmund's. In it he is described as "of Ratelsden, single man." James makes no mention of his brother William in his will, from which it is to be inferred, as above said, that William was then dead. I shall return to the provisions of James's will after quoting the entries of the baptism of his next brother, and of his three youngest sisters, the only members of the family living at the time he made his will.

* For procuring me this record of John Bedell's presentation to Rattlesden, and also for that of his father's presentation, as well as for the extract relating to his grandfather's presentation to Horninger, I am indebted to Mr. Cadge of Norwich.

† That is the December preceding February 1682-3.

V. Ambrose. In the P. R. of Rattlesden there are two entries relating to this son, one recording his birth, and one his baptism :—
"1653, February 5. Ambrose, the sonne of William Bedell and his wife, was born. February 19. Ambrose, the sonne of William Bedell and his wife, baptized."

VI. Penelope. The following is the entry of the baptism of this daughter in the P. R. of Rattlesden:—
"1656, October 12. Penelope, the daughter of William Bedell and his wife, baptized."

VII. Agnes. The following is the entry of the baptism of this daughter in the P. R. of Rattlesden :—
"1658, December 19. Agnes, daughter of William Bedell and his wife baptized."

VIII. Isabella. The following is the entry of the baptism of this daughter in the P. R. of Rattlesden:—
"1662, August 3. Isabella, ye daughter of William Bedell, Rector of this parish, baptized."

It is to be observed that Mrs. Mary Bedell, the mother, died the year after the birth of this daughter Isabella.

To return now to the provisions of James Bedell's will. To his brother Ambrose ("who liveth in the Kingdom of Ireland") he bequeaths his lands and other real property in the King's County. To his sister Agnes Bedell of Ratelsden he gives his real property in the County of Suffolk, including the "Grove," in his own occupation. To his other two sisters, Penelope and Isabella Bedell, in Ireland, he gives £50 each. His sister Agnes, to whom he gives the rest of his personalty, including his books at the time lying in the care of his "Uncle Barber," he appoints his sole executrix.

From this will we see that James Bedell, the elder surviving son of his father, in 1682 possessed lands and other real property in Ireland. This property may have been granted to the Rev. William Bedell in compensation for the losses sustained by his father the Bishop by the Rebellion. Or, it may have been acquired by James's eldest brother William, the Prebendary of Iniscattery, and, on his death, have come to James. It is not likely that James, himself resident in England, would have invested money in Irish property. However this may be, it is also seen that Ambrose, the youngest son of the Rev. William Bedell of Rattlesden, with his sisters Penelope and Isabella, had emigrated to Ireland, and were living there at the time their brother James made his will.

I have not been able to trace the history of Agnes Bedell who remained in Suffolk.

Before proceeding with the history of Ambrose, Penelope, and Isabella in Ireland, we have to recur to the will of Captain Ambrose Bedell. He devised his lands of inheritance known by the names of Carne and Listiernan, Dromheriffe and Uragh, Killerolyn with the two mills, Antner, Ardue, Clony, Clonachatige, and Creaghrahen, first to his nephew James Bedell and his heirs male; and failing such to his nephew Ambrose Bedell (James Bedell's next brother) and his heirs male; and, failing such, to his (the testator's) heirs next in blood to his father William, late Lord Bishop of Kilmore. The plate to go with the estate.

To his niece Isabella Bedell, the testator left 500*l.* to be paid out of the profits of his whole estate at the time of her marriage, and directed that until she is married 40*l.* a year be allowed her for her maintenance besides the 500*l.*

To his niece Agnes Bedell he gave 140*l.* to be raised out of his whole estate at the time of her marriage, and meanwhile 14*l.* a year.

To his "Cussin John Lowry and Penelope * his wife" he gave 250*l.* due upon Sir Charles Hamilton and his son Captain Francis Hamilton, with the deed of mortgage on the lands of Faransire, and on the land in the barony of Tullaghconcho.

James Bedell having died before his uncle, as above seen, his brother Ambrose Bedell succeeded to his uncle Ambrose's property.

Penelope Bedell was married in 1680 to John Lowry, vicar of Kinawly and Killinagh (1685), and afterwards (1704) of Arklow, in the co. Wicklow. Of this marriage there was a son named

* This was testator's niece Penelope.

Ambrose. Mrs. Penelope Lowry died in 1689. In 1721 the Rev. John Lowry and his son Ambrose, both ministers, were living at Callaghil near Belturbet.

Isabella Bedell was married, about 1689 or 1690, to Major Daniel French, and had a daughter Eleanor who married Mr. John Stanford of Belturbet. Major French died at the end of the year 1702.

Ambrose Bedell, who succeeded to his Uncle Ambrose's property, having joined the army of King William III. against James the Second, was attainted by King James's Irish Parliament of 1689. In the list of persons attainted in the county of Cavan, given in the Appendix to Archbishop King's " State of the Protestants of Ireland under King James's Government," Ambrose Bedell of Carndallan, Gent. appears.*

Ambrose Bedell, an officer, died in the camp at Dundalk in 1690, unmarried. He left a will, dated 1689, of which the following is the history:—

In 1721 the will had not been proved, but on April 6, 1693, administration of Mr. Ambrose Bedell's goods and chattels was granted at Dublin to Wm. Connolly, Esq. a principal creditor, on the supposition that Mr. Ambrose Bedell had died intestate. Mr. Connolly, the said administrator, gave 1,000*l.* security for administration.

The will of Mr. Ambrose Bedell remained in the hands of Richard Geering of Dublin, Esq. unproved. By the terms of his will Mr. Ambrose Bedell gave all his lands to his sister Isabella, the wife of Major Daniel French, and after her death to the next heir male of the name of Bedell. On the death of Mrs. Isabella French, which occurred some time between 1714 and 1721, the next heir male of the Bedell family was, in accordance with this provision, advertised for in the London Gazette, as follows: †—

* For reference to Abp. King's work I am indebted to C. S. K. in N. and Q. for June 18, 1870.

† Advertisement on the last page of the London Gazette, for Tuesday, April 12, to Saturday, April 16, 1721.

"Whereas Ambrose Bedell (incorrectly printed Bodell) formerly of Cairn in the county of Cavan and Kingdom of Ireland, Esq. by his last will did devise an estate in the said Kingdom to the heirs male of the name of Bedell under 30 years of age that should appear to be next in blood to William Bedell, sometime Rector of the parish of Ratlesden in Low Suffolk, in England, and to Mr. William Bedell, sometime Minister of Horningsheath in Essex (mistake for Suffolk), afterwards Provost of Trinity College, Dublin, and afterwards Bishop of Kilmore in Ireland, and to his heirs male for ever; therefore, if there be any person living entitled as aforesaid to the said estate, let him give notice thereof unto Richard Geering, Esq. one of the six Clerks in Chancery, in Dublin, in Ireland, or unto John Hamilton, Esq. of Castle Yard, in Holborn, London, and upon due proof of such his pedigree and qualification, his title to the said estate will be produced."

Mr. Thomas Bedell of Charles Square, Hoxton, London, the author of the MS. Genealogical Notes in the copy of Bishop Burnet's Life of Bishop Bedell,* above referred to at pp. 88, 89, 197, conceiving himself the next heir male of Bishop Bedell's family, made application in 1723 to Mr. Richard Geering, who, not being satisfied that Mr. Thomas Bedell had made out his pedigree and qualification, declined to produce the title.

Mr. John Stanford, who married Eleanor the daughter of Daniel and Isabella French, on the other hand, applied to Mr. R. Geering for surrender of the title deeds to him, but Mr. Geering declined. Whereupon Mr. Stanford, in right of his wife Eleanor, filed a Bill † against him. Mr. Richard Geering now acknowledged pos-

* This interesting volume was purchased by its present possessor of the late Mr. Lilly, the Bookseller, April 2, 1861.

† The Bill was filed in Chancery June 21, 1728, under the following title:—
John Stanford and Ellen his wife, the Rev. John Fletcher, Clerk, Mary his wife, and Susanna Britton, widow,
Plaintiffs;
Richard Geering, Thomas Bedell, Merchant, and Thomas Bedell Cooke,
Defendants.

session, and, July 18, 1729, deposited the title-deeds in the Court of Chancery. Mr. John Stanford and his wife Eleanor accordingly obtained the estate.

The Rev. John Lowry, the husband of Penelope, the elder sister and coheir of Mrs. Isabella French, in conjunction with his son Ambrose Lowry, had, in 1704, compounded, with Mrs. Isabella French, their claim for a consideration in money.

Mr. John Woodward Stanford, great-grandson in the third degree of Mrs. Isabella French, *née* Bedell, now enjoys the property.

In illustration of this history of William Bedell, Bishop of Kilmore, a tabular summary of the pedigree of his father's and mother's families is given in Appendix No. III. pp. 258-9.

CHAPTER XX.

Publication of the Old Testament in the Irish Language.

The translation of the Old Testament into Irish being completed, as above described in Chapter X., we have seen how Bishop Bedell's heart was set on its publication, but how he was thwarted, and how, like Moses, he was cut off without seeing the accomplishment of his cherished work. It was not until forty-three years after the Bishop's death that the Old Testament in Irish was published. The manuscript of the translation, which had been saved from the rebels by Mr. Denis Sheridan,* was by him committed to the care of Dr. Henry Jones, who, it will be remembered, was Dean of Kilmore at

* See Chapter XI. p. 188. In the text there is no mention of the manuscript of the Irish translation of the Old Testament having been saved from the rifling of the rebellion, nor is there any mention of it in Mr. Clogie's Memoir; and Isaak Walton (Reliquiæ Wottonianæ) says distinctly that the MS. was lost.

the time of the rebellion, but who was afterwards Bishop of Clogher, and latterly Bishop of Meath from 1661 till his death in 1681. With Dr. Jones the manuscript lay dormant, and was allowed to fall into the pitifully defaced and broken state in which Dr. Sall received it from him.

Dr. Andrew Sall, writing to the Hon. Robert Boyle,* from Christchurch in Oxford, December 17, 1678, says:—" I doubt not but it may conduce highly to the glory of God, good of those souls, and credit of our Government, if the other prelates and pastors of Ireland did use such endeavours as the good Archbishop of Cashell † does, by communing with the natives, and winning them to hear and read the Word of God, and specially if in the College (T. C. D.) there were a course taken for obliging or enticing candidates for holy orders to read and declare the Holy Scriptures in Irish, specially the New Testament, the historical and proverbial books of the Old, together with the old Psalms; of want of which I saw good men in both kingdoms give grievous complaints." In another letter to Mr. Boyle,‡ dated Dublin, May 20, 1680, Dr. Sall says:—" I conferred with my Lord Lieutenant, my Lord Bishop of Meath, and with the Provost of the College, upon the subject (of publishing a new edition of the New Testament in Irish), and I found all three very willing to countenance and further the matter . . . . . I find both my Lord Bishop of Meath and the Provost willing to continue the reading of it, and of Irish prayers in the College . . . . By preaching in Irish at Cashell and elsewhere, I will endeavour to prepare the way for the reading of your Irish Testament."

In a letter dated Dublin, August 4, 1680, to the Hon. Robert Boyle,§ Bishop Jones of Meath says:—" By Dr. Sall I understand,

* Letters from and to Mr. Boyle. In Dr. Thomas Birch's Life and Works of the Honourable Robert Boyle. Vol. v. folio, London, 1744, p. 603.

† Thomas Price, who had been Bishop Bedell's Archdeacon. See pp. 168, 201, 202, 213, 221.   ‡ Letters from and to Mr. Boyle, *ut supra*, p. 604.

§ Life of the Honourable Robert Boyle, *ut supra*. Appendix No. III. Letters relating to the edition of the Irish Bible, printed and distributed at the expense of Mr. Boyle.

Sir, your zeal for having this poor ignorant people, the *Irish*, informed in the true knowledge of God in their own language, by reprinting the New Testament and Common Prayer in Irish, these being now out of press, and the books of them extant hardly found. In addition whereunto is herein offered the publishing of the Old Testament also in Irish, together with the Psalms in metre fitted to our ordinary church tunes, translated by means and procurement of the learned and pious prelate Dr. Bedell, sometime Bishop of Kilmore in Ireland, and Provost of Trinity College in Dublin; whose heart God had stirred up thereunto zealously. This was by that learned Bishop himself compared with the original, and finished anno 1640; after whose death it came into mine hand, where it now continues in sheets and MSS. This compleating the Bible in Irish, and added to what is already printed, would be a work greatly to God's glory, in bringing by his grace many from darkness to light, and of deserved praise to the happy undertaker.

* * * * * *

"As for the Irish letters, stamped for the first printing here of the Common Prayer and New Testament, they had passed from hand to hand of many of His Majesty's printers in Dublin successively, until by coveteousness of one, into whose hands they fell, unhappily, they were by the Jesuits gotten away, and are now at Doway, for Irish prints; some of which I have seen to my grief sent hither, further corrupting the people. So as there is nothing left of what was formerly towards the printing of Irish here, if it should be required.

"I have dealt with our present Provost of the College of Dublin,* that he, according to what was sometimes by Dr. Bedell, his predecessor, practised, would encourage the reading Irish; and that Irish prayers, &c. as others, might be publicly used in the College for thereby fitting out labourers for that harvest of souls which may, by God's blessing such endeavours, be hopefully expected. But even for that are books wanting, or not sufficient to

* Dr. Narcissus Marsh.

be found for it. Therefore the reprinting what is now out of press, if there be no more, will be for that good work necessary."

* * * * * *

In another letter to Mr. Boyle,* dated September 3, 1681, Bishop Jones of Meath says:—" I am surprised in missing, in that our Common Prayer-book in Irish, the vulgar translation of the Psalms, which until now I never observed; it having been a strange omission that the Psalms, of such daily use in reading, should have been neglected. But I suppose that what of the Psalms we have in the body of the Old Testament in the Irish MS. (which I have) may supply that want, although it be not according to the vulgar, and may be added in the Common Prayer-book as the other.

* * * * * *

" I understand by Dr. Sall and others versed in the Irish, that it may be necessary that the Irish version of the Old Testament in MS. should be first revised before it be exposed to public view."

Mr. Boyle, in answer to the Bishop of Meath's observation as to the absence of the reading Psalms in the Irish Common Prayer-book, says:—" But perhaps it will not be for the worse, since it will be necessary to supply that omission out of your Irish Old Testament, in which it is hard if the Psalms be not better translated out of the original than if they had been out of the vulgate."

The Bishop of Meath, writing from Dublin, November 5, 1681, to Mr. Boyle, says:—" I shall forthwith put into his (Dr. Sall's) hand the Irish Old Testament in manuscript, to be by him revised."

Writing again to Mr. Boyle † from Dublin on the 8th of November, 1681, Dr. Andrew Sall says:—" I am daily and long time expecting the Old Testament in Irish to be sent to me to see what it is, and what it wants, that I may contribute my small endeavour, while those few live who have any zeal of the conversion of the natives here." In another letter to Mr. Boyle,‡ dated Dublin, De-

---

* Life, *ut supra*.   † Works, *ut supra*, vol. v. p. 605.
‡ Ibid. p. 606.

cember 13, 1681, Dr. Sall says:—" Some ten days ago, my Lord Bishop of Meath sent me the manuscript of the Old Testament in Irish, a confused heap, pitifully defaced and broken. It was a work of very great labour to bring it into some order. I sent for a bookbinder to bind up what I could gather, of which and another uncouth bulk, sent to me from the College, I hope to make up a complete Old Testament, by the help of Mr. Higgins the Irish lecturer, if he be encouraged by our Prelates, wherein I wish they may be more zealous than accustomed to be. It will be a work of great labour and no little time to draw up a clear copy of the whole, purged from errors and foolish additions or alterations, interlaced by some unlucky corrector, pretending to criticism in Irish."

Dr. Andrew Sall to Mr. Boyle,* Dublin, February 7, 1681-2, says:—" As soon as I received yours of January 21, I bestirred myself, with all care possible, to effect your pious desire of having the printing of the Old Testament in Irish to begin speedily, and having found out haply a very able person to write Irish, I brought him to my house, and set him to work, and already he has written out eight chapters of Genesis, in a very fair letter, as legible as any print, and within four days will have the twelve sheets, which Mr. Rely desires to be sent over, and as fast as the print can go I hope to send over sheets in the same manner.". . . In superintending the preparation of the transcript, Dr. Sall continues:—" My labour and industry I will not spare, and will lay aside other studies I was engaged in to attend this work, being persuaded that none other can be of more importance for the glory of God and the good of souls in this poor country."

The funds for the publication of the Old Testament in Irish were to be raised by subscription, and Bishop Jones of Meath exerted himself in procuring them. Mr. Boyle put 50*l*. at his disposal for the purpose. Bishop Jones, however, dying, his successor Dr. Anthony Dopping (previously Bishop of Kildare) undertook the

* Ibid. p. 607.

charge of the business. In a letter to Mr. Boyle, dated August 3, 1682, Bishop Dopping* of Meath says:—"As for the design on foot about the Irish Old Testament, it goes on, though by slow and leisurely steps; but I doubt not within a small time to procure (from some well-affected persons to the work) such subscriptions as may add a little more of life and briskness to the undertaking."

In regard to Dr. Dopping, the successor of Dr. H. Jones as Bishop of Meath, Dr. Sall in his letter of February 7, says:—" He is the only man, his predecessor a little before his death told me, he had gained to join with him in this work." It will be seen below, however, that the new Bishop of Meath was not steadfast in his support of the cause.

To return to Dr. Sall: " What I can offer," continues he, " is the drudgery of inspecting and correcting this confused chaos of papers put into my hands, with such auxiliaries as God shall be pleased to provide for me . . . . . I write a letter to Mr. Rely, in which I endeavour to encourage him for continuing the work of correcting the print, as I hope you will more effectually do by your authority; and truly I know none so able as he to do that work."

In a letter to Mr. Boyle,† dated April 8, 1682, Dr. Narcissus Marsh, then Provost of Trinity College, Dublin, says:—" The design of printing the Old Testament in the Irish language has received a great (though I hope not a fatal) stroke by the death of Dr. Sall, who departed this life April 5, in the evening. I intend that the revising of that old translation of the Old Testament and its transcription shall nevertheless go on with the help of Mr. Higgins and some other Irishmen whom I will call in to assist, if I can but discern that by God's help I may be able to guide and direct the management of the work, what pains soever it may cost me. And for subscriptions, I doubt not but enough might be easily gotten to so pious an undertaking, were it put into a due method." Dr. Narcissus Marsh again writing to Mr. Boyle ‡ from Dublin, June 23, 1682, says:—

* Appendix to Life, *ut supra*. † Works, *ut supra*, vol. v. p. 610.
‡ Ibid. p. 610.

"Since Dr. Sall's death I have taken upon me the care to see the Irish Bible transcribed and fitted for the press. The work goes on successfully, there being above a hundred and forty sheets transcribed already. All our care at present is, how to get the charges of transcribing and printing it to be defrayed, which must be done by subscription.". . . . "Mr. Higgins having gotten a good preferment," Dr. N. Marsh continues, " has put himself out of a capacity of being further serviceable towards the carrying on my design of teaching Irish in the College, by getting him a wife as soon as he had gotten himself preferment, so that 'he is very shortly leaving, and I must be at new charges to provide another to supply his place."

In another letter to Mr. Boyle,* dated Dublin, September 30, 1682, Dr. N. Marsh says:—" Lately understanding that my Lord Archbishop of Canterbury was very solicitous to know what is become of Bishop Bedell's Translation of the Old Testament into Irish, (because he is now about to write his Life,) and it being the copy that I have, I gave his Grace an account where it is and what is doing with it, and likewise that through your care, as well as at your present charges, it is begun to be printed." . . . . " I have ready transcribed as far as Ezra."

Again, Dr. N. Marsh to Mr. Boyle,† Dublin, February 17, 1682-3, says:—" The transcriber goes on with his work, having written as far as the end of Jeremiah's prophecy."

* * * * * *

" What Mr. Rely objects against the Irish translation, that it follows the English too much word for word, whereby the phrase many times is rendered less proper and more obscure, is confessed by those who well understand the language to have much of truth in it, as to the first part of the allegation; but they add that, though the Irish thereby may be less elegant, yet it is proper enough, and never the less intelligible by the vulgar people; yea, they think it

---

* Works, *ut supra*, vol. v. p. 612.   † Works, *ut supra*, vol. v. p. 612.

is a good, plain, familiar translation, and that if it were more elegant it would not be so fit as now it is for common use." . . . . . " The translation, I conceive, ought not lightly to be altered but where it is faulty, out of respect to the author of it, Bishop Bedell, whose memory I know that my Lord Archbishop of Canterbury does honour, and with what care he caused it to be made by Ulster men is sufficiently known."

Dr. Narcissus Marsh, now Bishop of Ferns and Leighlin, writing in conclusion of the subject to Mr. Boyle,* from Staplestown, on March 22, 1685-6, says:—" Upon the hint in your letter of my Lord Lieutenant's favourable thoughts of this design of publishing the Bible in the Irish tongue, I made bold to address to his Excellency about it (and that the rather because I have gotten a great deal of ill-will from some great men in this Kingdom for what I have done in promoting this good and charitable work, which has been no small discouragement to me). His Excellency was pleased to promise his encouragement and assistance towards the carrying it on, both by his purse and otherwise, but withall was surprised to hear what I related of the discouragements (and indeed threats †) that I have had on this account. The unwelcomeness of this undertaking to many in this country, I believe, was the reason why the Bishop of Meath (Dr. Dopping) flew off from prosecuting what he designed and promised, and has ever since been wholly unconcerned and sat neuter." . . . " The great charges and care that you have been at in printing the Old Testament will, I hope, find that acknowledgment, and the pious work find that acceptance amongst the generality of this Kingdom, as they really do deserve; and that a means will yet be found out to commit the Book of Common Prayer in the Irish tongue to the press also ; that so the design of the Canons of this Church, which require every

* Works, *ut supra*, vol. v. p. 614.

† What Dr. Narcissus Marsh here refers to was the utterance of the Lord Primate Boyle, then Lord Chancellor, and others, to the effect " that there was an Act of Parliament for abolishing the Irish language ; but that Dr. Marsh endeavoured to propagate it, for which he might be questioned in Parliament."

parish to have the Bible and Book of Common Prayer in Irish, may be answered."

At last, in the year 1685, the Old Testament in Irish was published in quarto, uniform with the new edition of the Irish New Testament which had been brought out in 1681. And thus was Ireland supplied with a complete version of the Holy Scriptures in the native language.

The Honourable Robert Boyle, in promoting the publication of the whole Bible in Irish with his influence and purse, so far made some return for the rich possessions which his family had acquired in Ireland ; and for this, as well as for his scientific labours, he is entitled to grateful remembrance. As the real labourers in the work, Archbishop Price of Cashel, Dr. Andrew Sall of Cashel, and Archbishop Marsh of Armagh, here deserve a special notice.

Thomas Price was Archdeacon of Kilmore in the time of Bedell, as we have seen. He was afterwards made Bishop of Kildare, and in 1667 was translated to the Archbishopric of Cashel. Having been trained under Bishop Bedell, he took great pains to instruct the native Irish in religion through the means of their own language. He died on the 4th of August, 1685, aged 85.

Andrew Sall was brought up a Roman Catholic, became a member of the Society of Jesus, and was for many years a Professor in in Spain. In 1664 he returned to Ireland as Superior of the Jesuits' Mission. Under the auspices of Archbishop Price he was led in 1674 to abjure popery, and on the 5th of June in that year he preached in Christ's Church, Dublin, declaring the reasons of his change. He was D.D. of T. C. D. and of Oxford. His preferments in the Established Church were the Prebend of Swords, the Rectory of Ardmulchan, and the Chancellorship of Cashel. He died at Cashel while revising the Irish translation of the Old Testament, as we have seen, on the 6th of April, 1682, aged about 70.

Narcissus Marsh, educated at Oxford, was the founder of the library in Dublin which bears his name. Seeing the efforts made

by Archbishop Price, above referred to, he was led, while Provost of Trinity College, Dublin, to use all his exertions towards encouraging the study of the Irish language among the scholars of that house. Provost Marsh was made Bishop of Ferns in 1683, Archbishop of Cashel in 1691, Archbishop of Dublin in 1694, and lastly Archbishop of Armagh in 1703.
He died in 1713, aged 75.

On learning that the language of the Highlanders of Scotland was similar to the Irish, and that they had neither Bibles nor Catechisms in their own language, Mr. Boyle sent a number of copies of the Irish Bible into Scotland, where they were most gladly received.* The following extract from a letter, dated March 5, 1687-8, written by Mr. Boyle to Mr. Kirkwood, gives some interesting particulars relative to the distribution of the Irish Bible both in Ireland and in Scotland :—" In the publication of the Irish Bible, my aim at first was, as I thought it became me to do some service to the country wherein I was born and have some little estate, though I have lived a great stranger to it; and especially to contribute to the conversion and instruction of those Irish natives that are most of them of the Romish religion. In pursuit of this design, I, with much ado, procured a version of the New Testament, made, as I remember in [1602]; and finding it to have been many years out of print, the copies having, as I have been informed, been bought up from time to time by some Romish ecclesiasticks, I caused a font of Irish letters to be cast, and the book to be here reprinted, of which I sent over some hundreds ready bound, to be distributed gratis among those to whom they should upon the place be judged the most likely to do good. These things I relate that you may not think it strange that I have not still by me any number of New Testaments in Irish, though I should not have so much disfurnished

* Life of the Hon. Robert Boyle, *ut supra*. Appendix No. iv. Letters and Papers relating to the distributing of the Irish Bibles in the Highlands of Scotland, at the expense of Mr. Boyle.

myself of them if I had been so informed, as now I am, that this language is still that of a great part of the North of Scotland. And my main design being, as I said above, to acquaint the native Irish with the Divine oracles, as soon as I had with the same characters caused an edition to be made of an Irish version of the Old Testament, which the excellent Bishop Bedell had long ago procured, and which, after the lately mentioned publication of the New Testament, divers of the reverend Protestant Clergy in Ireland, besides some worthy Prelates, intended to promote, but by various occurrences were hindered from accomplishing their good desires—as soon, I say, as the press had despatched this book—I sent a competent number of these books into Ireland to be distributed gratis by some pious and judicious persons there. By all which particulars you may easily discern that it was not, nor well could be, my principal design to provide for the Highlanders and other natives in Scotland that speak Irish; and that it never was my purpose that any of those that were printed at my charge should be set to sale. But yet, because it were great pity that the pious intentions and endeavours of your reverend ministers should be altogether disappointed, I shall acquaint you with what comes into my mind about it. Before I well knew the great extent of the Irish language in Scotland, I had caused several Old Testaments to be bound for the use of your nation, divers of which remain yet in my hands, so that, as to the one-and-thirty you mention, I can spare each of them a book, which I think you very discreetly advise should not be disposed of by the minister at his death, or removed, but be kept for the use of the parish. . . . . . I shall also send an hundred more unbound . . . .
With Irish New Testaments I formerly told you that I was not furnished, and I did not think fit to reprint them with the Old.
. . . . But, having caused inquiry to be made, I am informed that a bookseller, having with my leave printed a somewhat greater number of New Testaments than I had contracted for, he has yet in his hands about fifty Old Testaments, and about one hundred and fifty New ones. He can afford each whole Bible for a mark,

INTRODUCTION OF THE IRISH BIBLE INTO SCOTLAND. 251

provided the whole fifty be taken off his hands; and for the supernumerary hundred or thereabouts of New Testaments he can part with them at three shillings apiece in quires."

The Irish translation of the Scriptures, thus introduced into Scotland, was eventually superseded by a translation into the vernacular Gaelic. I am favoured by that eminent Gaelic scholar the Rev. Dr. M. Mackay, of Portobello, with the following short historical notice of the edition of the Irish Bible in a modified form which was long in use among Scotch-Gaelic readers, and of the subsequent publication of the pure Gaelic version.

The Irish character not being in use in Scotland, the Highlanders experienced some difficulty in reading the words in the Irish Bibles sent to them by the Hon. Robert Boyle from London, though they could understand the language, when decyphered, sufficiently well. It therefore became a desideratum to have an edition printed in the Roman character. Accordingly the Rev. Robert Kirke, then Minister of the Scottish Episcopal Church at Aberfoyle, and afterwards at Balquidder in Perthshire (author of the first metrical version of the Psalms in Gaelic), was employed to go to London to superintend the printing in Roman type of an edition of the Bible in Irish, comprising Archbishop Daniel's or O'Donell's New Testament and Bishop Bedell's Old Testament. In thus reprinting the Bible in Irish, the opportunity was taken to substitute, to some extent, Gaelic idioms for such Irish idioms as were not quite intelligible to the Scotch Highlanders. This edition of the Irish Bible by the Rev. Robert Kirke was published in 1690, and continued to be for a lengthened period the only Celtic version of the Scriptures to be found in the Highlands and Islands of Scotland.

In 1767 the Society for Propagating Christian Knowledge published a translation of the New Testament into pure Scotch Gaelic, and subsequently a translation of the Old Testament also. Several successive editions of this version of the whole Scriptures in Gaelic were published under the sanction of the General Assembly of the

Kirk of Scotland down to the year 1826, when a revised edition was brought out (in quarto) by the Society above-named. The revision was conducted by a committee consisting of several ministers in the Highlands, men of known classical learning, and this version of the Holy Scriptures is now considered as the standard of Gaelic orthographical correctness.

253

APPENDIX No. I.

I have been favoured by B. Beedham, Esq. of Ashfield House, Kimbolton, with the copy of a letter to Sir Nathaniel Riche, in which Bedell gives a graphic account of his first entrance on the duties of Provost of Trinity College, Dublin. The original letter is in the possession of the Duke of Manchester at Kimbolton Castle, and the transcript was made with his Grace's permission, some twelve years ago, by Mr. Beedham himself, who at the same time had leave to print it.

The appropriate place for this interesting letter, which has hitherto lain inedited, would have been in Chapter VI., page 143, but, the document not having been received in time, it finds a place here as Appendix No. 1.

The connection of the Montagu family with that of Riche, it may be observed, was by the marriage of Edward, second Earl of Manchester, with Anne, daughter of Robert, second Earl of Warwick, of the Riche creation.

The patronage of the Rectory of South Runcton, and of the Chapelry of Holme, co. Norfolk, was in the Riche family, and it may have been through Bedell's friendship with them that his cousin Dr. Joseph Alliston (p. 99) was in 1614 presented to these benefices. (See Blomfield's History of Norfolk, 8vo vol. vii.) It may, however, on the other hand, have been that Bedell became acquainted with the Riche family through Dr. Alliston.

Salutem in Chr'o Jesu.

S^r,

I am retourned from Dublin vpon Michaelmas day, whether I set forth vpon St. James day. My iorney I thanck God was prosperous, as farre as hitherto I can judge of it, if the vndertaking a place of y^t charge and burthen aboue my strength do not oppresse and crush me. At my comming I p^{r}sented my selfe to my Lord Deputy, by whom I was graciously vsed. The next day came to me M{r} Ussher, who was elected by y{e} junior fellowes, wishing me to be advised ere I entered a place whereto he had right ; He douted not but when His Ma{ty} should be informed he would administer indifferent justice to all his subjects, ec. I could not get of him the grownds of his p{r}tension, nor perswade him to goe w{t} me to Drogheda to my L. Primates, whether I went y{o} next day, & communicated with him of all Things. He to the point of M{r} Usher sayd he was sorry he would not be advised by his friends : wished me to proceede ec. I retourned, & having pervsed the Statutes, went to the Colledge, & took y{e} oath, yet w{t} Protestatiō y{t} I entended not to binde my selfe to every clause and phrase in the Statutes, but to the Substance : & where y{e} Provost might not hold any Benefice, except it were w{t} in three miles of Dublin, I did not intend presently to give over my Benefice, in as much as the place was litigious, & my family & affayres in England vnsettled, but would do it when w{t} conveniency I might. Thence forward, having taken vpō me y{e} place, I endeavoured to sow vp the rent betweene y{e} fellowes, & to y{t} end appointed a Communiō y{o} next Sonday (A Thing intermitted these 11 years). Then ordered the members of o{r} governing Senate, I meane y{e} Seniors; removing (as by o{r} charter we were bound) such as by tyme after their Degree of M{r} of Arts were to be removed. Next we chose officers, gave graces in the house for Degrees, reformed some abuses in the Chappell & Hall: as y{e} Evening Prayers were in the Hall, & Philosophical Acts in the Chappell. But my next care was about the Statutes, which, being part Latin, part English, & in sheetes of Paper, some stich'd together, some loose, a heape w{t}out order, w{t} long p{r}ambles, and sometyme vnnecessary, & in many thinges defective: w{t} the cōsent of y{e} greater part of the Seniors, I digested into a new forme, and and (*sic*) at last perfected, as I hope, & published in the Chappell. The state of the Colledge in respect of the Revenew and Treasure should have been the thing I would next have entered into consideratiō of. But it required a long tyme. And this, in short, I fownd, there was not money enough in the chest to pay y{e} Commons and the stipends when y{e} day should come. I consigned all the Bookes of former accounts into the handes of the Vice-Provost (M{r} Lloyd) and the Auditor (S{r} James Ware), desiring him to set me downe the Estate of the Colledge, especially in respect of Areares. Which hitherto he sayd he could never doe, in as much as he had not so much as a Rentall of the College revenewe, but had made vp every yeares account only out of what was taken out of the chest and disbursed. Wherein notw^{t}standing sundry Bursars had left in their hands large summes of the Colledge money, never satisfied. And to mend the matter a custome was brought in of giving to the Senior Fellowes at ther departing a *Viaticum* as they call it. Which also was demanded by those Fellows who now left their places. But to these Viaticums I have I hope given a Viaticum. And whenever I shall retorne to the house I hope to looke a litle better to the Accounts: & if it be possible to recover some of those hundreds wch I doe already by a superficiall view perceive are vnjustly w^{t}helde frō the Colledge, partly received & never accounted; partly lent (as is p^{r}tended) but w^{t}out assent of the greater part of ye Seniors; partly lent indeede, but never repayed; & as it is now hoped to be granted for a Viaticum to the form^r Provost. S^r, you may by this wch I have in short run over, conceive what a world of busines I am put into: yet I repent me not of my iorney, though I have not had there one houre voyd of paines, trouble, or thought, nor do looke to have when I shall retourne, for many moneths. But if I shalbe able to setle the Colledge in a good state, for their maners, lawes, revenew, & studies, whereof in respect of many difficulties in each I have great reason to doubt, yet, the state of ye country considered, now wholely assubjected to Romish superstition, &, as it seemes, in respect of religion, even abandoned by those y^t should have the care & charge of it, I have little hope euer to have comfortable day there. Vnlesse w^t the Ap'le I could rejoice in labours & troubles, & euen to be offered vp on the sacrifice & service of ye faith of God's people; which I do some tymes wish, & have some comfort I confesse euen in y^t very wishing. But I should enter into a Sea to goe about to relate vnto y^u the p^{r}sent state of religio' in Ireland. Your selfe I beleeve would scarce beleeve it possible y^t in a few yeares since y^r being there it should receive such a headlong downefall. I shall reserve y^t to o^r meeting, which shalbe I hope ere long, when I shall receive the Colledge, & my Lord Primates letters, or advice y^t they are in London for me. At wch tyme also I hope to make my excuse & satisfaction for my not seeing my Lord of Canterbury at my parting, being in truth required by my L. Primate to repair to Dublin w^t *all possible speede*. I hope y^u have in part made my excuse, & on any occasiō will further doe it. Meane while desiring y^u to remember my [hum]ble service to the Earle of Warwick, my ever honoured Lord, I committ y^u to the protection of o^r good God, & rest,

S^r,
Yours ever in Christ to be commanded,
W. BEDELL.

Horningerth, October the 9th, 1627.

Indorsed: To the Worsh^ll and my Very good friend Sr Nathaneell Riche at Warwick House d^r these in London.

APPENDIX No. II.

In the Cotton MS. Julius, C. III. (British Museum), there is an original letter from Bedell to Sir Robert Cotton from which the following extract is here given as an addition to the note at pp. 193-4, respecting Ricemarch's Psalter. It may be here observed that "the manuscript Psalter in the Irish letter," which Bedell, writing to Ussher, August 12, 1628 (p. 145), asks to have the use of, was no doubt his own Ricemarcus' Psalter, which, from this letter to Sir Robert Cotton, it is seen Bedell had lent Ussher. The Rev. Dr. Reeves suggests that, the book having again been lent to Abp. Ussher, it was in that Prelate's library at the time of the Rebellion, and thus escaped destruction. Finally, by Bedell's will, use was converted into possession.

Sir Robert Cotton was educated at Trinity College, Cambridge, and being only about a year or two older than Bedell the two had no doubt become acquainted at the University.

Salutem in Chr'o Jesu.

S^r,
I received this other day by Sr E. Askew a note from you, wherein you claime a promise of me of the Psalter of David written by Ricemarcus in ye Irish hand, and a Roll of the Evidences of Bury Abbey. For the

former of them it is yet in the hands of my L. Primate of Armagh, to whom I sent it by Dr. Warde while he was here in England, and, at my being w^t him at Drogheda this summer, he told me he did esteeme it even for the translatiō's sake (being not the Vulgar, but according to ye Hebrew Verity). And in truth, S^r, besides ye use y^t I conceived he had of the Tables and Kalender in the begin'ing, being in hand w^t something about the Ecclesiastical Compt, that poore Kingdome as I am perswaded may have special use of it in ye new translatiō of ye Psalter, wch may be well countenanced w^t a monum^t of y^t antiquity, justifying the not resting in ye Vulgar, even by ye opinion of those tymes. (Here follow observations respecting the " Roll of the Evidences of Bury Abbey.")

Your affectionate frend and servant,
W. BEDELL.

Horningerth, near Bury, Decem. 10, 1627.
To Sir Robert Cotton.

APPENDIX No. III.

PEDIGREE OF THE BEDELL AND ELLISTON FAMILIES OF ESSEX.

Thomas Bedyll, of=Johan. Black Notley, will dated 1550.

...... Aliston or Elliston.

John Bedell, of=Elizabeth Elliston or Aliston, died in March 1623-4. Black Notley, co. Essex; d. in 1600.

Mathew Elliston or=Anna Whighte, mar. in 1570, died in 1597. Aliston, of Castle Hedingham, co. Essex; d. in 1625.

WILLIAM BEDELL,=Leah, dau. of John Bowles, and relict of Robt. Mawe, married in 1611-12; died in 1638, aged 57. 2nd surviving son, and only son who left issue. Died Bishop of Kilmore in 1641-2, aged 70.

John Elliston or Alliston,=Alice, dau. of Thos. Pilgrim, of Halstead, co. Essex. of Guestingthorpe and Black Notley, co. Essex; second son, and the only one of six of whom descendants are known to exist; died 1625, aged 52.

Grace, b.1614, died 1624; bur. at Hornings-hearth.

John, born 1616, died 1635, bur. at Kilmore.

Ambrose, born 1618, a Captain in the army in Ireland; married Mary Hill, daughter of Peter Hill, eldest son of Sir Moyses Hill. Died in 1683, s. p.

Peter Elliston, Rector=Mary Fuller, dau. of Richd. Fuller, of Heathfield, co. Sussex; died in 1712, aged 94.ᵈ of Sandhurst, co. Kent, sixth son, and the only one of seven of whom descendants are known to exist; d. 1660.ᵉ

William Bedell, born Feb.=Mary (Barber?) died at Rattlesden in 1663. 1612-13. Was instituted vicar of Kinawley in the Diocese of Kilmore in 1634, died Rector of Rattlesden, co. Suffolk, in 1670.

John Elliston of West=Elizabeth ...., died in 1711. Malling, eldest son and the only child of whom descendants are known to exist; born in 1648, died in 1707-8.

William, b. 1645, Prebendary of Inniscattery and Tullagh, ob. s. p. John, born 1648, died Rector of Rattlesden in 1672, s. p. James, b. 1651, d. 1682-3, unmarried. Ambrose, born 1653-4, d. unmar. in 1690, in the army of K. William III. at Dundalk.

Leah, born 1643, died 1671 unmar. Penelope b. 1656, mar. in 1680 the Rev. John Lowry, of Arklow, and had a son Ambrose. She died in 1689. Agnes, b. 1658.

Isabella, born 1662, mar. about 1689 or 1690, died between 1714 and 1721.

=Major Daniel French, of Belturbet, died in 1702.

Martha El-=Richard Philips, of Great Queen Street, Lincoln's-Inn-Fields, portrait painter, b. 1680, second son of Charles Philips, of Chesham, co. Bucks, who was eldest son of Charles Philips of Nashleigh, parish of Chesham. Richard Philips was the only child of his father who had issue; died in 1741 in Great Queen Street, Lincoln's-Inn-Fields.ᵉ liston, 3rd dau. born 1683, m. in 1702. The only one of the Elliston family of whom descendants are known to exist; died in 1743.

PEDIGREE OF THE BEDELL AND ELLISTON FAMILIES.

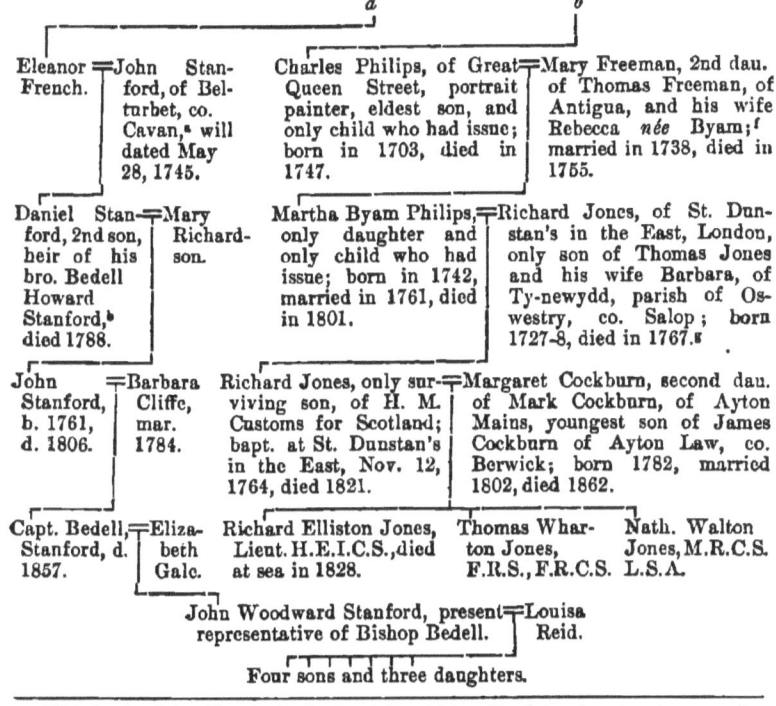

```
         a                                           b
         |                                           |
 ┌───────┴───────┐                        ┌──────────┴──────────┐
Eleanor =John Stan-   Charles Philips, of Great=Mary Freeman, 2nd dau.
French. | ford, of Bel-  Queen Street, portrait | of Thomas Freeman, of
        | turbet, co.    painter, eldest son, and| Antigua, and his wife
        | Cavan,ᵃ will   only child who had issue;| Rebecca née Byam;ᶠ
        | dated May      born in 1703, died in   | married in 1738, died in
        | 28, 1745.      1747.                   | 1755.

Daniel Stan-=Mary      Martha Byam Philips,=Richard Jones, of St. Dun-
ford, 2nd son,| Richard- only daughter and  | stan's in the East, London,
heir of his   | son.    only child who had  | only son of Thomas Jones
bro. Bedell   |         issue; born in 1742,| and his wife Barbara, of
Howard        |         married in 1761, died| Ty-newydd, parish of Os-
Stanford,ᵇ    |         in 1801.            | westry, co. Salop; born
died 1788.    |                             | 1727-8, died in 1767.ᵍ

John      =Barbara   Richard Jones, only sur-=Margaret Cockburn, second dau.
Stanford, | Cliffe,  viving son, of H. M.    | of Mark Cockburn, of Ayton
b. 1761,  | mar.     Customs for Scotland;   | Mains, youngest son of James
d. 1806.  | 1784.    bapt. at St. Dunstan's  | Cockburn of Ayton Law, co.
          |          in the East, Nov. 12,   | Berwick; born 1782, married
          |          1764, died 1821.        | 1802, died 1862.

Capt. Bedell,=Eliza-  Richard Elliston Jones,  Thomas Whar-  Nath. Walton
Stanford, d. | beth   Lieut. H.E.I.C.S., died  ton Jones,    Jones, M.R.C.S.
1857.        | Gale.  at sea in 1828.          F.R.S.,F.R.C.S. L.S.A.

       John Woodward Stanford, present=Louisa
       representative of Bishop Bedell.| Reid.

           Four sons and three daughters.
```

ᵃ This is the John Stanford who in right of his wife claimed and got possession of the Bedell property.

ᵇ This had been the Mr. Bedell Stanford who communicated the anecdote of Mr. Edmund Ferrely's prayer at Bishop Bedell's funeral to the publisher of the Dublin Edition of Burnet's Life of Bedell, 1758. (See p. 195.)

ᶜ For obituary notice, see Calamy's Life and Times of Richard Baxter, under "Horsmonden" and "Sandhurst," in Kent.

ᵈ See Herald and Genealogist for 1870.

ᵉ For obituary notice, see "The London Daily Post and General Advertiser" Newspaper, for Thursday, Sept. 10, 1741. For obituary notice of his brother Nathaniel, also, see "The Public Advertiser" newspaper for Friday, May 20, 1757.

ᶠ See Pedigree of Byam of Antigua, in the College of Arms, and that of Freeman, Philips, and Jones, in connection therewith.

ᵍ For obituary notice, see Lloyd's Evening Post Newspaper, London, Feb. 25-27, 1767.

*** See Visitations of Essex, 1634 and 1664, for Elliston; also entry at the College of Arms, in 1868, of the pedigree of Alliston or Elliston, of Essex and Kent, and of Philipps of Chesham, Bucks, with that of Jones in continuation thereof.

INDEX.

Abbot, Archbishop of Canterbury, 24, 143
Aliston or Alliston, or Elliston, Bedell's mother's family name, 2, 86, 93
Alistone, Mathew, of Castle Hedingham, Bp. Bedell's mother's brother, 86, 87; his will, 233
Alliston, John, of Black Notley, Bedell's cousin, his will, 233
——— Dr. Joseph, rector of South Runcton, Bishop Bedell's cousin, 99, 104, 124, 130. 253; his will, 99
Alliston or Elliston, pedigree of, 86, 258
Ardagh, Bedell's resignation of the Bishopric of, 46, 156, 157
——— Dr. John Richardson made Bp. of, 159
——— improvement of the revenue of, under Bp. Richardson, 159
——— Bp. Richardson of, and the rebellion, 189
Ardfert, Bp. Fulwer of, and the rebellion, 188
Armagh, Abp. James Ussher of, and the rebellion, 188
——— see Ussher.
——— Abp. M. G. Beresford of, previously Bp. of Kilmore, erects the new Cathedral of Kilmore, 201
Arthur, the Christian name of, derived by the Duke of Wellington from his great-grandfather in the fourth degree, Col. Arthur Hill, 224, 225
Ash, Mr. Richard, registrar of Kilmore, 56
Augustine St., saying of, "Fruit, not leaves, I seek," 172
Authorship of this "Life and Death" of Bp. Bedell attributed to William, Bp. Bedell's eldest son, viii., 232.
Autograph initials of the Rev. Dr. Joseph Alliston, Fellow of Emmanuel College, Cambridge, 99
Autograph of Capt Ambrose Bedell, viii.
——— of Bedell, while resident in Venice, 104
——— while Provost of T.C.D. 146

Autograph while Bp. of Kilmore and Ardagh, 160
——— when Bp. of Kilmore alone, 160
——— of the Rev. William Bedell, the Bp.'s eldest son, 231
——— of the Rev. Alexander Clogie, 217

Bagshaw, Sir Edward, Bp. Bedell's proceedings against, for the recovery of episcopal lands, 155
Baldi, Ottavio, see Ottavio Baldi
Bayly, Mr. William, his unjust conduct to Mr. Murtach King, 163, 177-180
——— made Bp. of Clonfert, 180
Beast, the, number of, 115, 116
Bedell, Ambrose, his deposition respecting the sufferings and losses of his family in the rebellion, 221-224
——— in his will, directs that he be buried beside his father, 226
——— Captain, as one of the "Forty-nine officers," receives a grant of lands, 224, 225
——— his letter to Abp. Sancroft, vii.
——— the testamentary disposition of his property, 237
——— in conjunction with Archdeacon Price, holds out Croghan Castle against the rebels, 201, 202, 221
Bedell, Ambrose, junr., attainted by King James the Second's Parliament in Ireland, 238
——— dies in the camp of King William III. before Dundalk, 238
——— the history of his will, 238
Bedell, Bp., his correspondence with Laud, see Laud
——— his letters to Dr. Samuel Warde, x., 94, 102, 124, 127, 130, 149, 159, 160-1, 174
Bedell, Mrs. Elizabeth, the Bp.'s mother, her maiden name of Elliston, 2, 86, 93
——— her will, 87

INDEX.

Bedell, James, of Rattlesden, his will, 235, 6
Bedell, John, the Bishop's father, his will 87
——— John, the Bishop's second son, his death, 160
Bedell, John, the Bp.'s grandson, succeeds his father as Rector of Rattlesden, 234; his death, 235
Bedell, Mrs. Leah, her family by her first husband Robert Mawe, Esq., and family by Mr. Bedell, 129
Bedell, pedigree of, 258
Bedell, pronunciation and derivation of the name, 85
Bedell, Thomas, of Charles Square, Hoxton, claims to be heir-male of Bishop Bedell's family, 89, 197, 239; his MS. genealogical notes, 88, 89, 197
"Bedell's Statutes," T.C.D. 27, 145
Bedell, the Rev. Wlliam, his collation and induction to the Vicarage of Kinawley, 226, 227
——— and his family 226-232 et seq.
——— his letter to his godfather Dr. Samuel Warde, 229, 230, 231
——— his presentation to the Rectory of Rattlesden, 231
——— his visit to England in 1637, 228
Bedell, William, Prebendary of Iniscattery and Tullagh, 234
Belturbet, vi., 62, 258-9
Beresford, M. G., Abp. of Armagh, see Armagh and Kilmore
Bernard, Dr. Nicholas, his "Character of Bishop Bedell," 40, 147, 148
Bible in Gaelic, first publication of the, 251
Bible in Irish, publication of the, 175-181, 240
Birth and Parentage of Bp. Bedell, 1, 2, 85, 91, 92
Bishops of Ireland and the rebellion, 188, 189
Black Notley, 1, 85 et seq.
Boyle, Hon. Robert, publishes a new edition of Daniel's Irish New Testament and promotes the first publication of Bedell's Irish Old Testament, 248
Braintry or Braintree, William Bedell and his elder brother John attend the school of Mr. Denman at, 2, 92
Burnet, Gilbert, afterwards Bishop of Salisbury, supplied by the Rev. Alexander Clogie with the materials for his Life of Bp. Bedell, 217, 218, 219
Burnet and Clogie censured for their inaccuracies respecting Bp. Bedell, 186, 187, 219

Cambridge, Emmanuel College, Bedell's education at, 3 et seq; 93 et seq.
Canterbury, Abbot, Abp. of, 24, 143
Canterbury, Laud, Abp. of, see Laud
Canterbury, Sancroft, Abp. of, see Sancroft
Caraffa, the family of, 114
Caraffa, Fra. T. M., his Theses, 115
Carne Hill, the residence of Capt. Ambrose Bedell, vi., 225
Cashel, Abp. Hamilton of, and the rebellion, 188
Cashel, Thos. Price, Abp. of, formerly Archdeacon of Kilmore, forwards the publication of the Irish Old Testament, 248,
Cavan, 62
Chaderton, Dr., Master of Emmanuel College, Cambridge, 4, 94
Chancellor of the Dioceses of Kilmore and Ardagh, Mr. Alane Cook, Bishop Bedell's protracted litigation with, 34, 35, 36, 55, 56, 152, 155
——— his unjust jurisdiction, 32, 33, 151, 154
Charles I., his letter to the fellows of T. C. D., 146
——— Sir Henry Wotton's letter to, recommending Mr. Bedell for the Provostship of T. C. D., 25
Chirurgery, Mrs. Elizabeth Bedell, the Bishop's mother, famous and expert in, 2
Churches, Bp. Bedell's labours in repairing and building, 60
Clogher, Bp. Spottiswoode of, and the rebellion, 189
Clogie, the Rev. Alexander, his biography, 211-220
——— description of the person of Bp. Bedell by, 191
——— his first marriage to Miss Leah Mawe, 212
——— his letter to Abp. Sancroft, 216, 217
——— his family by his second marriage 215
Clogie and Burnet censured for their inaccuracy as to a connexion of Bp.

INDEX. 263

Bedell with the "Remonstrance" of the Rebels, 186, 187; and for other inaccuracies, 219
Clonfert and Kilmacduagh, Bp. Dawson of, and the rebellion, 188
Cloyne, Bp. Synge of, and the rebellion, 188
Condé, Prince of, his visit to Father Paulo in Venice, 139, 140
Contemporaries, College, Bedell's, 94-100
Convocation, Bedell chosen Member of, for Suffolk, 22, 23
Cooke, Mr. Alane, the Chancellor of the Dioceses of Kilmore and Ardagh, Bishop Bedell's protracted litigation with, 34, 35, 36, 55, 56, 152, 155; his unjust jurisdiction, 32, 33, 151, 154
Cork and Ross, Bp. Chappell of, and the rebellion, 188
Cotton, Sir Robert, Bedell's letter to, about Ricemarchus's Psalter, 256
Courts Ecclesiastical, extortions of the, Bishop Bedell labours to reform, 38, 39, 40, 42, 151-2-3-4-5-6
Craig, Sir James, of Croghan Castle, 181, 201, 221
Croghan Castle, held against the rebels by Ambrose Bedell and Archdeacon Price after Sir James Craig's death, 201, 202
Croghan and Keilagh Castles capitulate to the rebels, 202
Cumberland, Dr. Denison, Bishop of Kilmore, desires to be buried beside Bishop Bedell, 196

Daniel or O'Donell, Wm., Abp. of Tuam, translator of New Testament and Book of Common Prayer into Irish, 60, 175
Daru's Histoire de la Republique de Venise, 110
Deafness, the cause of Bp. Bedell's, 3
Death of Bishop Bedell, 79, 80, 81, 189
―――― of Bishop Bedell's wife Leah, 161
De Dominis, Archbishop of Spalato, 135, 136
―――― his dead body burnt, 136
Denman, Mr., William Bedell's schoolmaster at Braintry, or Braintree, a good teacher but harsh master, 2, 3, 92
Derry, Bp. Bramhall of, 174
―――― and the rebellion, 188

Despotine, Dr. Jasper, of Venice, makes the acquaintance of Bedell, 10, 12
―――― his adventure with the friar in Venice, 10, 11, 12
―――― accompanies Bedell on the return of the latter to England from Venice, 13, 124, 125
―――― is established in Bury St. Edmund's as a physician, and marries there, 13, 14, 125, 126, 128
―――― Sir Henry Wotton and, 126, 127
―――― an elder of the Presbyterian Church in Bury St. Edmund's, ix.
Diodati, John, 110, 111, 141, 142
Diodati family, the, 142
Diocesan Synod, 41, 162
Divines, the Seven, of Venice, and their tractate on the Papal Interdict, 108
Dodwell, Dr. Henry, his letter to Abp. Sancroft, vii.
Dopping, Dr. Anthony, Bp. of Meath, 174
―――― and Bedell's Irish Old Testament, 245, 247
Down and Connor, Bp. Leslie of, and the rebellion, 189
Dromore, Bp. Buckworth of, and the rebellion, 189
Drum Corr, Mr. Denis Sheridan's residence at, 189, 207
Dublin, Abp. Lancelot Bulkeley of, 56, 185
―――― and the rebellion, 188
Dublin, Trinity College near, Bedell Provost of, 23, 24, 25, 26, 27, 28, 142, 143, 144, 145
―――― Bedell's letter to Sir Nathaniel Riche on state of, 253

Education and entrance into Holy Orders, Bedell's, 3, 4, 5, 92, 93, 94
Elizabeth, Queen, recommends an Irish translation of the New Testament to be made, 171, 175
Elliston, or Alliston, Bedell's mother's family name, 2, 86, 93
―――― pedigree of, 86, 258; wills of, 99, 233
Elphin, Bp. Tilson of, and the rebellion, 188
Emmanuel College, Cambridge, Bedell's education at, 3 et seq., 93 et seq.
Estey, or Estye, the Rev. George, preacher at St. Mary's, Bury St. Edmund's, succeeded by Bedell, 7, 100
Extortions of the Court Ecclesiastical, 33,

34, 35, 36, 38, 39, 40, 42, 151, 152, 153, 154, 155

Falkland, the Lord Deputy, 26, 58
Family bereavements, Bp. Bedell's, 160, 161
Ferns and Leighlin, Bp. Andrews of, and the rebellion, 188
Fletcher, the Rev. Nathaniel, Sir Henry Wotton's first chaplain in Venice, 102
" Forty-nine Officers," Capt. Ambrose Bedell as one of the, receives a grant of lands, 224, 225
French, Major Daniel, marries Isabella Bedell, the youngest daughter of the Rev. William Bedell of Rattlesden, 238
" Fruit, not leaves, I seek," St. Augustine's saying, 172
Fulgentio, the Franciscan Friar of Venice, burnt at Rome for alleged heresy, 112, 113
Fulgentio, the Servite Friar of Venice, 108, 110, 111
Funeral of Bishop Bedell, 80, 81, 195

Gaelic Bible, first publication of the, 251
Griselini, his Life of Father Paulo, 106, 107, 123

Hall, Joseph, Bishop of Norwich, 97, 98, 196
Hamilton, Sir Francis, Bp. Bedell's proceedings against, for the recovery of episcopal lands, 155
Harley family of Brampton Bryan, 141, 217
Hickes, Dr. George, deprived Dean of Worcester, consecrated titular Bishop of Thetford by the deprived Bishops of Norwich, Peterborough, and Ely, xvii., 105
—— his strictures on Burnet's Life of Bedell, 105, 123, 134, 138, 139, 219
Hill, Colonel Arthur, 221, 224. The name Arthur derived from him by his descendant the late Duke of Wellington, 224, 225
—— Mary, only daughter of Peter, and grand-daughter of Sir Moyses Hill, wife of Capt. Ambrose Bedell, 221
—— Sir Moyses, and his family, 221
Holland, Earl of, and Sir Thomas Jermin, friends of Bedell, 57, 58
Horninger, see Horningshearth
Horningshearth, Sir Thomas Jermin presents Bedell to the Rectory of, 15, 16, 131
Horningshearth, Bedell's Incumbency of 16, 17, 18, 19, 20, 21, 22, 130
—— Bedell's literary labours during his incumbency of, 131-141
Hoyle, Dr. Joshua, 28

Illness, last, of Bishop Bedell, 78, 79, 189, 190, 191
Iniscattery and Tullagh, William Bedell (son of the Rev. William of Rattlesden), prebendary of, 234
Institution of a Christian in English and Irish, description of the book, 172, 173
Interdict, Papal, against Venice, 8, 101
—— tractate on the, by the Seven Divines, 108
—— History of the, by Father Paulo, 140
Ireland, Bedell's removal to, 23 et seq., 142, 143 et seq.
Irish language, Bp. Bedell's efforts to spread the Gospel through the medium of, 44, 45, 171 et seq.
—— translation of the New Testament into the, 175
—— translation of the Old Testament into the, 60, 61, 175-180, 240
Irish Old Testament, Bedell's, the publication of, obstructed and delayed, 175-181
—— MS. of, entrusted by Denis Sheridan to Henry Jones, Dean of Kilmore, and afterwards Bp. of Meath, 240, 242
—— eventual publication of, 240
Irish Rebellion of 1641, 65 et seq., 181 et seq.

James I, King, 8, 25
—— his " Apologie " and " Premonition," 25 ; presentation of, to the Doge of Venice, 117-123
—— autograph letter of, 121, 122
—— orders the Irish New Testament to be read in "the Parishes of the Irishrie," 175
James II. and Thomas Sheridan, 208, 209, 210
Jegon, Dr., Bishop of Norwich, Bedell refuses to pay the fees demanded by the officers of, 16
Jermin, Sir Thomas, friend and patron of Bedell, 15, 29, 58, 59, 143
—— presents Mr. Bedell to the Rectory of Gt. Horningshearth, 15, 16

Jews in Venice, Bedell's acquaintance with, 9
Jones, Henry, Dean of Kilmore, his narrative of the rebellion, 182
—— afterwards Bp. of Meath, and Bedell's Irish Old Testament, 240 *et seq.*

Keilagh Castle, held against the rebels by Sir Francis Hamilton, at last is surrendered to the rebels, 201, 202
Kildare, Bp. Ussher of, and the rebellion, 188
Kilfenora, Bp. Sibthorp of, and the rebellion, 188
Killala, Bishop Adair of, unjustly deprived, 52, 53, 54
—— alleged secret cause of the proceedings against, 180
Killala, Bp. John Maxwell of, and the rebellion, 188
Killaloe, Bp. Jones of, and the rebellion, 188
Kilmore and Ardagh, Bedell's elevation to the Bishoprics of, 29 *et seq.*, 147-150
Kilmore, Episcopal house of, 62; lines written on one of the windows of, by Dean Swift and Dr. Thomas Sheridan, 211
—— New Cathedral of, erected by Dr. M. G. Beresford, now Abp. of Armagh, 201
—— Dr. Swiney, Popish Bishop of, 71, 72, 91, 92, 187, 195
—— topographical description of, 62, 63
Kinawley, William Bedell collated to the vicarage of, 227
King, Rev. Murtach, employed in the work of translating the Old Testament into Irish, 61, 176, 180
—— articles against, 177
" King's Evil," Capt. Ambrose Bedell touched by the King for the, 225, 226
Kirke, Rev. Robert, supervises the printing of an edition of the Irish Scriptures in Roman type for use in Scotland, 251

Laud, Bp. of London and afterwards Abp. of Canterbury, Bedell's letters to, about the Chancellor, Mr. Alane Cook, 35, 151-154, 155 ; and Laud's reply, 154
—— his uncourteous letter to Bp.

Bedell about the petition of the Protestants of Cavan, 51
—— to Abp. Ussher on Bedell's resignation of the Provostship of T. C. D., 145, 146
—— Bedell's letter to, recommending a deputation of Fellows of T. C. D., 146
—— Bedell's letter to, about resigning the see of Ardagh and recommendation of Dr. Richardson, 156
—— Bedell's letter to, about the improvement of the revenue of the see of Ardagh under Bp. Richardson, 159
—— Bp. Bedell's letter to, in explanation of his Diocesan Synod, 170
—— Bp. Bedell's letter to, about the persecution of Mr. Murtach King, 177
—— letters on Popery in Ireland, from Bp. Bedell to him, and to the Lord Deputy Wentworth, read in the House of Lords at Laud's trial, 150
Lecasserio, James, Father Paulo's letter to, about King James's Book, 120
Limerick, Bp. Webb of, and the rebellion, 188
Loughoughter Castle, Bishop Bedell and sons imprisoned in, 73, 74, 187
—— liberation of Bp. Bedell and his sons from imprisonment in, 75, 76, 189
Lowry, the Rev. John, marries Penelope Bedell, third youngest daughter of the Rev. William Bedell, of Rattlesden, 237
Lucas, Wm. Esq., Bedell's suit with, for the recovery of lands belonging to the Rectory of Great Horningshearth, 21

Mant's, Bp., history, description of Bp. Bedell's tomb in, 198, 199, 200
Marriage, Rev. William Bedell's to Mrs. Leah Mawe, widow, 14, 128
Marsh, Narcissus, Abp. of Armagh, forwards the publication of Bedell's Irish Old Testament, 246-7-8.
Mawe, Edward, Bp. Bedell catches fever from, 78, 190
—— Mrs. Leah, widow, her marriage with the Rev. William Bedell, 14, 128
—— Dr. Nicholas, 15, 129, 161
Meath, Bp. Dopping of, 174, 245, 247
Meath, Bp. Martin of, and the rebellion, 189
Ministers, able to speak Irish collated to Benefices by Bishop Bedell, 43, 44, 45, 176

Moigne, Dr. Thomas, Bedell's predecessor as Bishop, 149, 155
—— Mrs., Bp. Bedell's law-suit with, 48, 155, 194, 195
Moreton, Bp. of Durham, 141, 143
Morosini's Historia Veneta referred to, 123
Morton, Sir Albertus, 102
M.P. for the University of Dublin, Provost Bedell elected as, 145

Nangle, Mr. James, employed in the work of translating the Psalms into Irish, 61, 171.
Newton, Mr., afterwards Sir Adam, Bedell's correspondence with, 103, 104
Non-conformists in the north of Ireland, their petition to the House of Commons in 1641 against Episcopal rule, 151

O'Donell, or Daniel, Wm. Abp. of Tuam, completes the translation of New Testament into Irish, and also translates the Book of Common Prayer, 60, 175
O'Donnellan, Abp. of Tuam, continues Bp. Walsh's work of translating the New Testament into Irish, 175
Old Testament, translation of the, into the Irish language procured by Bp. Bedell, 60, 61, 175, 176, 242
Ossory, Bp. Walsh of, commences the translation of the New Testament into Irish, 175
Ossory, Bp. Williams of, and the rebellion, 188
Ottavio Baldi, Sir Henry Wotton's first introduction to King James in Stirling Castle under this name, 118

Pale, the English, rebels of, 223
Palliser, Dr. William, afterwards Abp. of Cashel, his letter to Capt. Ambrose Bedell, v.
Parentage, birth and, of Bishop Bedell, 1, 2, 85, 91, 92
Paulo, Father, the Servite Friar of Venice, 8, 9, 103, 106, 107, 108, 109, 110, 111, 113, 114
—— attempted assassination of, 103, 109
—— his History of the Council of Trent, 135, 137, 138, 139; his History of the Venetian Interdict, 140
—— his life translated into English, 8

Paulus V. Pope, his interdict against the state of Venice, 8, 101, 103
Pedigree of the Bedell and Elliston families, 258, 259
Perkins, the Rev. William, 4, 6, 94
—— his work on the Government of the Tongue, 19
Pestilence in Ireland in 1641, 190
Plessis-Mornay, du, 111
Pluralities, Bishop Bedell's discountenance of, 43, 147, 159
Pope, Paul V. his interdict against Venice, 8, 101, 103
Price, Thos., Archdeacon of Kilmore, assists Ambrose Bedell in the defence of Croghan Castle, 201, 202, 221
—— Abp. of Cashel, formerly Archdeacon of Kilmore, forwards the publication of Bedell's Irish Old Testament, 241, 248
Protestant Petition of the county of Cavan, complaint against Bedell on account of, 49, 50, 51
—— Bp. Bedell's part in, erroneously applied by Mr. Clogie to the remonstrance of the rebels of Cavan, 186
Provostship of T.C.D., Bedell's, 23-29, 142-146, 253
Prynne, William, his Life of Abp. Laud, 49, 150

Radcliffe, Sir George, his account of Bp. Adair of Killala's trial, 54
Raphoe, Bp. Lesley of, and the rebellion, 189
Rattlesden, John 2nd son of the Rev. William Bedell of Rattlesden presented to the rectory of, 235
—— William, eldest son of Bp. Bedell, presented to the rectory of, 231
—— extracts from the P.R. of, relating to the Rev. William Bedell's family, 232 et seq.
Rebellion, Irish, of 1641, outbreak of, 65 181
Rebels, the, Protestants escaping from, are protected by Bishop Bedell, 65, 66, 67, 69, 181
—— rob the Bishop himself, 70, 71, 72
—— imprison Bishop Bedell and his sons in Loughoughter Castle, 73, 74, 187, 189

Reeves, the Rev. Dr. William, dedication of this volume to, xi.
Reilly, Relly, or O'Reilly, the names of the Clan signing "Remonstrance" of the rebels of the county of Cavan, 184
"Remonstrance" of the rebels of Cavan to the Lords Justices and Council, 181, 182, 183, 184
—— answer of the Lords Justices and Council thereto, 185
Republic, Sir Henry Wotton's opinion of a, 119
Ricemarchus's Psalter, 193-4, 256
Riche, Sir Nathaniel, Bedell's letter to, on the state of T.C.D., 253

St. Edmondsbury, Preachership at St. Mary's, 5, 7, 13, 100
Sall, Dr. Andrew, aids in revising for the press the MS. of Bedell's Irish Old Testament, 241-5
—— his life and death, 248
Sancroft, William, Archbishop of Canterbury, his intention to write a life of Bp. Bedell, vi., 100, 216, 217, 218, 246
—— his opinion of Bp. Burnet, 133
Sancroft, William, Master of Emmanuel College, Cambridge, uncle of Archbishop Sancroft, 99
S. Maria of Vangadezza, the Abbacy of, 121
Sarpi, Francis, the father, and Isabella, née Morelli, the mother of Father Paulo, the Servite Friar of Venice, 108
Scriptures, the, in a language understood by the people, judged by Bishop Bedell to be as essential to the Church as the building of stone walls, 60
Seal, Bp. Bedell's, with the figure of a crucible, and a Hebrew motto, 81, 82
Sheridan, the Rev. Denis, ordained and collated to the vicarage of Killasser by Bp. Bedell, 204
—— presented to the vicarages of Drunge and Larra, 204
—— Bishop Bedell takes up his abode in the house of, 76, 77, 189
—— saves Bedell's MS. Hebrew Bible and the MS. of the Irish translation of the Old Testament, 76, 77, 188, 240
Sheridan Family, 203-211
Sheridan, Dr. Thomas, and Dr. Jonathan Swift, Dean of St. Patrick's, their lines written on a window of the Episcopal Palace of Kilmore, 211

Spalato, De Dominis, Archbishop of, 135, 136; his dead body burnt, 136
Stanford, John, marries Eleanor French, 238, 239
—— claims and obtains the Bedell property in right of his wife, 239, 240
Stanford, Pedigree of, 259
Statutes of T. C. D., Bedell's, 27, 145
Stern, Dr. John, Bishop- Suffragan of Colchester, Bedell ordained by, 5
Stokes, Professor Dr. William, dedication of this volume to, xi.
—— on the fever of which Bp. Bedell died, 190
Strafford, Earl of, see Wentworth
Swift, Dr. Jonathan, Dean of St. Patrick's, and Dr. Thomas Sheridan, their lines written on a window of the Episcopal Palace of Kilmore, 211
Swiney, Dr., Roman Catholic Bp. of Kilmore, 71, 72, 91, 92, 187, 195
Synod, Diocesan, 41, 162-169
—— names of Ministers present at, 169
—— Bp. Bedell's letter to Abp. Laud in explanation of, 170

Tate or Teate, Dr. Faithfull, 169; succeeded by Denis Sheridan in the benefices of Drunge and Larra, 204
Templeport, Rev. Murtach King, disseized of his living of, 177
Tirconnell, Richd. Talbot, Earl of, and Thomas Sheridan, 209
Tomb of Bp. Bedell, 197-200
Trent, History of the Council of, by Father Paulo, 135, 137, 138, 139
Tuam, Abp. Boyle of, and the rebellion, 188
Tullagh, William Bedell, Prebendary of, 234

Ussher, James, Archbishop of Armagh, 24, 26, 30, 34, 143, 145, 188, 193, 256,

Venice, Mr. Bedell's residence in, 8-13, 100-124
Venice, the State of, controversy with Rome, 8, 101, 103
Vox Corvi, Mr. Clogie's sermon, entitled, 219-220

Waddesworth, James, 10, 95-97
—— Bedell's correspondence with, 131
Waldron, Mr. John, of Farnham, 182, 185

Walsh, Bp. of Ossory, commences the translation of the New Testament into Irish, 175

Walton, Isaak, his notices of Bedell in his Life of Sir Henry Wotton, 101, 102, 216

―――― his account of the writing of Father Paulo's History of the Council of Trent, 138

Ward, Dr. Seth, Bp. of Salisbury, 95

Warde, Dr. Samuel, Master of Sidney College, Cambridge, 94-95

―――― Bishop Bedell's letters to, x., 94, 102, 124, 127, 130, 149, 159, 160, 161, 174

―――― his character of Bedell, 144

―――― godfather of William, Bishop Bedell's eldest son, 226

Waterford and Lismore, Bp. Adair of, and the rebellion, 188

Wentworth, Lord Deputy, his ill-feeling to Bishop Bedell about the petition of the Protestants of Cavan, 49-51

―――― interferes to delay the publication of the Old Testament in Irish, 175

―――― Bp. Bedell's letter to him about the persecution of Mr. Murtach King, 177-180

Wettenhall, Bishop of Kilmore, desires to be buried beside Bishop Bedell, 196; his disapprobation of Burnet's Life of Bedell, 218

Whepstead, William Bedell, the Bishop's eldest son, does clerical duty at, 229, 230

Will of John Alliston of Black Notley, Bedell's cousin, 233

―――― Dr. Joseph Alliston, Bedell's cousin, 99

―――― Mathew Alliston, or Elliston, Bp. Bedell's uncle, 233

―――― Capt. Ambrose Bedell, 237

―――― Ambrose Bedell, Junr., 238

―――― Bp. Bedell, 192-195

―――― Bp. Bedell's father, 87

―――― Bp. Bedell's mother, 87

―――― James Bedell 235, 236

Wotton, Sir Henry, English Ambassador at Venice, 8, 101-123

―――― invites Mr. Bedell to join him as Chaplain at Venice, in succession to the Rev. Nathaniel Fletcher, 8, 101, 102

―――― his first introduction to King James in Stirling Castle under the name of OTTAVIO BALDI, 118

―――― his letter to Charles I. recommending the Rev. Mr. Bedell to the Provostship of T. C. D., 25

www.ingramcontent.com/pod-product-compliance
Lightning Source LLC
Chambersburg PA
CBHW032108230426
43672CB00009B/1672